Towards Sustainable Consumption and Lifestyles

About the Editors

Prof. Suresh Misra a well-known expert on consumer issues is currently Professor (Consumer Affairs) and Coordinator, Centre for Consumer Studies, a Think Tank and Knowledge Partner of the Department of Consumer Affairs, GoI at the Indian Institute of Public Administration, New Delhi. He holds his Master's in Political Science from Jawaharlal Nehru University, New Delhi, Masters in Human Resource Management from Pondicherry Central University, D.Phil. from Allahabad Central University and Post-Graduate Diploma in Journalism and Mass Communication from Calcutta. He had his advance training in Corporate Governance at AOTS, Tokyo, Japan; in Total Quality Management at UK Civil Service College, Sunningdale, UK; and in Public Policy Management at Development Study Centre, Rehovot, Israel. He participated in the Public Administration programme for senior officers at ENA, Paris, France and also attended advance Training of Trainers programme on Training Techniques and Methodology at Thames Valley University, Slough, UK. Prof. Misra has been associated with consumer studies for the last twenty-five years and carried out a number of research and evaluation studies sponsored by national and international agencies. Prof. Misra is a member of the Central Consumer Protection Council, GoI. He is the Project Director of the National Consumer Helpline and the State Consumer Knowledge Resource Management Portal set-up by the Department of Consumer Affairs, GoI at IIPA.

Dr. Sapna Chadah is currently working as Assistant Professor in Constitutional and Administrative Law at the Indian Institute of Public Administration, New Delhi. She holds her Masters in Law (LL.M.) from University of Delhi and Ph.D. from Jamia Millia Islamia, New Delhi. Her major areas of interest include Constitutional Law, Administrative Law, Consumer Protection Law and Policy, Environmental Management, Laws in Urban Management, Regulation of Service Sectors and Privatisation. She was associated with a number of research studies in the area of consumer protection and consumer welfare. She has also been associated with Consultancy Project on "Promoting Involvement of Research Institutions/Universities/Colleges in Consumer Protection and Consumer Welfare" sponsored by Department of Consumer Affairs. She has nine books, four monographs to her credit and published more than 30 papers in journals of repute.

Towards Sustainable Consumption and Lifestyles

Some Insights

Edited by
Suresh Misra
Sapna Chadah

CONCEPT PUBLISHING COMPANY PVT. LTD.
NEW DELHI-110059

ISBN-13: 978-93-86682-28-4

First Published 2018

Published and Printed by

Concept
Since 1974

Concept Publishing Company Pvt. Ltd.
A/15-16, Commercial Block, Mohan Garden,
New Delhi-110059 (INDIA)
T : +91 11 25351460, +91 11 25351794
E : publishing@conceptpub.com, *W* : www.conceptpub.com

Cataloging in Publication Data--Courtesy: D.K. Agencies (P) Ltd. <docinfo@dkagencies.com>

Towards sustainable consumption and lifestyles : some insights / edited by Suresh Misra, Sapna Chadah.
pages cm
Contributed articles.
Includes bibliographical references and index.
ISBN 9789386682284

1. Consumption (Economics)—India. 2. Lifestyles—India. 3. Sustainable development—India. I. Misra, Suresh, editor. II. Chadah, Sapna, editor.

LCC HB820.T69 2018 DDC 339.470954 23

Preface

Consumption is the reason why anything gets produced. Billions of people are now being drawn into a consumer culture of increased consumption with growing focus on acquisition of a wide array of consumer products. Technological changes coupled with strive of consumers for identity, distinction, and status through the purchase of marketed products and services has given rise to changes in the consumption pattern and growth in total consumption. Increasing incomes and falling prices have made these status symbols accessible even to the general public. The present consumption and production patterns together are reason for all man-made stress on natural environment. Consumerism may be the single greatest threat to environmental and social stability on the planet. The Earth's natural capital, on which our social and economic prosperity is built, is finite. We urgently need to halt the depletion of natural resources, restore damaged ecosystems, conserve biodiversity and maintain essential ecosystem services. At the same time, we need to provide equitable access to natural resources and provide food, water and energy for a growing global population.

Three main groups of actors who influence the sustainability of private consumption are consumers, governments and business. The decisions made by these actors often have little or no consideration regarding preservation of our natural resources. Policies at governmental level have myopic focus on economic growth and narrow interests. Business models focus on short-term profits and fail to account for externalities and long-term costs. Excessive consumption at individual level makes only few happier or healthier. This all adds up to immense costs to the planet, and its inhabitants. In each case, there is need to adopt a better choice.

Sustainable consumption is not necessarily about consuming less; it is about consuming better, i.e. more efficiently, with less risk to our health and environment. Changing our course and finding alternative pathways though not easy; but is the only way to protect our planet. There is an urgent need for systematic change. Consumers need to increasingly take an active part in the creation of the sustainable economy, demanding greater transparency over the origin and contents of the goods they consume. They should be ever more aware of the broad sustainability challenge facing the world. It is necessary to connect the intentions of individuals as citizens with their actions as consumers. A better understanding of social behaviours and clarity on how individual actions contribute to social goods is need of the hour. Many businesses are now looking to transform demand through the way they interact with the consumer. They must recognize the need to reshape demand by making sustainable consumption more personal and relevant to consumers, leveraging the power of technology to drive engagement and transparency, and redesigning products and services to deliver increased value with fewer resources to make the sustainable choice the default choice.

In addition to the environmental strategies relying on improvement of resource productivity and eco-efficiency of processes and products, the concept of sustainable consumption calls for changing the levels and patterns of consumption, which require complimentary approaches. However, so far, there has been a noticeable lack of strategies that conceive ways of shifting from a material-intensive consumer culture to a society with less materialistic aspirations. It has to be realized by all the stakeholders in the society that the costs of inaction will be too high. The governments, industry, civil society and consumers are key stakeholders whose initiatives can reduce poverty and drive sustainable economic growth in both developed and developing countries. We need a renewed and positive focus on the connection between lifestyles, consumption and aspirations, cultures and social norms. Then, we will have the potential to mobilize and unlock people's consumption and lifestyles as real drivers for change and sustainable development. As market "values" reflect society's preferences, the general public will have to campaign, both in their role as consumers and citizens, for a "greener" economy. If society prefers a more conserving and sustainable economy, then business will have an incentive to develop "green" technologies and products. If consumers are "green", then it will be profitable for business to become "green".

September 1st, 2016
New Delhi

Suresh Misra
Sapna Chadah
Editors

Contents

List of Contributors

Anand Acharya, Senior Officer (Corporate Planning Department: Sustainability Team) Gail India Ltd., C.O. New Delhi Office-16, Bikha Ji Cama Place, New Delhi-66, Ph: +91-11-26182955; Extn: 2767 (M) 91 95602 13130
Email: *anandacharya.mission@gmail.com o-aacharya@gail. co.in*

Dr. Badruddin, Associate Professor, PES's Shri Ravi Sitaram Naik College of Arts and Science, Ponda, Goa-403401, (O) 0832-2335171, (R) 08322319786, (M): 09823647950
Email: *drbadar@rediffmail.com, drbadar786@gmail.com*

Bansuri Das, Student, Flat No. 7412, B-10, Vasant Kunj, New Delhi-110070, (M): 9716770553
Email: *bansuridas@gmail.com*

Prof. D.S. Poornananda, Professor, Department of Mass Communication and Journalism, Kuvempu University, Jnana Sahyadri, Shankaraghatta-577451, Shivamogga District, Karnataka, Ph: 91-8282-256324, Fax: 91-8282-256262
Email: *poornananda@yahoo.com*

Dr. Henrique Dsouza, Assistant Professor, Villa Sousa, B/249, Sousa Complex, Betim, Bardez, Goa-403101, (M): 9960280404,
Email: *hesoza@ gmail.com*

Dr. Indramohan Jha, Associate Professor, ARSD College, University of Delhi, Dhaula Kuan, New Delhi-21 (M): 9818490377,
Email: *imjhaa@ gmail.com*

Dr. Jayashree Pillai, Associate Professor, Miranda House, University of Delhi, C-304, Kaveri Apartment, Plot 11, Sector 3, Dwarka, New Delhi-110075, (M) 09818194505
Email: *jayashree.pillai@gmail.com*

Dr. Joseph Benjamin, Associate Professor, Department of Political Science, S F S College (RTM Nagpur University), Seminary Hills, Nagpur-440006, Maharashtra, (M) 09422807587
Email: *joseph.sfscollege@gmail.com*

Dr. Jyoti Marwah, Associate Professor, G.B. Pant Social Science Institute, Jhusi, Allahabad-211019, (O): 0532-2569214, (M): 09336899726, Fax: 0532-2569214
Email: *knbhatt1@rediffmail.com*

K. Shailaja Rao, 70-70-40-44/2, Siddharth Nagar, Kakinada, Andhra Pradesh-533003, (O) 2377120, (M): 098485 53331
Email: *shailajakoka @gmail.com*

K.G. Vasuki, Special Correspondent, The Pioneer, No. 81, 11th Main, 14th Cross, 6th Sector, H S R Layout, Bangalore-560102, Karnataka, (O) 080-25729191, (M) 09845032321
Email: *kgvasuki@yahoo.com*

Dr. Mamta Pathania, Assistant Professor of Public Administration, Centre for Consumer Studies, Indian Institute of Public Administration, Indraprastha Estate, Ring Road, New Delhi-110002, (O): 011-23468392, (M): 9958422873
Email: *mamtapathania@gmail.com*

Pawan Kumar Rose, Teaching Associate, Department of Energy and Environmental Science, Chaudhary Devi Lal University, Sirsa, Haryana, (M): 0966246725
Email: *pawankumarrose@gmail.com*

Praveen Goyal, Research Scholar, Department of Management Studies, Indian Institute of Technology, Roorkee-247667, Uttarakhand, (M): 91-9548030015
Email: *praveeng23@gmail.com*

Ramaben R. Mavani, President, Rajkot Saher Jilla Grahak Suraksha Mandal, 329, Popatbhai Sorathia Bhavan, Sadar Bazar, Rajkot-360001, Gujarat, (R) 0281-2471122/ 2471120, (M) 09426201611, 09898398035, Telefax: 0281-2471122
Email: *mavaniramb@sancharnet.in, ramjibhaimavani@gmail.com*

Ramjibhai B. Mavani, Founder President, Rajkot Saher Jilla Grahak Suraksha Mandal, 329, Popatbhai Sorathia Bhavan, Sadar Bazar, Rajkot-360001, Gujarat (R) 0281-2471122/ 2471120, (M) 09426201611, 09898398035, Telefax: 0281-2471122
Email: *mavaniramb@ sancharnet.in, ramjibhaimavani@gmail.com*

Rani Devi, Department of Energy and Environmental Science, Chaudhary Devi Lal University, Sirsa, Haryana.

Dr. Rashmi Tripathi, Assistant Professor, Graphic Era University, Clement Town, Bell Road Dehradun, Uttarakhand, M: 09415171324
Email: *rtripathi@ddn.upes.ac.in, tripathirashmi79@yahoo.com*

Roopa Vajpeyi, Academic and Consumer Activist, Consumers India, Res: D-203, Saket, New Delhi-110017, Ph: 91-11-26866032, Mobile: +9810366706
Email: *roopa.vajpeyi@gmail.com*

Santosh B. Patkar, Principal, S.V.S. Sridora Caculo College of Commerce and Management Studies, Khorlim, Mapusa, Goa, (O) 0832-2250042, (R) 0832-2910051, (M) 9421157379
Email: *patkar_santosh@ rediffmail.com*

Dr. Sapna Chadah, Assistant Professor, Centre for Consumer Studies, Indian Institute of Public Administration, Indraprastha Estate, Ring Road, New Delhi-110002, (O): 011-23468348, (M): 9810657989
Email: *sapnachadah@yahoo.co.in*

Dr. Sheetal Kapoor, Associate Professor, Department of Commerce, Kamala Nehru College, University of Delhi, (M): 9810751903, (R) 011-25259404,
Email: *sheetal_kpr@hotmail.com*

Prof. Shrikrishna Mahajan, Professor and Head, Department of Commerce and Management, Shivaji University, Kolhapur-416004, Maharashtra, India, (O): 0231-2609173, (R): 0231-2694863, M: 09420133818
Email: *ssm_commerce@unishivaji.ac.in,ssmahajan_suk@ rediffmail.com*

Shruti Mittal, Associate Manager Sustainability, E-43/1, Okhla, Ph-2, New Delhi-110020; Residence Address: 142, Engineer's Estate, Plot No. 21, IP Extension, Patparganj, New Delhi-110092, (M) 91-8800194999
Email: *shruti.mittal1@gmail.com*

Prof. Suresh Misra, Chair-Professor (Consumer Affairs) and Coordinator, Centre for Consumer Studies, Indian Institute of Public Administration, Indraprastha Estate, Ring Road, New Delhi-110 002, (M): 9312413955, (O): 011-23766136, 23468349
Email: *drsureshmisra@gmail.com*

Suresh Prasad Singh, Policy Analyst, CUTS International, D-217, Bhaskar Marg, Bani Park, Jaipur-302016, (M): 91-9460736459, Ph: 0141-2282821, Fax: 91 141 2282485
Email: *sps@cuts.org, ssingh@eepcindia.net*

Dr. Zillur Rahman, Associate Professor, Department of Management Studies, Indian Institute of Technology, Roorkee-247667, Uttarakhand, (M): +91-9897052333
Email: *yusuffdm@iitr.acnet.in*

1
Introduction

Suresh Misra and *Sapna Chadah*

Introduction

The importance of consumption is constantly growing in the modern societies. Increased consumption is used as key indicator of economic growth. Resultantly, consumption has become a central feature of our society. The connection between consumption and other development goals has mostly been approached from a purely economic perspective. This has led to the misconception that any kind of increased consumption is good for the economy and thereby for the society as a whole. Development today means material prosperity and conspicuous consumption even at the cost of human development. High standard of living means more goods and services unmindful of their implications for environment, health and hygiene. However, there is a global recognition that unsustainable patterns of consumption have extreme serious social and environmental impacts worldwide. Ever increasing and irresponsible consumption is putting a catastrophic strain on the environment, by causing pollution and global warming inducing climate change; destroying the ecosystem, and undermining sustainable lifestyles.

The global Living Planet Index (LPI) shows a decline of 52 per cent in vertebrate species populations between 1970 and 2010; that is vertebrate species populations across the globe are, on average, about half the size they were 40 years ago. The Ecological Footprint shows that 1.5 Earths would be required to meet the demands humanity makes on nature each year. These demands include the renewable resources we consume for food, fuel and fibre, the land we build on, and the forests we need to absorb our carbon emissions. For more than 40 years, humanity's demand has exceeded the planet's biocapacity. Further complexity is that demand is not evenly distributed, with people in industrialized countries consuming resources and services at a much faster rate. The biodiversity is declining far faster than any natural rate; the concentration of carbon dioxide in the atmosphere is already causing significant changes to our climate and ecosystems; and—while converting nitrogen from the air into fertilizer has helped feed the world—nitrogen pollution has become a significant environmental threat. As the LPI declines and the Ecological Footprint increases, the planet's capacity to supply and replenish vital natural resources diminishes. Today, almost a billion people suffer from hunger, 768 million live without a safe and clean water supply and 1.4 billion lack access to a reliable electricity supply. Securing resilient, healthy communities where people can thrive will become an even greater challenge than it is today as population and consumption increase, and climate change and ecosystem degradation take their toll.[1]

Promoting sustainable consumption and production are important aspects of sustainable development, which depends on achieving long-term economic growth that is consistent with environmental and social needs. However, till recently the environmental impact has primarily been approached as an issue for producers and regulating authorities to deal with. The environmental, social and economic costs derived from consumption and production patterns are significant and mounting. All the environmental problems including water scarcity, land degradation, deforestation, loss of biodiversity and pollution are all connected with the consumption and production patterns. Without reorienting current consumption and production patterns there can be no genuine mitigation of climate change. Since the late 1980s, we have been in "overshoot"—the Ecological Footprint has exceeded the Earth's biocapacity—as of 2003 by about 25 per cent. According to the WWF, "effectively, the Earth's regenerative capacity can no longer keep up with demand—people are turning resources into waste faster than nature can turn waste back into resources. Humanity is no longer living off nature's interest, but drawing down its capital. This growing pressure on ecosystems is causing habitat destruction or degradation and permanent loss of productivity, threatening both biodiversity and human well-being.[2]

The cause and effect is also connected to the advancing prosperity in many parts of the globe. More and more natural resources are needed to fuel this new demand putting both renewable and non-renewable resources under pressure. While some non-renewable resources are at risk of complete exhaustion, while many renewable resources such as water, soil and forests are under extreme stress. The 12 per cent of the world living in North America and Western Europe account for 60 per cent of global private consumption spending, while the one-third living in South Asia and sub-Saharan Africa account for only 3.2 per cent.[3] If the present scenario continues, by 2050 we will need more than two planets due to unsustainable patterns of consumption and production.[4]

Traditionally, the people living in developed countries are the world's largest consumer of natural resources. The 20 per cent of the world's population living in OECD countries earn 85 per cent of the world's annual income; consume 75 per cent of global energy; and over 80 per cent of other resources annually. They also generate 75 per cent of annual global pollution.[5] However, with increasing affluence, the number of consumers in the developing countries is also increasing rapidly. Besides this, the peoples' spending on the common household goods is decreasing and they are spending more on the luxuries such as mobile and takeaway meals. Thus, while consumer class numbers are already large, there is still ample potential for growth. The major emerging economies' capacity to consume is enormous. As the Background Chapter to the Yogyakarta meeting (2003) pointed out "If car ownership in China, India and Indonesia reached the world average, 200M vehicles would be added to the global fleet—twice the number of cars in the United States today."[6]

Global warming and climate change is not a myth; it is something that is already here. This problem of global warming and climate change has now acquired such serious proportions that unless corrective steps are taken sooner than later, the very survival of humanity would be jeopardized. Man would become an endangered species. Our very survival and development is at stake. Fortunately, it is still within the powers of man to stop any further contamination of the atmosphere, and thereby, any increase in earth's temperatures and other changes before it is too late. Thus, the pertinent question before us is: what should we do as individuals, communities, and societies to take any concrete and time-bound corrective action before it is too late? The belief that 'scientific' thinking is capable of solving all problems all the times is so deeply ingrained in our minds that we tend to overdepend on it and ignore the feedback control mechanism that keeps a system functioning smoothly. We forget that in all living and health systems the 'scientific' thinking and the feedback control mechanism exist interdependently. [7]

To turn away from the basic human values such as truth, non-violence, love, compassion, human brotherhood, and respect for nature on which most great civilizations were built, is another trait of modernity. Nature becomes the resource for exploitation as do the fellow human beings.

Want based conspicuous consumption does not produce happiness; and if it does, it is not for all. The need based consumption on the other hand leads to *Sarvodaya* (development of all). We have seen how nature is being robbed of its inherent capacity to regenerate. If we continue to tread on the path set by modern civilization, we are sure to destroy ourselves. We can either opt for higher GNH (Gross National Happiness) and usher in a new civilization or continue to pursue the mirage of higher GDP and be the dying generation of the so-called modern civilization. The Earth gives enough scope for progress provided that its culture and nurture go together and it is used with difference and within the limits of what its carrying capacities.[8]

Sustainable Consumption—Concept and Definition

Sustainable consumption has repeatedly been identified as a cornerstone for achieving sustainable development in society. Sustainable consumption is a significant element and is part of policies and strategies for sustainable development. Sustainable consumption and production is a practical implementation strategy to achieve sustainable development, which addresses economic, societal and environmental problems. Sustainable consumption gives consumers the opportunity to consume products and services that meet their needs in an efficient and effective way, while minimizing the negative environmental, social and economic impact. The ultimate goal of sustainable consumption is to improve quality of life for all consumers in our and future generations, while minimizing associated environmental impacts.

In such a scenario addressing the issue of consumption is of vital importance in reducing the impact of society on its environment. In this context, the statement of Mahatma Gandhi becomes quite significant: "The Earth has resources for meeting man's every need, but not his every greed". Therefore, sustainable consumption is both a challenge and an opportunity. Ever increasing and irresponsible consumption is putting a catastrophic strain on the environment, by causing pollution and global warming induced by climate change; destroying the ecosystem, and undermining sustainable lifestyles. Promoting sustainable consumption and production are important aspects of sustainable development, which depends on achieving long-term economic growth that is consistent with environmental and social needs. A key issue in such a scenario will not be just reducing the volume of goods and services consumed, but also the extent to which improvement in environmental quality can be achieved through the substitution of more efficient and less polluting goods and services.

"Sustainable" here refers to a level and pattern of consumption which meets the needs of the present without compromising the ability of future generations to meet their own needs.[9] Sustainable consumption has been defined by the 1994 Oslo Symposium on Sustainable Consumption as ".... the use of services and related products which respond to basic needs and bring a better quality of life while minimising the use of natural resources and toxic materials as well as emissions of waste and pollutants over the life cycle of the service or product so as not to jeopardise the needs of future generations."[10] Sustainable consumption is an umbrella term that brings together a number of key issues, such as meeting needs, enhancing the quality of life, improving resource efficiency, increasing the use of renewable energy sources, minimising waste, taking a life cycle perspective and taking into account the equity dimension. Integrating these component parts is the central question of how to provide the same or better services to meet the basic requirements of life and the aspirations for improvement for both current and future generations, while continually reducing environmental damage and risks to human health. A key issue is, therefore, the extent to which necessary improvements in environmental quality can be achieved through the substitution of more efficient and less polluting goods and services (patterns of consumption), rather than through reductions in the volumes of goods and services consumed (levels of consumption).[11]

Sustainable consumption should, therefore, be understood as a situation where consumer needs and demands are fulfilled in an as efficient and resource lean way as possible, resulting in a minimized negative environmental, social and economic impact. The ultimate goal of sustainable consumption is improved quality of life for all consumers.[12] Although there is no common understanding of sustainable consumption, it is undisputed that negative impacts of dominating consumption patterns in affluent countries need to be substantially reduced to achieve sustainability.

Sustainable consumption lays an emphasis on satisfying basic human needs (not the desire for 'wants' and 'luxuries'); favouring quality of life over material standards of living; minimising resource use, waste and pollution; taking a life cycle perspective in consumer decision-making; and acting with concern for future generations. Sustainable consumption integrates a range of social, economic and political practices at the individual, household, community, business and government level that support and encourage: reducing the direct environmental burden of producing, using and disposing goods and services; meeting basic needs for key consumption goods and services, such as food, water, health, education and shelter; maximising opportunities for sustainable livelihoods in the South; consuming goods and services that contribute positively to the health and well-being of women and children; increasing the development and adoption of energy and water efficient appliances, public transport and other demand-side measures; the production and sale of new goods and services adapted to global environmental constraints; and lifestyles that place greater value on social cohesion, local traditions and non-material values.[13]

Transforming the World through Sustainable Development Goals

At the United Nations Sustainable Development Summit on September 25, 2015, countries have adopted the 2030 Agenda for Sustainable Development, and global agreement on climate change. This new development agenda applies to all countries, promotes peaceful and inclusive societies, creates better jobs and tackles the environmental challenges particularly climate change. The Agenda includes a set of 17 Sustainable Development Goals (SDGs) to end poverty, fight inequality and injustice, and tackle climate change by 2030.

The new Goals and targets which have come into effect from January 1, 2016 will guide the decisions for the next 15 years. SDGs also known as the Global Goals, are built on the Millennium Development Goals (MDGs), adopted in 2000, eight anti-poverty targets that the world committed to achieving by 2015. The MDGs aimed at an array of issues that included slashing poverty, hunger, disease, gender inequality, and access to water and sanitation. Though enormous progress was made on the MDGs; however, the indignity of poverty could not be ended for all. That is why new SDGs, and the broader sustainability agenda, that is much broader than the MDGs, has been adopted to address the root causes of poverty and the universal need for development that works for all people.[14]

The 17 Sustainable Development Goals are as follows:[15]

1. *No poverty*—End Poverty in all its forms everywhere;
2. *Zero hunger*––End hunger, achieve food security and improved nutrition and promote sustainable agriculture;
3. *Good health and well-being*—Ensure healthy lives and promote well-being for all;

4. *Quality education*—Ensure inclusive and equitable quality education and promote lifelong learning opportunities for all;
5. *Gender equality*—Achieve gender equality and empower all women and girls;
6. *Clean water and sanitation*—Ensure access to water and sanitation for all;
7. *Affordable and clean energy*—Ensure access to affordable, reliable, sustainable and modern energy for all;
8. *Decent work and economic growth*—Promote inclusive and sustainable economic growth, employment and decent work for all;
9. *Industry, innovation, infrastructure*—Build resilient infrastructure, promote sustainable industrialization and foster innovation;
10. *Reduced inequalities*—Reduce inequality within and among countries;
11. *Sustainable cities and communities*—Make cities inclusive, safe, resilient and sustainable;
12. *Responsible consumption and production*—Ensure sustainable consumption and production patterns;
13. *Climate action*—Take urgent action to combat climate change and its impacts;
14. *Life below water*—Conserve and sustainably use the oceans, seas and marine resources;
15. *Life on land*—Sustainably manage forests, combat desertification, halt and reverse land degradation, halt biodiversity loss;
16. *Peace, justice and strong institutions*—Promote just, peaceful and inclusive societies; and
17. *Partnerships for the goals*—Revitalize the global partnership for sustainable development.

Responsible production and consumption is one of the 17 Global Goals that make-up the 2030 Agenda for Sustainable Development. As achieving economic growth and sustainable development requires that we urgently reduce our ecological footprint by changing the way we produce and consume goods and resources. The efficient management of our shared natural resources, and the way we dispose of toxic waste and pollutants, are important targets to achieve this goal. Encouraging industries, businesses and consumers to recycle and reduce waste is equally important, as is supporting developing countries to move towards more sustainable patterns of consumption by 2030.[16]

Sustainable Consumption and Development Goals

It is important to recognize sustainable consumption as a strategy to meet other development goals such as access to basic services, economic development and poverty eradication. There is need for "sustainable economic development". "Sustainable economic development" denotes a situation where the national economy is able to ensure that the basic needs are fulfilled for all. In a sense it is more ambitious than the traditional ambition of"economic growth" as it also implies that the economic growth of a country should not be allowed to infringe on the access to basic needs and services of its population.[17] If successfully adopted sustainable consumption should ultimately result in a better quality of life. The main goal for sustainable consumption is to achieve a better quality of life for all. To achieve the goal of better quality of life through sustainable consumption there is need for governments to take action in nine specific areas as recognized by the UN Guidelines on Consumer Protection, viz. Environmentally, sound products, services and technologies; Recycling programmes for waste and products; Regulatory mechanism; Economic instruments; Public (product) information; Impartial testing of products, Research on consumer behaviour, Sustainable practices (e.g. public green procurement) and Awareness and information campaigns.

Due to the wide disparities between countries and even more within countries, sustainable consumption would imply that consumption would have to increase for those without access to basic needs, whereas the more affluent consumers would have to change their patterns and levels of consumption. In the developing world at least two billion people need to increase their consumption in a sustainable manner to escape poverty. In contrast, millions of new consumers in developing countries, like their counterparts in the developed regions, need to reorient their consumption patterns towards sustainability. So, for the developing world, it can mean both more and less (or more sustainable) consumption. The developing world has the opportunity to meet its increasing consumption and production needs in a more sustainable manner than the developed countries have done so in the past.[18]

This dual complexity has made the consumption issue difficult for many countries to deal with. Sustainable consumption should, therefore, be understood as a situation where consumer needs and demands are fulfilled in an efficient and resource lean way as possible, resulting in a minimized negative environmental, social and economic impact. The ultimate goal of sustainable consumption is improved quality of life for all consumers. Sustainable consumption is directly linked with many other development priorities, such as poverty alleviation, economic growth, health and education, and environmental protection, all of them contributing to an improved quality of life. Sustainable consumption is not a prescription for how to consume less, but for how to meet the consumers' needs in a smart way. The need is for adoption of more efficient, less resource consuming and less polluting technologies like hybrid cars.[19]

The awareness on sustainable consumption is in general quite low and the concept is often misunderstood by both governments as well as civil society stakeholders. Sustainable consumption merely appears on the political agenda in countries as part of policies and strategies for sustainable development. Higher priority and relevance is usually accorded to in national development goals to sustainable production instead of sustainable consumption. Still most of the sustainable consumption activities are identified and carried out as part of environment projects rather than sustainable consumption projects. The consumer movement on the other hand basically focuses on consumer rights and consumer protection issues for getting redressal for substandard products as the means to seek compensation for such goods are limited. Sustainable consumption is generally a lower priority area for most consumer groups.

Sustainable Consumption and Production (SCP) needs an active involvement of all stakeholders and a wide range of locally-adapted policy responses. A key element of the SCP approach is the use of a range of public policies, private sector actions and investments which influence both the supply of and demand for goods and services, thus, reducing the negative impacts of both their production and consumption in an integrated manner.

Sustainable Consumption—Global Concerns

Sustainable Consumption and Production has been recognized in a number of International Summits as an important ingredient and integral part of the sustainable development. Principle 8 of the Rio Declaration on Environment and Development highlights the responsibility of nations to "reduce and eliminate unsustainable patterns of production and consumption". The principle clearly points out that this task is necessary "to achieve sustainable development and a higher quality of life for all people". The principle of common but differentiated responsibilities, as defined in Principle 7 of the Rio Declaration, focuses specific attention on the imbalances in global patterns of consumption and production and the need for governments to specify their role and responsibility in establishing the proper balance.

Chapter 4 of Agenda 21 explicitly identifies unsustainable production and consumption patterns, "particularly in industrialized countries", as "the major cause of the continued deterioration of the global environment".[20] The situation is described as "a matter of grave concern, aggravating poverty and imbalances". The chapter identifies two broad tasks for responding to this concern: (1) focusing on unsustainable patterns of production and consumption; and (2) national governments to develop national policies and strategies to encourage changes in unsustainable consumption patterns. Chapter 4 then points out the need for the developed countries to "take the lead" and developing countries to include sustainable consumption in their development process. The chapter further highlights the need for policies and strategies to address unsustainability ranging from the excessive demands and lifestyles of the rich to the lack of access to food, clean water, healthcare, shelter and education by the poor.

Agenda 21 asks each country to "develop a domestic policy framework that will encourage a shift to more sustainable patterns of production and consumption."[21] A national policy framework on sustainable production and consumption implies an understanding and appreciation of the linkages involved in balancing demand and supply-side approaches. Such a framework requires integrating various concepts such as product life cycle, environmental space, ecological footprints, and environmental cost internalization into a concrete interdepartmental plan with measurable targets and timetables and indicators to monitor and report on progress.

To achieve these objectives, Agenda 21 recommends the following activities: use of new and renewable energy sources[22]; recycling by industry and consumers[23]; reducing wasteful product packaging[24]; expanding environmental labelling and other environmentally related product information programmes designed to assist consumers to make informed choices[25]; providing information on the consequences of consumption choices and behaviour[26]; making consumers aware of the health and environmental impacts of products, through such means as consumer legislation and environmental labelling[27]; reviewing and improving government procurement policies[28]; using appropriate economic instruments to influence consumer behaviour[29]; promoting more positive attitudes towards sustainable consumption through education, public awareness programmes and other means.[30]

Since Rio, a number of international conferences, seminars, workshops, programmes etc. have been organized to implement the various recommendations made in Agenda 21. Following the Earth Summit, the OECD began its exploration of the relationship between production and consumption patterns and sustainable development.[31] It was the Oslo Ministerial Roundtable (Norwegian Ministry of Environment, 1995) which established the most commonly accepted definition of sustainable consumption as: "the use of goods and services that respond to basic needs and bring a better quality of life, while minimizing the use of natural resources, toxic materials and emissions of waste and pollutants over the life cycle, so as not to jeopardise the needs of future generations."[32] These and other activities contributed to the mandate by the second and third sessions of the UN Commission on Sustainable Development to develop an international work programme on sustainable production and consumption,[33] the first such global framework of programmes for implementing Agenda 21 objectives. The agreed upon programme of work consisted of five tasks:[34]

1. Identifying the policy implications of projected trends in consumption and production patterns.
2. Assessing the impact on developing countries, especially the least developed countries and small island developing States, of changes in consumption and production in developed countries.
3. Evaluating the effectiveness of policy measures intended to change consumption and production patterns, such as command-and-control, economic and social instruments, government procurement policies and guidelines.
4. Eliciting time bound voluntary commitment from countries to make measurable progress on those sustainable development goals that have an especially high priority at the national level.
5. Revising the guidelines for consumer protection, with regard to sustainable consumption.

In the International Programme of Work on Sustainable Production and Consumption, the task of revising the UN Guidelines on Consumer Protection, with regard to sustainable consumption, represents an important contribution to meeting the Agenda 21 objectives of developing domestic policy frameworks. The evolution of these revised guidelines—their development, adoption, and use—offers useful insights in assessing governments' progress achieving the policy framework objective, not to mention the overall goal of promoting sustainable production and consumption patterns. In January 1998, the Government of Brazil hosted the UN Inter-Regional Expert Group Meeting on "Consumer Protection and Sustainable Consumption", producing recommendations for revising the Guidelines discussed at the CSD's Sixth, Seventh and Eighth Sessions and finally adopted by the General Assembly in December 1999.

The United Nations Guidelines for Consumer Protection sets out valuable principles for effective consumer protection legislation, enforcement institutions and redress systems. The Guidelines assist interested Member States in formulating and enforcing domestic and regional laws, rules and regulations that are suitable to their own economic, social and environmental circumstances, as well as promoting international enforcement cooperation among Member States and encouraging the sharing of experiences in consumer protection. The Guidelines were first adopted by the General Assembly in Resolution 39/248 of 16 April, 1985, later expanded by the Economic and Social Council in Resolution 1999/7 of 26 July, 1999, and revised and adopted by the General Assembly in Resolution 70/186 of 22 December, 2015. The 2015 revised Guidelines make specific reference to the needs of developing countries, to the setting of the Sustainable Development Goals as the successors to the Millennium Development Goals, and the need for governments to cooperate across borders.[35]

In 1999, the UN Guidelines for Consumer Protection were expanded to include elements on sustainable consumption. The expanded guidelines provide an important opportunity to include environmental protection and sustainable development and to strengthen the linkage between consumer interests and sustainable consumption, thereby stimulating national policy-making to promote more sustainable consumption. The guidelines recommend governments to take action in nine specific areas: (1) Environmentally sound products services and technologies; (2) Recycling programmes for waste and products; (3) Regulatory mechanism; (4) Economic instruments; (5) Public (product) information; (6) Impartial testing of products; (7) Research on consumer behaviour; (8) Sustainable practices (e.g. public green procurement); and (9) Awareness and information campaigns.

In addition to specific policy recommendations on consumer information (e.g., on the impacts of consumption patterns and benefits of changes), education, eco-labelling, product testing, research on consumer behaviour, subsidy and tax reform, the Guidelines stressed the importance of government promotion of consumer empowerment and public participation in policy making, as well as the responsibility of developed country governments to support developing countries in promoting sustainable consumption and development. In particular, the revised Guidelines on sustainable consumption supported efforts to develop domestic policy frameworks on sustainable production and consumption shaped through informed partnership with all members of society.

While the environmental, social and economic aspects of production processes have been in the focus for various efforts to attain sustainable development for many years, it is only recently that the intricate interaction with the consumption side has come into focus. The Plan of Implementation, adopted at the World Summit for Sustainable Development in Johannesburg in 2002, notes in Chapter 3 that *"fundamental changes in the way societies produce and consume are indispensable for achieving global sustainable development"*. The Plan also calls for a number of more specific actions to be taken by international organizations and governments to achieve such changes.[36]

On that occasion, sustainable consumption and production was identified as one of the three overarching objectives of, and essential requirements for, sustainable development, together with poverty eradication and the management of natural resources in order to foster economic and social development. The Johannesburg Plan of Implementation also called for all countries to promote sustainable consumption and production patterns, with the developed countries taking the lead and with all countries benefiting from the process, taking into account the Rio principles, including, *inter alia*, the principle of common, but differentiated responsibilities as set out in Principle 7 of the Rio Declaration on Environment and Development. Furthermore, the Plan called for governments, relevant international organizations, the private sector and all major groups to play an active role in changing unsustainable consumption and production patterns and more specifically, through its Paragraph 15, to "*Encourage and promote the development of a 10-Year Framework of Programmes (10 YFP) in support of regional and national initiatives to accelerate the shift towards sustainable consumption and production to promote social and economic development within the carrying capacity of ecosystems.*"[37]

Marrakech Process named after the city where the First International Expert Meeting on the 10-Year Framework Programme (YFP) took place in 2003. It was a global platform that brought together all stakeholders to work jointly in the promotion and implementation of SCP patterns. The Marrakech Process has provided significant inputs for the elaboration of a "Global Framework for Action on SCP"; the so-called 10-Year Framework of Programmes on SCP. The United Nations Environment Programme (UNEP) and the United Nations Department for Economic and Social Affairs (UN-DESA) acted as the Secretariat of this global process, with an active participation of national governments, private sector, civil society, development agencies, UN Agencies and other stakeholders. The Marrakech Process involved the following four phases, which were implemented simultaneously: (1) Organising regional consultations in all regions to promote awareness and identify priorities and needs for SCP; (2) Building regional strategies and implementation mechanisms with regional and national ownership; (3) Implementing concrete projects and programmes on the regional, national and local levels; and (4) Monitoring and evaluating progress as well as exchanging information and experience at the international level. The Marrakech Process identified regional SCP needs and priorities, and supported the development of regional SCP strategies in most regions as well as the implementation of 33 demonstration projects worldwide. These included national SCP action plans, capacity building and SCP tool kits in the areas of sustainable procurement, tourism, buildings and construction, products, education and lifestyles, as well as various communication tools and awareness raising activities. The Marrakech Process informed the elaboration of the 10-YFP, which was one of the five themes at CSD 18 and CSD 19.[38]

The United Nations Conference on Sustainable Development—or Rio+20—took place in Rio de Janeiro, Brazil on 20-22 June, 2012 also adopted ground-breaking guidelines on green economy policies. The Rio+20 Conference reaffirmed that Sustainable Consumption and Production is a cornerstone of sustainable development. The well-being of humanity, the environment, and the functioning of the economy, ultimately depend upon the responsible management of the planet's natural resources. It recognised that poverty eradication, changing unsustainable and promoting sustainable patterns of consumption and production and protecting and managing the natural resource base of economic and social development are the overarching objectives of and essential requirements for sustainable development. It reaffirmed the need to achieve sustainable development by promoting sustained, inclusive and equitable economic growth, creating greater opportunities for all, reducing inequalities, raising basic standards of living, fostering equitable social development and inclusion, and promoting integrated and sustainable management of natural resources and ecosystems that supports, *inter alia*, economic, social and human development while facilitating ecosystem conservation, regeneration and restoration and resilience in the face of new and emerging challenges. It accepted green economy in the context of sustainable development and poverty eradication as one of the important tools available for achieving sustainable development and that it could provide options for policy-making.[39] The United Nations Conference on Sustainable Development (Rio+20) in 2012, Heads of States adopted the 10-Year Framework of Programmes on Sustainable Consumption and Production Patterns (10-YFP), reaffirming that SCP is one of the overarching objectives of, and essential requirements for, sustainable development. The '10-YFP' is a global framework for action to enhance international cooperation and advance the implementation of SCP in all countries and regions. It generates collective impact through multi-stakeholder programmes and partnerships, which develop and scale-up SCP policies and initiatives at all levels, fostering knowledge and experience sharing, and facilitating access to technical and financial resources for developing countries.

Strategies for Sustainable Consumption

For many in the private sector, the idea of sustainable consumption is controversial for its implications of less consumption. While consuming less will surely lower environmental impact, less consumption could also imply less economic activity, which would deliver less growth, lower incomes and fewer jobs. It is not about consuming less, but about consuming differently—consuming right. It is important to look for opportunities beyond just the manufacturing of a product, to the full life cycle, from conception and design through production, use, service and all the way to disposal or end of life. Life cycle thinking and the metrics that inform it have a powerful role in accelerating the shift from more consumption to a more strategic design and delivery of products and services.[40]

It is important to understand that sustainable consumption is not necessarily about consuming less; it is about consuming better, i.e. more efficiently, with less risk to our health and environment. It recognizes that current consumption patterns are drivers for unsustainable production and resource degradation. Sustainable consumption implies not only purchasing behaviours, but includes all types of interactions between individuals and infrastructures (mobility, leisure, housing), which together make-up lifestyles and livelihoods. Sustainable consumption requires a convergence of current consumption patterns, and a need for all to consume responsibly. It can be promoted through a mix of policy, economic and voluntary instruments, including formal and informal education. Sustainable consumption can generate economic benefits, social well-being and social inclusion (access to markets, innovation, job creation, healthier livelihoods and lifestyles), in addition to reducing environmental risks and capitalizing on environmental opportunities. Achieving sustainable consumption patterns is more technically and politically complex than changing production patterns, because it raises important issues such as human values, equity and lifestyle choices. The sustainable consumption challenge has generated fewer policy initiatives than those seen on sustainable production. There are, however, some large-scale initiatives aimed at improving and spreading the use of energy-efficient appliances and on promoting access to cleaner, affordable forms of energy and related energy services (e.g. Sustainable Energy for All) or reducing food loss and waste. Elevating sustainable consumption to the necessary level of policy and decision-making will require work on education and awareness-raising among consumers, civil society, private sector and policy-makers. At an international level it may also require negotiations which, in an inclusive and objective manner, take account of current imbalances in and impacts of unsustainable consumption patterns.[41]

The One Planet Perspective (WWF 2012)[42] outlines better choices for managing, using and sharing natural resources within the planet's capacity. It requires that we:

- **Preserve natural capital**: restore damaged ecosystems, halt the loss of priority habitats, significantly expand protected areas.
- **Produce better**: reduce inputs and waste, manage resources sustainably, scale-up renewable energy production.
- **Consume more wisely**: through low-footprint lifestyles, sustainable energy use and healthier food consumption patterns.

It also suggests two essential enabling conditions:

- **Redirect financial flows:** value nature, account for environmental and social costs, support and reward conservation, sustainable resource management and innovation.

- **Equitable resource governance:** share available resources, make fair and ecologically informed choices, measure success beyond GDP.

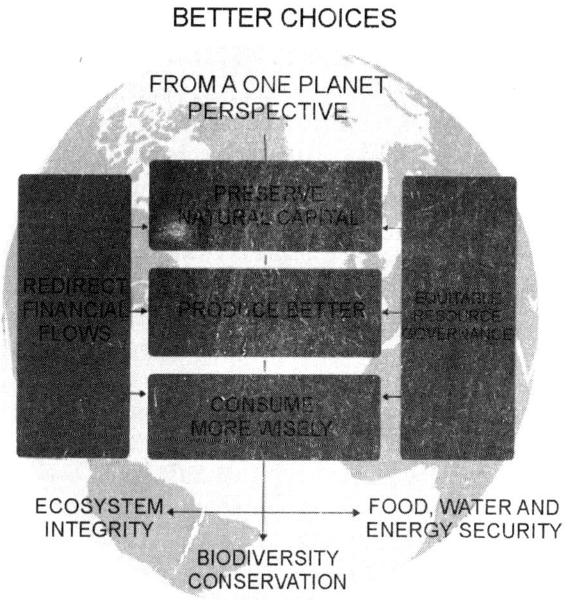

Fig. 1: One Planet Perspective.

Source: WWF, *Living Planet Report 2014.*

Role of Various Stakeholders in Sustainable Consumption

UN Guidelines for Consumer Protection, 1985 mandates that the Governments, in partnership with business and relevant organisations of civil society, should develop and implement strategies that promote sustainable consumption through a mix of policies that could include regulations; economic and social instruments; sectoral policies in such areas as land-use, transport, energy and housing; information programmes to raise awareness of the impact of consumption patterns; removal of subsidies that promote unsustainable patterns of consumption and production; and promotion of sector specific environmental-management best practices.[43] It has to be realized by all the stakeholders in the society that the costs of inaction will be too high. The governments, industry, civil society and consumers are key stakeholders whose initiatives can reduce poverty and drive sustainable economic growth in both developed and developing countries.

(i) Consumers

Green consumers can be defined as those who care sufficiently about the environment to make a conscious effort to buy products that avoid environmental damage. Criteria for defining "green" products include organic, durable, non-toxic, recyclable and using production methods that do not threaten important ecosystems. The majority of consumers pay little attention to environmental issues. Their main interest is "value for money". Since, "green" products tend to be more expensive, price "resistance" is a major constraint on market demand. Either the consumer must be persuaded by better product information or encouraged by more competitive prices. The former might be achieved by a comprehensive system of eco-labelling; the latter, by a comprehensive system of environmental taxation.[44]

Consumer decisions can play an important role in countering unsustainable trends in the following three ways: Firstly, by deciding what products are to be bought, e.g. conventional *vs.* energy-efficient light bulbs. Secondly, by deciding how products are to be used, e.g. by turning the light off when leaving a room or by double-sided printing. Here, consumers exert substantial influence on the ecological and social efficiency of the economy. Thirdly, by deciding how many products are to be bought, e.g. if mobile phones are used until they are out of order instead of buying new ones every year—consumers can increase economic sufficiency, another important lever of sustainability. Consumers have to initiate structural changes towards sustainability by demanding ecologically, socially and ethically produced products. [45]

Consumers' low willingness to act, i.e. to change their purchasing decision and their use and disposal behaviour, can be attributed to several factors. These include perception of the characteristics of sustainable products, societal norms, personal habits and emotions, and lack of information. Consumer behaviour differs in importance depending on the product under consideration. It is easier to communicate the sustainable nature of functional products (e.g. the energy-efficiency of household appliances) than of emotive products (e.g. cars) that are often linked to a certain lifestyle and frequently feature specific product characteristics. Most consumers make their purchasing decisions based on price and fail to consider the potential downside of cheaper products over their entire life cycle leading to high maintenance, high energy and high disposal cost. Consumer purchase decisions are mostly based on: (1) Level of private utility (e.g. convenience, functionality), and (2) Emotivity.[46]

Alongside product characteristics, information plays a key role in affecting consumer behaviour. Consumption choices depend on variety of aspects like price, quality, personal preference, culture, values. It is, therefore, necessary that reliable and understandable product information about the quality, price, health and safety, environmental and social impacts regarding the products and services should be provided to consumers. In this testing and certification tools like impartial product testing, independent product certification and Eco-labelling can play an important role.

The majority of consumers are poorly informed for several reasons:

(1) *Ignorance of Environmental and social issues*, such as climate change and consumers tend to perceive all products as reasonably "sound" in terms of their environmental and social implications.
(2) *Complexity*: Some issues such as climate change and the concept of sustainable development are very complex and diffuse, making them difficult for consumers to grasp from their perspective. This makes it hard to make the "right" purchasing decisions or to adopt sustainable use or disposal behaviour.
(3) *Short product life cycles*: Particularly in the market of fast-moving electronic consumer goods (PCs, cameras etc.), life cycles are so short that product information becomes obsolete very quickly.

In addition to testing of products on certain environmental and social criteria, sustainability labels (eco-labels, fair trade labels, etc.) provide guidance to consumers and are thus an effective means of building credibility and brands. However, having too many labels tends to confuse consumers, which necessitates consolidation of labelling schemes in some product categories through government initiatives. Consumer behaviour is not only highly fragmented, varying across different categories (e.g. energy use, waste, housing, tourism and leisure), but it is also often subject to habits. These habits, which may be associated with certain societal norms, are particularly difficult to change, if they are deeply engrained. It may be possible to convince some consumers to buy more fuel-efficient cars, but it is considerably more difficult to "make" them cycle short distances or to use public transport more.[47]

(ii) Government

Mainly due to an increasing population, changing life styles and rapid development, there has been a phenomenal increase in waste production. There is need to adopt "3R" approach to deal with the problems—reduction, reuse, and recycle. Government needs to develop the right policy framework and legislation that provide incentives to producers to reduce the generation of waste at the source. This includes changing the regulations on packaging and implementing an eco-tax on packaging and/or disposable products which would encourage producers to reduce the packaging or utilize returnable or biodegradable packaging. Producers can very much influence waste minimization/generation for example by reducing unnecessary packaging, and by avoiding the inclusion of substances/components that are difficult to recycle. Likewise, some of the responsibilities for waste minimization lie on consumers. For example, consumers could be motivated to repair faulty products rather than replacing them, reuse products/materials (e.g. exchange of clothes), avoid disposable products such as disposable razors, chopsticks etc. Also, based on the availability and competitive cost, consumers could engage in product substitution to use those products that offer lower resource use (e.g. energy efficient light bulbs) or produce less waste.

Also, governments could intervene on the demand side by providing the right information to consumers about products with less packaging and more environment-friendly products. As regards the waste minimization is concerned production merely focusing on the production aspects alone is insufficient there is need to take into consideration consumption phase also. To prevent environment degradation, recycling of waste also needs to be encouraged. For this, the principles like producer "take back" responsibility are important. Consumers must also take the responsibility for ensuring that the used products are returned to recovery system. Communities have an important role to play in ensuring that community-generated organics (food waste, yard trimmings) are composted and returned safely back into the environment.

Governments as both consumers and policy-setters have an instrumental role to play in SCP. Decision-makers directly and indirectly influence consumer behaviour and the sustainability of production. Information and education campaigns, economic instruments (taxes and rebate schemes) or regulation (standard-setting) can influence consumption and production patterns. Government is also one of the biggest consumers of products and services. It can leverage its support for sustainable procurement to promote change. Further, there is a need to establish incentives for the creation and improvement of markets for sustainable goods and services, to reduce the barriers to trade, improve access to markets and promote fair trade. This is key to ensuring the competitiveness of sustainable goods and services.

However, the policies and instruments used in this respect should take into account local context, cultural values and religions. This would make it possible to recognize a region-specific approach for sustainable consumption and to develop solutions adapted to local circumstances, rather than copying Western models. For countries like India energy, waste, food and agriculture, transport and health are key action areas to implement sustainable consumption policies.[48]

(a) Standards and Mandatory Labels

Mandatory government actions to promote sustainable consumption include performance standards and mandatory labels to limit damages from products when they are consumed or used. In terms of changing consumption patterns, these tools are the most direct policy instruments for eliminating unsustainable products from the market. As the range of consumer concerns widens, governments are being called on to regulate more products in the interest of the environment and general welfare. The most common sustainability-related performance standards arc those aimed at reducing energy use, e.g. promoting energy efficiency in household appliances, effectiveness of home insulation, and fuel economy in motor vehicles. Labels are also used to provide information to consumers on their recycling obligations to encourage greater involvement in the collection and recycling of products and packaging waste. Labels often show the collection and recovery systems available to consumers, the meaning of markings on the packaging itself, and the consumer role in recovery and recycling. Symbols may be required which indicate the type of materials a product is made of, whether it is composed of recycled parts, whether it can be recycled, and/or compliance with a recognised recycling scheme. Mandatory labelling on consumer products for health reasons includes warning labels on cigarettes, health-declaration requirements for nutritional values of food products, labelling of foods with genetically modified contents, and labelling rules for organic food. Nutritional labelling is a main tool for preventing increasing rates of obesity and unhealthy diets.[49]

(b) Voluntary Labelling

One of the most commonly used instruments for influencing sustainable consumer choices is voluntary labelling which has expanded to more products and countries in recent years. The most viable labels are those where environmental or social claims are verified by a third party, including governments and non-governmental organisations. These can be multi-criteria labels, which compare products with others in the same category on a number of impacts throughout their life cycle, or single issue labels which refer to a specific environmental or social characteristic of a product. These labels are most useful when they communicate complex information on sustainability in a simple way and provide transparency which enables consumers to make informed choices. However, the proliferation of voluntary labels on the market has also led to consumer confusion between self-declarations and third-party certified labels.[50]

The Bureau of Energy Efficiency, Ministry of Power has developed a scheme for energy efficiency labelling of equipment. The Objectives of Standards and Labelling Programme is to provide the consumer an informed choice about the energy saving, and thereby the cost saving potential of the marketed household and other equipment. This is expected to impact the energy savings in the medium and long run while at the same time it will position domestic industry to compete in such markets where norms for energy efficiency are mandatory. The scheme currently invoked for equipments/appliances like Frost Free (No-Frost) refrigerator, Tubular Fluorescent Lamps, Room Air Conditioners, Direct Cool Refrigerator, Distribution Transformer, Induction Motors, Pump Sets, Ceiling Fans, LPG, Electric Geysers and Colour TV. The Bureau will appoint an independent agency to evaluate the programme impact and process of implementation on a periodic basis. The scope of evaluation will include the impact on sales, energy consumption, cost, consumer purchasing behaviour, manufacturing, national energy use and the environment. The user of label shall extend full cooperation by providing the relevant data for the purpose.

Eco-labels also play an important role in policy frameworks to implement sustainable consumption. Eco-labelling is a voluntary method of environmental performance of a product or service, within a specific product or service category based on life cycle considerations, e.g. India's Ecomark, Green Food China etc. Eco-labels are always awarded by an impartial third-party that authorizes the use of the label on products in a certain product category. They exist to reward and promote environmentally superior goods and services and offer information on quality and performance with respect to issues such as health and energy consumption.

(c) Taxes and Charges

Taxes and charges can be effective in influencing consumer behaviour towards sustainability by raising prices on less sustainable products. Taxes and charges can be more cost effective than regulations, which may require intensive monitoring efforts, in terms of enforcement and control. Taxes are more efficient than regulations from an economic point of view and give more flexibility to households and firms to adapt. Generally, taxes and charges will influence consumers only, if the financial stimulus is strong enough to enter the decision-making process. Too often, taxes and charges to promote sustainable consumption are not set at a sufficiently high level. When targeting consumers and households, taxes and charges can help limit car emissions (e.g. fuel taxes, purchase or registration taxes, and congestion charges), household energy consumption (e.g. CO_2 taxes, electricity taxes), water-use, and household waste (e.g. waste disposal taxes, packaging taxes). In the health area, taxation is most commonly used to reduce tobacco and alcohol consumption.[51]

(d) Subsidies and Incentives

Subsidies and incentives are given by many governments as "carrots" to encourage consumers and households to make more sustainable product and service selections. These include monetary grants, donations of goods and fiscal incentives in the form of tax reductions. These instruments influence consumer behaviour by making sustainable choices less expensive. Though the amount of these sustainable consumption incentives is small; still, they are valuable in encouraging households to make more sustainable choices and can help counteract "stick" measures for more disadvantaged groups in society. Many OECD countries offer financial incentives for sustainable transport, sustainable household energy investments, such as boilers, energy-efficient windows, insulation, water and space heaters etc.[52]

(e) Consumer Education and Awareness

Communication and awareness raising activities on sustainable consumption should contribute to ensuring smarter and more accessible information on consumption choices to consumers. The guiding principle is that "better informed citizens can make informed choices to bring about concrete changes in their attitudes and behaviour" with beneficial impacts on environmental protection and social cohesion. There are three key means to convey information to consumers where governments can play an active role to reorient consumption patterns towards sustainability, these areas are: awareness raising, consumer education and marketing. Governments, consumer organizations and NGOs working in environment and development can undertake campaigns to raise awareness of consumers on issues related to sustainable consumption.

Consumer education offers more than knowledge and skills on how to buy; it promotes critical thinking, problem solving, and action. Consumer education in the context of sustainable consumption is essentially about empowering consumers to choose sustainable products based on an informed choice or to use some products in a more sustainable way. It is also about helping consumers realize their responsibilities as citizens, both locally and globally. For this, there is need to introduce education for sustainable consumption in the formal education sector. Till now, the education has mainly focused on environment or consumer issues, now it needs to incorporate sustainable consumption. Marketing has a direct impact on the consumption side. Marketing products to encourage sustainable consumption is about providing consumers with information on products or services that satisfy consumer demands without damaging the social fabric or environment along the value chain, e.g. marketing products which are organically grown and purchased directly from farmers.

(f) Sustainable Government Practices—Green Procurement

The government and its various agencies form the biggest single purchaser of goods and services, ranging from basic commodities to high technology equipment. The impact of their purchasing on the market is, therefore, potentially one of the major leverages supporting sustainable production and consumption. Governments purchase products and hire services in very large quantities, thus are in a position to negotiate a good price for a good quality and push companies to adapt their offers to the orders. By defining the conditions and specifications for the products or services, Government procurement can also foster sustainability innovation. In this regard, the local authorities have to be at the forefront in taking some environmental sustainable procurement initiatives.

(g) Regulation of Advertising

Commercial advertising is a powerful force for promoting sustainable consumption in highlighting the sustainability dimensions of goods and services and convincing consumers to purchase these products, sometimes regardless of price. Regulations governing truth in advertising are a basic consumer protection tool in OECD countries, usually contained in fair trading legislation and policed by consumer protection agencies. These generally cover advertising claims made regarding the environmental, social or ethical attributes of products and services.[53]

(h) Legal Framework

In 1999, the UN General Assembly revised the United Nations Guidelines on Consumer Protection to include sustainable consumption in the Objectives and General Principles as well as in a specific new section. The UN Guidelines now encompass conducting sustainable consumption research, promoting recycling and sustainable government practices, encouraging life cycle thinking and eco-products, and developing standards for regulating and verifying environmental claims. The new section on "Promotion of Sustainable Consumption" (Section G) encourages governments "to create or strengthen effective regulatory mechanisms for the protection of consumers, including aspects of sustainable consumption." Most of the consumer protection legislations at present cover false marketing claims related to the environmental and other characteristics of products. However, yet the legislations have not incorporated the UN language in their consumer protection laws and guidelines. There is need to incorporate national sustainable development strategies in the legal framework which apply to sustainable consumption and also facilitate right to environmental information.

(i) Sustainable Consumption Programmes

To make Sustainable Consumption and Production (SCP) a reality, coordinated and integrated programmes are essential, considering in particular the cross-sectoral nature of consumption and production patterns. A strategic programmatic approach can help balance the necessary interventions for the consumption and production of and market for goods and services. It should connect long-term vision to medium-term targets and short-term action. A multi-stakeholder approach is an important prerequisite for implementing SCP. An effective SCP programme should be flexible enough to withstand a process of continuous improvement. Sustainable consumption programmes can promote coherence and realise synergies across a range of policies: consumer, education, economic, social, environmental etc. In the absence of an integrated strategy, disconnected initiatives not only lack cohesion, but also the full force of a range of government ministries and their policy tools. Without coherent approaches to sustainable consumption in terms of sectors (food, energy), actors (households, women, youth) and instruments (regulations, taxes, communications), initiatives may have inconsistencies or significant gaps and be generally ineffective.[54]

(iii) Business Initiatives

Free market economics dictates that companies seek to minimize costs in order to maximize profits regardless of any environmental damage that might be caused. Unless compelled by law, companies have a strong incentive to externalize some costs by exploiting the "free" services of the natural environment. Competitive markets compel companies to cut costs to stay in business even when this damages the environment, e.g. pollution. Indeed, there is an incentive to pollute because it is cheaper to discharge waste materials in the local environment than to invest in pollution abatement. As market prices reflect private (costs and benefits), business decisions are based on faulty and inadequate assessments. By ignoring environmental costs, market prices provide the wrong signals for resource management, leading to an overuse of the environment. Short-term profitability rather than long-term sustainability is the motivating force behind private enterprise. The ethos of economic growth has created a materialistic culture and a society preoccupied with "economic progress". Business has a vested interest in promoting this "culture", thus commercializing more and more of our everyday life. As market "values" reflect society's preferences, the general public will have to campaign, both in their role as consumers and citizens, for a "greener" economy. Further, the push from government in the form of higher environmental standards is forcing more companies to invest in new products and technologies to satisfy stricter environmental regulations on better pollution control, waste management and new product design. While legislation forces companies to change, few companies go beyond satisfying the minimum requirements because of the costs involved. This is when the pull of the market can become a decisive factor and help to reinforce new laws on environmental protection.[55]

A precondition of "greenness" is a corporate philosophy which explicitly incorporates environmental criteria in management decision making. The corporate strategy will include environmental as well as financial objectives, and indicate how these objectives will be monitored and achieved. The following criteria can be used to determine how "green" a company has become:

- **Product criterion**: A company making products which are environment-friendly, e.g. durable, non-polluting, made from recycled materials.
- **Technology criterion**: A company using production/assembly methods that minimize environmental damage, e.g. minimizing waste and pollution, conserving energy.
- **Business ethics criterion**: A corporate philosophy that embraces environmental values, made effective by an environmental policy with specific objectives, e.g. procurement policy to buy components/services from other "green" companies.

Although all three criteria are important, the essential characteristic of a "green" company is the last one. Corporate values must change so that environmental protection becomes an integral part of the corporate strategy.[56]

The transformation imperative is clearly an opportunity for business; if more businesses adopt the principles of sustainable consumption, we have the potential to increase global prosperity while avoiding the depletion of our natural resources and still preserving the ecosystems that underpin our lives. It is equally clear that this transformation can be beneficial for business. Sustainability can and should be thought of as a way to create opportunities and become a substantial source of competitive advantage, not solely as a way to mitigate risk. An economy transformed by sustainable consumption principles will allow companies to explore new business models and design strategies that can open up new market opportunities by promoting radical innovative solutions.[57]

The WBCSD (World Business Council for Sustainable Development) has proposed a seven-point blueprint for corporations: (1) Develop technological and social innovations to improve quality of life and tackle depletion of resources; (2) Practice eco-efficiency to create more value with less impact, growing qualitatively, not quantitatively; (3) Build alliances and move towards partnerships for progress based on common goals, empathy, open feedback, flexibility, ability to compromise and share rewards; (4) Provide and inform consumer choice; (5) Improve market conditions; (6) Establish the worth of the Earth; and (7) Make the market work for everyone.[58]

Design choices about things like material weight and packaging have direct impacts on transportation costs and fuel use, while choices about energy efficiency directly impact energy consumption in a product's use phase. Good design is generally judged based on its ability to meet a need. The challenge is to develop frameworks that allow people to design with the needs of sustainability in mind. For consumer electronics in particular, most business efforts have focused on lowering the energy consumption of products through renewable energy sources and increasing energy efficiency with technological solutions. More than 80 per cent of a product's environmental impact is determined during its design phase. Products should be designed using material that could be easily reused or repaired when they have outlived their usefulness. In some cases, a focus on sustainable consumption may result in the radical redesign of familiar products, and in other cases, there may be an opportunity to deliver the same value through services (such as car-sharing) rather than products (such as car sales).[59]

Consumers do not always have actionable information to make the best choices or use products and services in the best way in terms of sustainability, or in terms of delivering the basic value they seek. Business has many opportunities to engage consumers to increase overall awareness with regard to their consumption choices and behaviour. Products, services, policies, programmes, and communications that reflect user characteristics, needs, and skills can serve to improve, support, and sustain behaviour. The type of communication falls into the four focus areas: (1) Information about social and environmental attributes of products; (2) Information about social and environmental performance of corporate operations; (3) Information on how to reduce impacts during product use; and (4) Information about extending product life cycle and/or end-of-life actions.[60] Corporate sustainability reporting is used by companies to inform consumers of their social and environmental values and practices beyond the sustainability characteristics of individual products, which are usually covered by labelling. Such information disclosure is now one of the main mechanisms by which consumers are informed of the environmental and social conditions under which products have been produced. In addition to goods-producing companies, sustainability reporting is being adopted by firms providing services, including financial (e.g. investments, insurance, pensions), tourism, and transport. Reporting topics include corporate governance, environmental performance, health and safety of employees, community contributions, and supply chain management. The gap between corporate reporting and most notions of sustainable consumption is still large, e.g. not many reports look at how the company's product range supports sustainable consumption in terms of life cycle and social impacts. While many companies have a good track record on corporate reporting, this may not necessarily match actual sustainability practices. Only few countries impose legal obligation regarding sustainability reporting; in most of the countries, it is voluntary with approaches varying by country, sector and company.[61]

At the end of their use, many products are discarded and end-up in landfills. There is a long way to go as regards waste management, such as waste reduction, product reuse, and recycling. The huge amount of waste generated by society today is nothing more than inefficient product design, materials selection and manufacturing, and service-delivery systems. These inefficiencies equate to lost capital and revenue for companies, as a tremendous investment of money and resources is required to extract raw materials, process them, turn them into manufactured products, and then deliver them to the consumer. Design for environment programmes focus on energy efficiency, materials innovation, and design for recyclability. Today, leading companies are striving for zero emissions, which means that all materials currently ending-up in landfills or incinerators are returned "upstream" to the materials and production cycle as feedstock for new products or services, or they are created to naturally decompose and be reintegrated into nature without environmental impacts.

Conclusion

It is amply clear that the world cannot achieve sustainable economic growth with old fashioned consumption and production patterns. Modern civilization now constitutes a dense network of sub-units which has become huge and highly complex and is unable to form a well-functioning system. Unless it conforms to the law of the nature and evolves a feedback mechanism to get over the systemic problems as and when they arise, it is sure to crash, sooner or later. Decoupling environmental impact from economic growth is an essential prerequisite for sustainable development. For this, all the stakeholders need to join hand and take steps in maintaining the environmental balance and promote sustainable lifestyles. Government must clarify the objectives for consumer action, reinforce existing policies and laws, and support the initiatives of private sector and civic actors to develop sustainable life styles. Companies have to accelerate the trends of polluting less and of designing, producing and marketing better products and services. Consumers have to get used to the fact that environmental considerations are as important in their daily choices as considerations of price, convenience and quality. Governments and civil society have a key role to play in, there is thus need for innovative and concerted efforts to decouple economic growth from natural resource extraction and environmental degradation inspiring such a process.

In the chapter "*Sustainable Consumption—A Gandhian Perspective*", by Dr. Sapna Chadah has highlighted the Gandhian philosophy that offers a practical way to a peaceful social revolution to improve the quality of life and protect environment. Mahatma Gandhi is perhaps the only great thinker who could foresee the social and ecological consequences of the exploitative model of development and offer an alternative model. If we look at Gandhian views on sustainable development, non-violence, the rural lifestyle, the agrarian lifestyle, and sustainability are far more relevant today than they ever were. He identified with the poor, took-up issues of the poor, realized that consumerism and people who try to enrich themselves are not a good thing. Gandhiji saw economic reasoning based on people rather than on consumer goods as the way to social and environmental sustainability. Gandhi abhorred the profit motive which is the main characteristic of modern industrialism. He rejected the view that profit was the source of pleasure and the lack of it the source of pain. Gandhi's philosophy offers a practical way to a peaceful social revolution to improve the quality of life. What he preached was not only for the Indian masses, but for the entire deprived people of the world. His message was not for a particular time, but for the future of the mankind, especially his theory of non-violence and peaceful co-existence. Gandhiji with his commonsense approach to technology, production and consumption can surely be relied upon as guide with regard to sustainable production and consumption. Environmental protection found place of importance in his scheme. According to him, society has to limit its wants. Greed will destroy the world and in this way he focused on sustainable consumption.

The chapter "*Challenges of Sustainable Consumption: Indian Context*" by Dr. Sheetal Kapoor attempts to study the challenges of sustainable consumption in the Indian context. The idea is not to thwart the juggernaut of Indian consumerism, but to change the direction towards sustainable consumption. The perspectives of various stakeholders have been analysed and recommendations made. Rapid industrialization and globalization has lead to the emergence of transnationals and multinationals that in turn are leading to environmental damage in many ways. Ethical consumption has become imperative for consumers, as well as businesses around the world. Every single purchase decision has an effect on the environment, business, consumers and the workers who manufacture the products. Therefore, what is required is a responsible behaviour from all stakeholders in preserving the environment. In the Indian society, life styles have largely been regulated by long-standing practices. Since, ancient times Indians have believed in *Aparigraha* (non-possession), conservation of resources, and in need-based consumption, not want-based. Economic reforms carried on since 1991 have produced remarkable results, making India one of the most exciting prospects among the emerging markets. The Indian middle class has become wealthy and there is a major shift in consumer behaviour. An Indian consumer who at one point of time was saving for the rainy day is not hesitant in taking home loans, car loans and does not shy away from spending on the life's luxury. Whereas the West which is already facing a consumerist society, the governments and the social organizations are educating business and the consumers about ethical consumption, will thc Indian consumer with its new found wealth think about sustainable consumption?

In the chapter "*Corsumption: Need vs. Greed—Gandhian Alternative*", Dr. Indramchan Jha has highlighted the Gandian way of living which focused on need-based consumption. For Gandhi, greed is the root cause of all ills of humanity. He was not opposed to a machine necessary for human well-being. He despised only the craze for machine geared to more and more production only for hoarding and making profit to be amassed by a few. Such a mindless production process is based on the principle that an ever-increasing consumption is good for economy. This, in turn, is sustained by a new modernist value system emphasizing the unlimited desires of human beings and their overweening ambitions to achieve rare goals. Every human action is directed towards physical pleasure, power and strong positions to dominate. Such a social culture produced a large-scale industrialization and mushrooming of urban slums as centres of all vices. This has caused an irreparable ecological imbalance. The twenty-first century witnessed the culmination of machine and modernity. However, it has its horrendous pitfalls as well. Existence of threatening environmental crises are already there. Billions are spent on leisure and pleasure while millions die of hunger and disease. What a paradox of development! Thus, a modern man lives under the brutal tyranny of artificial wants and desires. This has alienated him from his species being and the society as well.

Certain initiatives, such as value education and ethical consumerism are taken to salvage the situation. Undoubtedly, there is a growing concern for ethical consumerism attaching economic values to concern for human rights, animal rights and environment. Ethical consumer market has grown as people are opting for green house-cars, local shopping, organic foods, energy-efficient boilers and bulbs, ethical cosmetics etc. However, they have made little impact to address to the root cause of greed. Follies of capitalism-communism have brought Gandhism to the fore as a hope for humanity. Other 'isms' rely upon external-institutional control whereas Gandhi preached and practiced internal-spiritual limits. He emphasized the values of non-stealing, detachment, contentment etc. for people living in small village communities having self-sufficient economy to fulfil their basic needs. Thus, there can be a meaningful life with a balance of rights and duties as a societal goal instead of individual pursuit.

Dr. Roopa Vajpeyi in "*Cultural Dimensions of Sustainability*" has explored cultural dimensions of sustainable consumption especially significant from the Indian perspective. Despite a vast amount of available discussions on sustainability, a universally acceptable definition or an understanding of what it involves when applied to the day-to-day life, and to raising the quality of life for an average consumer, no clear indicators are available. This chapter tries to build focus on the relevant areas of concern in this field for Indian consumers and other stakeholders, and how these can be used or reconnected with, in their existing modes or reinvented for common use. Currently two tracks concerning Sustainability have emerged. One emanating from the West which incorporates words like 'Green', 'Ethical', 'Organic' etc. which focuses on production processes and the marketed consumption patterns. This track, though emerging in urban spaces is mostly irrelevant for the common consumers as they either lack familiarity with the jargon or can simply not afford to participate in it. The other which needs clear articulation and documentation, is the Asian, or more specifically, the Indian track. This has certain specificities, like culture, tradition, experiential knowledge, conventional good practices, a life skills base and informal sectors, which are managed locally and are also people centric, rather than machine centric. This can and should reconnect to the Gandhian concepts of commerce and its role in day-to-day life-choices. How, Is, What this chapter tries to explore. Differences in literacy levels and access to purchasing power are also responsible for marked differences in the two approaches. A recent Global survey has rated Indian consumers as the greenest consumers of the year, with a marked and steady increase in sustainable practices and preferences adopted even by urban Indian consumers. What are the factors responsible for this and what are the steps that are needed to endorse, retain and improve the sustainable profile of the Indian consumer. Specific roles need to be defined for the various stake-holders and highlighted. The chapter also touches upon the role of consumer education, with specific focus on the role of sustainability in the formal education streams. This will focus on how to build on, and incorporate exposure to and understanding of the role of culture and tradition in sustainable consumption and production for the young. In conclusion, the threats to the Indian model of sustainability due to forces of urbanization, aggressive marketing, lack of connectivity with tradition and culture are highlighted. Solutions, if any are also suggested.

In chapter "*Towards Ethical Sustainable Consumption*", Dr. Mamta Pathania has highlighted the increased levels of consumption that have accompanied our consumer-oriented culture. The consumers have also started questioning their individual consumption choices, with many options for greater consumption simplicity. This link between consideration of actual consumption levels and consumer choices is evident among a group of consumers known as *ethical consumers*. Ethical consumers consider a range of ethical issues in their consumer behavioural choices. Particularly prevalent is voluntary simplification due to concerns for the extent and nature of consumption. The present chapter brings out the relationship of consumer attitudes to consumption levels, and how these attitudes impact approaches to consumer behaviour. Taking commodity consumption as a field in which the ethics, morality, and politics of responsibility has been problematical, it is argued that existing research on consumption fails to register the full complexity of the practices, motivations and mechanisms through which the working-up of moral selves is undertaken in relation to consumption practices. Rather than assuming that ethical decision-making works through the rational calculation of obligations, one witnesses the emergence of ethical consumption as ways in which everyday practical moral behaviours are re-articulated by policies, campaigns and practices. Ethical consumption, then, involves both a governing of consumption and a governing of the consuming self. The sustainable consumption in the market place cannot be achieved unless the target market's ethical concerns are addressed. This chapter provides a coherent synthesis of aspects dealing with consumption and sustainability. It offers an invaluable 'route map' through the complex intellectual terrain relevant to the pursuit of sustainable consumption.

In *"Consumers and Sustainable Consumption: Towards a Sustainable Global Society"*, Dr. Jayashree Pillai has tried to present issues facing the society in the context of consumerism. The lure of consumption is leading us to a never before scenario of wastage and pollution, at the cost of several traditional values. The last few decades have seen dramatic changes on a global scale due to political developments, changing consumer patterns and rapid progress in information and communication technology. Globalization has emerged as a key word leading to the emergence of a global village and community. In the wake of consumerism, we are witnessing unforeseen social, environmental and cultural changes. On the one hand, the developed nations are trying to lead other countries with manufactured goods, while on the other, the developing nations are struggling to cope with the emerging market changes. In our incessant effort to buy and accumulate things, consumers today have neglected concern for health or environment. This process has grown into threats for the very existence of the human race. The so-called progress is adding to the environmental degradation the world has been facing. The consumers today have to induce significant changes. The proliferation of technology and the ease of manufacturing goods should also show responsibility towards the future of the planet. Sustainable consumption should be the preferred option. Development in harmony with nature and sustainable consumption only will lead to a better future, not reckless shopping for unnecessary things just to have the satisfaction of something fashionable or to fulfil our insatiable lust for accumulation.

In *"Transforming Unsustainable Lifestyles—Key to Sustainable Consumption"*, Ms. Shruti Mittal and Mr. Suresh Prasad Singh have assessed the ways through which consumer ecological footprint can be minimized. This can be achieved by increasing the consumption of green goods. But there is an obstacle as their cost of production is higher than the non-green variants. This can be tackled with a two-pronged approach—reduction in cost of production and increasing consumer willingness to pay a premium for environment friendly goods. Production cost can be reduced by government subsidies and development of relevant technology. Simultaneously, consumers, whose consumption decisions are driven by utility gains, can be educated about the value addition from green consumption such as better physical health and quality of life, lower stress, simplicity in consumption patterns, along with long term economic and environmental benefits, i.e. lower pollution and cleaner atmosphere. This will encourage them to pay an environmental premium, i.e. the price differential between green and non-green products. Eventually, with economies of scale, the differential will shrink and larger masses will have access to these goods. A holistic approach with active involvement of various stakeholders—the government, producers, CSOs, media, and the people at large—will be essential. This research chapter analyses how the movement towards sustainable consumption could be strengthened.

The chapter "*Rethinking Development: People Centred Approach to Sustainable Consumption*" by Ms. Rashmi Tripathi is a systematic effort towards assessing the sustainable consumption initiatives specifically recycling programmes, energy efficient living, and organic food systems in terms of what they represent, what they may lead to, where they came from, and whether they are or can be successful. The chapter concludes with some reflections on how sustainable consumption initiatives can be made more effective using people centric approach. Despite many mistakes and failed initiatives in the past, we can see just as many signs of hope and some clear paths to a brighter future. We need to rethink development, building upon what has worked and rigorously rejecting failed approaches. One lesson learnt is that people must be at the centre of development—not only in the traditional sense that people are the engine of change, but also in the less traditional sense of development that puts people first. People are the critical factor in development: firstly, in terms of their numbers and the social, health, economic and environmental consequences of their actions; and secondly, in terms of the decisions they make concerning the size of their families and the way they live their lives. People-centred development also means full community participation at both decision-making and implementation levels. A second lesson is that development must be sustainable and environmentally sound. If economic development destroys the earth's natural resource base in the process, it is self-defeating. The other aspect of sustainable development is population growth; the number of people must be in balance with the resources to sustain them, otherwise the whole system will collapse.

Ms. K. Shailaja Rao in "*Sustainable Consumption or Sustainable Resource Management—Whose Responsibility*?" has emphasized that it is very difficult to get individuals, families, schools, hospitals, companies and government departments to think critically about the impact of their consumption patterns, especially in the days of inflation, low economic progress and overflowing expenses. However, it has become imperative for government agencies and non-government agencies alike to encourage consumers to think on the lines of changing their consumer activities for sustainable consumption. Change is necessary in their thinking patterns, both 'Top-Down' and 'Bottom-Up'. It is a matter of grave concern that, because of the inequalities of the advanced countries of the world, their unsustainable consumption practices and the underdeveloped and developing nations where the basic consumer needs are not being met, the planet is getting to a point of no return. These affluent lifestyles and excessive demands place great stress on governments. The governments of the affluent nations, therefore, should take a posture towards encouraging efficiency in production patterns, reduce wasteful consumption in the name of economic growth, and encourage sustainable methods of production and consumption, to accommodate developing nations. The key issues of consumerism have to be brought to the fore-front, along with health, citizenship, ecological conservation and the need for education in sustainability. Illogical consumerism has become a part of contemporary life, and its effects on social, economic and ecological trends need to be analyzed thoughtfully. If we cannot change consumption patterns, we have to look at other ways of sustaining the resources. This is where efficient waste management plays an important role.

In his chapter "*Contributory Role of Panchayati Raj in Facilitating Sustainable Economic Development*", Dr. Joseph Benjamin has highlighted the importance of Panchayati Raj Institutions in sustainable development at grassroots level and role of people's participation in preserving the environment not only for today, but also for the future generations. Any strategy for sustainable development must involve the people at all levels. For this, there is a need for revitalizing Panchayati Raj Institutions. The Panchayati Raj Institution can be recognized as a catalyst for participative planning and implementation of various development programmes especially sustainable development at grass-roots level. Panchayats have been the backbone of the Indian villages since the very beginning of the history. They are engines of growth, agents of change and sustainable development. Sustainable development is a pattern of resource use that aims to meet human needs while preserving the environment so that these needs can be met not only in the present, but also for future generations. Sustainable development can be defined as "the kind of human activity that nourishes and perpetuates the whole community of life on Earth." How the environment can be preserved? How the human needs can be met not only for the present generation, but also for the future? Here the role of Panchayati Raj would be very vital. People's participation and planning in rural areas in sustainable development is very important. The present chapter focuses on the role of Panchayati Raj in sustainable development also. This chapter highlights the role of Panchayati Raj and at the same time studies the various governmental schemes launched in rural areas for preserving the natural resources like water, mountains, riverbeds, soil, and land etc. which are to be used by future generations too.

In chapter "*Sustainable Consumption: Consumer Education and Awareness*", Ms. Ramaben R. Mavani and Mr. Ramjibhai B. Mavani have discussed the ways to achieve the aim of consumer education and awareness and how to give an outreach to the movement so that sustainable consumption patterns are adhered to by all. The consumption in olden days and modern day consumption differs a lot. Effect of industrialization, overpopulation, capitalism, super markets and malls, greed to possess and have more and more, advertisements, shopping, instincts etc., on consumption have led to a different picture of Consumption. Consumption of depleting natural resources, effect of corruption on sustainable consumption and exploitation of natural resources, use of disposable and use and throw goods even when other sustainable alternatives are available are some of the examples of declining consumption patterns. With all this, is it possible to achieve sustainability? To inculcate the habit of sustainable consumption there is need for mass education programmes at enormous scale, covering urban and rural population. The present chapter talks about programmes at urban and rural levels, inclusion of subject in schools and colleges curriculum, role of Government agencies and NGOs in generating awareness, awareness through street plays, media, slide shows, seminars, workshops, are some of the means to achieve the desired results.

"*Trend Analysis of Sustainable Consumption in Corporate Reporting*" by Mr. Anand Acharya and Ms. Bansuri Das intends to examine the sustainable consumption in context of social justice in two spheres—society and international community. The chapter has been attempted in the backdrop of the following predominant assumptions: (1) Sustainable consumption needs to be discussed in the interest of half of the world's population that are poor; and (2) Equity in consumption is a major challenge of the international community that seeks to regulate unsustainable consumption pattern. The important aspects need to be taken care of. Firstly, the high incidence of poverty and ignorance are the salient features of the Indian society, particularly rural society. Thus, the main objective and goal of sustainable consumption in India is creating well-being and happiness among all the people. The main challenge is to improve the 'living standards' of all. Secondly, studies have shown that the developed countries are harsher in disturbing the environmental equilibrium by emitting large scale green house gases to the atmosphere. As the atmosphere knows no political boundaries, the adverse impacts in the shape of global warming, ozone depletion, acid rain have affected poor developing countries like India. The chapter suggests that there is need of raising awareness and educating people about marketing campaigns; educating people about management of waste in terms of reduction, reusing, recover and recycling the waste; monitoring on certification and product information; implementing sustainable practices; and provisions for independent testing of products.

Dr. Jyoti Marwah in "*Promoting Business Enabling Medicinal and Aromatic Plants in the Indian Himalayan Region: Role of Government, Non-Government and Community Based Organizations*" has highlighted some of the measures taken by governmental and non-governmental organizations in maintaining the biodiversity in the Himalayan region. The conflict between man and eco-systems and socio-cultural matrices has a direct impact on the bio-diversity of any region. To add to this is a major concern related to climate change. The Indian Himalayan region has been directly impacted for all the reasons mentioned above. This naturally leads to depletion and marginalization of natural resources through loss of vegetation, degradation of soil and water quality and quantity. The importance of maintaining Himalayan bio-diversity becomes imperative not only for the present, but for posterity. Recognizing this need, government research institutions like HRDI, FRI and CIMAP have developed short term and long term programmes; to this is added private initiative. Accordingly, the Government of Uttarakhand issued a G.O. 913/gv/2003 regarding conservation, development and sustainable harvesting of medicinal plants. Thereafter, the government institutions of Uttarakhand collected 534 species of medicinal and aromatic plants including the endangered ones from various parts of the region to develop a herbarium. For documentation of the extent of systematic cultivation of medicinal and aromatic plants, the Government of Uttarakhand issued another order in May 2005 for registration of farmers participating in the development of medicinal and aromatic plants sector in the State. Civil Society Organisations, CBOs and Self-Help Groups (SHGs) are also contributing in sustainable conservation, domestication and propagation of MAPs. Paravatiya Jadi Booti Sansthan, Mussoorie, a registered NGOs works for the conservation and commercial use of a large number of medicinal and aromatic plants in Mussoorie. The Sansthan also promotes the prospects of these plants for economic enhancement among the women and villages in and around Mussoorie by conducting workshops and training programmes. The Sansthan has undertaken efforts in the domestication of wild species of *kapoor kacheri* from its own forest land which has resulted in generation of a cultivar. The Sansthan's future plans are to give a new life to the rocky and bare mountain stetches of Mussoorie ranges through an environmentally sound and sustainable programme to green these hills with MAPs. This will also provide the people with an option for sustainable benefits.

In chapter "*Awareness of Organic Farming in Promotion of Sustainable Agricultural Produce and Environment Protection: A Study With Reference to Goa*", Mr. Santosh B. Patkar and Mr. Henrique Dsouza have focused on the importance of organic farming, its benefits to farmers in getting higher price and also promoting environment balance. The present competitive market compels farmers to produce better quality of products in lesser time so that they can get advantage of market. This is possible by using high yielding variety of seeds quality, fertilizers and pesticides which are health hazardous. Today's consumer prefers to pay a higher price if the produce is safe and hazard free. The customers in rural areas may prefer low quality and higher quantity of produce at lower price, but in urban areas consumer are becoming more health conscious. They do not mind purchasing goods at higher prices. Hence, there is a tremendous demand for organic produce. Farmers, however, are not aware of the demand for organic produce. Organic farming reduces the use of fertilizers, chemicals and pesticides which benefits to the end users. In this study, the researchers selected Goa as a case study for organic farming. In Goa mining and tourism industry provides large number of employment opportunities. The Government has taken various measures to promote agriculture sector. There is growth of organic farms in Goa for which awareness among the consumers and farmers is required so that more and more farmers are educated about importance of organic farming. The consumers will also benefit from the development of organic farming and consumption of agriculture produce. Since, organic produce has high demands, it can also fetch a high price which will benefit farmers in increasing their revenue. The study tries to develop relationship between growth of organic farms and environmental issues. The researchers have suggested some measures to create awareness about organic produce and to educate farmers in managing sustainable consumption of agricultural produce.

Tourism is a multi-dimensional activity that brings enormous impact on the society by creating a meaningful employment, economic assets, socio-cultural affinities and environmental benefits to the indigenous population. However, it can cause considerable damage to the environment.

In "*Eco-Tourism: A Case Study of Beaches in Goa*", Dr. Badruddin has highlighted the concept of Eco-Tourism which is responsible travel to fragile, pristine, and usually protected areas that strives to be low impact and often small in scale. It helps to educate the travellers, provide funds for ecological conservation, benefit the community development, enhances the political empowerment of locals, and foster respect for different cultures. Eco-Tourism is held as important by those who participate in it so that future generations may experience aspects of the environment relatively untouched by human intervention. Generally, it focuses on volunteering, personal growth and environmental responsibility. Such process typically involves travel to destinations where flora, fauna, and cultural heritage are the primary attractions. One of the goals of eco-Tourism is to offer tourists insight into the impact of human beings on the environment, and to foster a greater appreciation of our natural habitats. This he has highlighted through the case study of Goa where Goa Tourism Development Corporation with assistance of Beach Management Support and local NGOs continue to emphasize on enlightening, participatory travel experience and welfare of local villagers near the coast. Emphasis is given "Keep Beaches Clean, Healthy, Wealthy, Wise and Natural" so as to maintain the ethics of "Green Principles". Incentives are also given for sale of eco-friendly products, inhabitants in cottages built with bamboos and naturally filtered resources, collection of articles in natural museums, organization of open air *yoga* camps, hiking, trekking, birds watching, boat cruise water sports and host of more attractions. Maintenance of turtle nest sites, water springs, medicinal plants, unattended palm trees, coral reefs, hillocks, waterfalls and springs, naturally preserved animals are important for eco-tourism. The unexplored 106 kilometre beaches in Goa have vast potential for conservation and preservation, blessed with variety of flora and fauna. The beaches provide effective arena for conduct of eco-tourism. The local administration in Goa has already given guidelines for water treatment and waste management based on WTO Directives. Prominent organizations organize workshops, conferences, seminars and public meetings to discuss the ethics of Beach Management and promotion of environmental awareness with the help of integrated holistic approach.

Metal ions presence in natural or industrial wastewater, their potential impact and removal has become major area of research in environmental science from the last few decades. Increased knowledge about toxicological effects of heavy metals on the environment is well recognized and therefore, priority is given to regulate heavy metal concentration at the discharge level.

In the chapter "*Fungal Biosorbents and Biosorption: A Review Article*", Mr. Pawan Kumar Rose and Ms. Rani Devi have suggested that there are number of treatment methods for the removal of heavy metals from metal-bearing wastewater as reduction, ion exchange, electrodialysis, electrochemical precipitation, evaporation, solvent extraction, reverse osmosis, chemical precipitation and adsorption. Most of these methods have their own limitations like high capital and operation cost, incomplete metal removal, low selectivity, high energy consumption and they generate toxic slurries that are difficult to eliminate. A variety of biomaterials are showing heavy metal removal potential including fungi, algae, bacteria, actinomycetes, yeast etc. along with some biopolymers and biowaste materials. In this review, the biosorption abilities of fungal biomass towards metal ions removal are emphasized. Effect of parameters such as *p*H, contact time, biomass and metal ion concentration, temperature, physical or chemical pre-treatment of biomass, presence of many ligands in solution, are covered in this study. Available data recommends more advance research and development of the fungal biosorption technology.

For a problem to enter into the arena of public discourse or become part of the political process media coverage is crucial. The mass media have been attributed a major role as a forum for public debate in general, where "*various social groups, institutions, and ideologies struggle over the definition and construction of social reality*". It is the mass-media, which are often held-up as the cause for the higher awareness of environmental issues. People had been aware of the environmental deterioration in a limited localised context for a long time, but in the recent past the media have played an important role in broadening that awareness and transforming many discrete problems into a major public issue. What had previously been perceived as individual difficulties were redefined as part of a more general problem of 'the environment'. The Indian media that rejected the claims of environmental groups as a Western fad irrelevant to India in the 1970s began paying attention to their claims by the 1980s. It was found that the 'environment' frame was inconsistent with the media perception of 'development'. Several environmental organizations and civil society groups in India have been making claims and influencing media frames of environmental problems.

In "*Media and Environmentalism: Coverage, Claims-Making and Framing of Environmental Issues*", Dr. D.S. Poornananda and Mr. K.G. Vasuki have examined how claims-makers are treated and how the mainstream media frame key environmental issues. It also analyzes whether the treatment of claims-makers and media frames change through time. A content analysis of major national daily newspapers has been made along with a case study of coverage of climate change as an environmental issue. The study helps in understanding the association between claims-making by environmental and civil society groups and framing of the environmental issues in media.

The challenge of sustainable development is a global phenomenon. Businesses can play vital role in fostering more sustainable levels and patterns of consumption, to meet this global challenge. The business has important opportunity to help consumers to choose and use their goods and services sustainable. As a social responsibility of business on one hand and the corporate ethics (or commitment with stakeholders) on the other hand, business must create sustainable value for consumers and simultaneously they should respect environmental limits and common values. The role of business in mainstreaming the sustainable consumption is to be analysed and for this purpose, the business approaches to sustainable consumption may be categorized into three groups: (i) Innovation, (ii) Choice Influencing, and (iii) Choice Editing.

In chapter "*Business Approaches to Sustainable Consumption with Reference to Entrepreneurship Development and Innovation Perspective*", Dr. Shrikrishna S. Mahajan has discussed the business approaches to sustainable consumption in the context of climate change. He has also tried to cover the entrepreneurship development and innovation perspective of this issue. The sustainable business practices in terms of corporate social responsibility, corporate governance, business ethics, environment management, environmental accounting etc. have been analysed.

In chapter "*Greening the Marketing Mix: Rethinking Competition during Climate Change*", Mr. Praveen Goyal and Dr. Zillur Rahman have dealt with the comparison of green marketing mix adopted by the various companies in FMCG group. We have taken a sample of companies that fall in the list of listed with BSE FMCG Index and CNX FMCG Index, with some adjustments, using CMIE Database. Through statistical analysis we have presented the relationship between the four Ps in promoting and competing with other companies. The chapter aims to investigate the marketing mix adopted by the companies in order to position and promote their products in the competitive markets during climate change. It describes the status of FMCG companies, discusses critical areas of marketing concerns by examining and comparing the marketing mix, and concludes with lessons that the managers can take from this study in order to adopt better green strategy.

Notes

1. WWF, *Living Planet Report 2014,* Geneva, WWF, (2014), http://wwf.panda.org/about_our_earth/all_publications/living_planet_report/ accessed on December 22, 2015, pp. 8-12.
2. WWF, (2006) *Living Planet Report 2006*, Geneva, WWF.
3. Worldwatch Institute (2004), *State of the World,* Washington DC, Norton.
4. Addis Ababa Meeting of the Marrakech Process, June 2006,
5. UNDP (1998). *Human Development Report*, 1998. New York: UNDP.
6. UNEP (2003). "*Forging New Paths to Sustainable Development*", UNEP Background Paper, Asia Pacific Expert Meeting on Promoting Sustainable Consumption and Production Patterns, Yogyakarta, Indonesia, 21-23 May.
7. R.P. Misra, "Facing Environmental Challenges: The Gandhian Way", *Anasakti Darshan*, Vol. 5, No. 2, July–December 2009, pp. 1-47 at pp. 10, 26-27.
8. R.P. Misra, "Facing Environmental Challenges: The Gandhian Way", *Anasakti Darshan*, Vol. 5, No. 2, July–December 2009, pp.1-47, at p. 9, 19-20.
9. World Commission on Environment and Development, 1987.
10. Norwegian Ministry of the Environment, Oslo Roundtable on Sustainable Production and Consumption. (1994).
11. *Oslo Rountable on Sustainable Production and Consumption, http://www.iisd.ca/consume/oslo004.html* accesed on November 13, 2015.
12. *Introduction to Sustainable Consumption in Europe and Asia—Background paper for SC. Asia cross-learning seminar*, pp. *2-3, http://www.unep.fr/scp/nap/pdf/BackgroundSC.pdf*
13. "*What is Sustainable Consumption?*", www.unesco.org/education/tlfs/TLFS/theme
14. Sustainable Development Goals (SDGs), http://www.undp.org/content/undp/en/home/sdgoverview/post-2015-development-agenda.html
15. http://www.undp.org/content/undp/en/home/sdgoverview/post-2015-development-agenda.html
16. http://www.undp.org/content/undp/en/home/sdgoverview/post-2015-development-agenda/goal-12.html
17. *Introduction to Sustainable Consumption in Europe and Asia—Background paper for SC. Asia cross-learning seminar,* p. 13. *http://www.unep.fr/scp/nap/pdf/BackgroundSC.pdf*
18. UNEP, "*Planning for Change – Guidelines for National Programme on Sustainable Consumption and Production*", United Nations Environment Programme, 2008, p. 20.

19. *Introduction to Sustainable Consumption in Europe and Asia—Background paper for SC. Asia cross-learning seminar*, pp. 2-3, *http://www.unep.fr/scp/nap/pdf/BackgroundSC.pdf*
20. UN, 1992: para 4.3
21. UN, 1992: para 4.17.
22. *Ibid.*, para 4.18d.
23. *Ibid.*, para 4.19b.
24. *Ibid.*, para 4.19b.
25. *Ibid.*, para 4.21.
26. *Ibid.*, para 4.22a.
27. *Ibid.*, para 4.22b.
28. *Ibid.*, para 4.23.
29. *Ibid.*, para 4.25.
30. *Ibid.*, para 4.26.
31. OECD—Organisation for Economic Cooperation and Development, *Sustainable Consumption and Production: Clarifying the Concepts*, Organisation for Economic Cooperation and Development, Paris (1997).
32. Norwegian Ministry of Environment, *Oslo Ministerial Roundtable Conference on Sustainable Production and Consumption*, Government of Norway, Oslo, (1995).
33. UNCSD—United Nations Commission on Sustainable Development, *Report of the Commission on Sustainable Development on its Second Session, 16-27 May, 1994*, United Nations, New York,(1994); and UNCSD—United Nations Commission on Sustainable Development, *Changing Consumption and Production Patterns: Report of the Secretary General, Commission on Sustainable Development, Third Session, 11-28 April, 1995*, United Nations, New York (1995).
34. UNCSD—United Nations Commission on Sustainable Development (1995b), *Report on the Third Session,* 11-28 April, 1995, United Nations Commission on Sustainable Development, United Nations, New York.
35. http://unctad.org/en/Pages/DITC/CompetitionLaw/UN-Guidelines-on-Consumer-Protection.aspx accessed on August 25, 2016.
36. *Introduction to Sustainable Consumption in Europe and Asia—Background paper for SC. Asia cross-learning seminar*, p. 4, http://www.unep.fr/scp/nap/pdf/BackgroundSC.pdf
37. Sustainable consumption and production, https://sustainabledevelopment.un.org/topics/sustainableconsumption and production accessed on November 13, 2015.
38. UNEP, *Planning for Change – Guidelines for National Programme on Sustainable Consumption and Production*, United Nations Environment Programme, 2008, pp. 10, 20-21 and Sustainable consumption and production, https://sustainabledevelopment.un.org/topics/sustainable consumptionandproduction accessed on November 13, 2015.
39. Report of the United Nations Conference on Sustainable Development, Rio de Janeiro, Brazil, 20–22 June, 2012, United Nations, New York, 2012.

http://www.uncsd2012.org/content/documents/814UNCSD%20REPORT%20final%20revs.pdf
40. Sustainable Consumption: Stakeholder Perspectives, p. 12, http://www3.weforum.org/docs/WEF_ENV_SustainableConsumption_Book_2013.pdf
41. UNEP Post 2015 Note #2: Sustainable Consumption and Production and the SDGs, http://www.unep.org/post2015/Portals/50240/Documents/UNEP%20Publications/UNEPBriefingNote2.pdf
42. WWF, *Living Planet Report 2014* Geneva, WWF, (2014), http://wwf.panda.org/about_our_earth/all_publications/living_planet_report/ accessed on December 22, 2015, p.100.
43. UN Guidelines for Consumer Protection, Section G SC.
44. Roarty, Michael; Greening business in a market economy; *European Business Review*, Bradford: 1997, Vol. 97, Iss. 5, p. 244.
45. Regina Schwegler, Burcu Tuncer, Daniel Peter: CSCP Background Paper—Sustainable Consumption Consumers as Trendsetters for Sustainability? *INRATE,* Zurich, March, 2008, p. 5; http://www.inrate.com/Inrate/media/Documents/Studies/2008-03-Study_Sustainable-Consumption_EN.pdf
46. Oliver Salzmann, Heike Leitschuh Fecht, Ulrich Steger, and Aileen Ionescu-Somers: *The Challenge of Sustainable Consumption and the Role of Business as a Solution,* Forum for Corporate Sustainability Management, 2006, pp. 3-6. https://www.imd.org/research/publications/upload/CSM_Salzmann_Fecht_Steger_Inoescu_Somers_WP_2006_09.pdf accessed on December 25, 2015
47. *Ibid.*
48. For Sustainable Consumption Tools see UNEP, *Advancing Sustainable Consumption in Asia—A Guidance Manual*, Division of Technology Industry and Economics, UNEP, 2005, pp. 15-19.
49. Promoting Sustainable Consumption—Good Practices in OECD Countries, OECD 2008, pp.9-11, http://www.oecd.org/greengrowth/40317373.pdf / 62 accessed on December 25, 2015.
50. Promoting Sustainable Consumption—Good Practices in OECD Countries, OECD 2008, pp. 29-31; http://www.oecd.org/greengrowth/40317373.pdf / 62 accessed on December 25, 2015.
51. *Ibid.*, pp.13-15.
52. *Ibid.*, pp. 17-19.
53. *Ibid.*, pp. 37-38.
54. Planning for Change—Guidelines for National Programmes on Sustainable Consumption and Production, United Nations Environment Programme, 2008, pp. 21-22; http://www.unep.org/pdf/UNEP_Planning_for_change_2008.pdf; Promoting Sustainable Consumption—Good Practices in OECD Countries, OECD 2008, pp. 53-54, http://www.oecd.org/greengrowth/40317373.pdf / 62 accessed on December 25, 2015.
55. Roarty, Michael: Greening business in a market economy, *European Business Review*; Bradford: 1997, Vol. 97, Iss. 5, p. 244.

56. *Ibid.*
57. *The New Frontier in Sustainability—the Business Opportunity in Tackling Sustainable Consumption*, BER, July 2010, www.bsr.org
58. UNEP, Advancing Sustainable Consumpion in Asia—A Guidance Manual, UNEP Division of Technology, Industry and Economics, 2005, p. 47.
59. *The New Frontier in Sustainability—the Business Opportunity in Tackling Sustainable Consumption*, BER, July 2010, www.bsr.org
60. *Ibid.*
61. Promoting Sustainable Consumption—Good Practices in OECD Countries, OECD 2008, pp. 33-35. http://www.oecd.org/greengrowth/40317373.pdf / 62 accessed on December 25, 2015.

2

Sustainable Consumption

A Gandhian Perspective

Sapna Chadah

Introduction

Today the world faces an unprecedented challenge from interlinked economic, social and environmental crises. Climate change is one of the most important global challenges, with implications for food production, water supply, health, energy etc. The resources such as air, water, soil and other natural resources are being depleted. There has been destruction of ecosystems and the extinction of wildlife. This destruction of natural habitats and depletion of natural resources is leading to degradation of the environment. This environmental crisis is the result of unsustainable patterns of consumption and production. There is broad global consensus that we need a fundamental shift in the way goods and services are produced and consumed if we are to avoid worsening development and resources/environmental crises. There is a clear need to rethink how we pursue economic growth, as well as the business models we use, in order to shift towards sustainable ways of living that are in harmony with communities, our ecosystems and natural resources.

Mahatma Gandhi is perhaps the only great thinker who could foresee the social and ecological consequences of the exploitative model of development and offer an alternative model. Gandhi was not only a pioneer, but also very original; he was not an academic theoretician, but a man of unparalleled wisdom. The gap between this man of wisdom and the men of knowledge that this century has produced in plenty still remains unbridled. If we look at Gandhian views on sustainable development, non-violence, the rural lifestyle, the agrarian lifestyle, and sustainability;

they are far more relevant today than they ever were. He identified with the poor, took-up issues of the poor, realized that consumerism and people who try to enrich themselves is not a good thing. In this context, the statement of Mahatma Gandhi becomes quite significant: "The Earth has resources for meeting man's every need, but not his every greed". Gandhi saw economic reasoning based on people rather than on consumer goods as the way to social and environmental sustainability. He said that whenever in doubt, recall the face of the poorest and the weakest person you may have seen, and ask yourself if the consumption activity you contemplate is going to be of any use to that person? Will that person gain anything? Will it restore that person's control over his or her own life and destiny? This approach considers actions that correct things for the most disproportionately impacted people in a community. Gandhi abhorred the profit motive which is the main characteristic of modern industrialism. He rejected the view that profit was the source of pleasure and the lack of it the source of pain.

Limitation of Wants

The present world is reeling in the fallacious belief that progress and development consist in the ever-growing multiplication of wants and the production of more and more goods to satisfy them. However, Gandhi strongly objected to this idea of wants. The Gandhian economic order was founded on "simple living and high thinking" enunciating the philosophy of limited wants, which promotes the elimination of exploitation of man by man. Gandhi's objection to the idea of the multiplication of wants and his insistence on their limitation were based on his conviction that the former obstructed while the latter facilitated moral and spiritual development of the individuals which was the highest Gandhian criterion for acceptability of any human activity. According to him, a certain degree of physical harmony and comfort is necessary, but above a certain level it becomes a hindrance instead of help. Gandhi was of the opinion that progress of materialism does not promote true happiness and instead engenders and nourishes social discontent. He asserted that civilization consisted not in the multiplication, but in the deliberate and voluntary reduction of wants. It alone promoted happiness and contentment and increased capacity for service. The control of the mind in relation to material wants alone leads us to happiness. Gandhiji said "The mind is a restless bird; the more it gets the more it wants and still remains unsatisfied. The more we indulge in our passions, the more unbridled they become. Our ancestors, therefore, set a limit to our indulgences. They saw that happiness was largely a mental condition. It was not that we did not know how to invent machinery, but our forefathers knew that if we set our mind after such needs, we would become slaves and lose our moral fibre."[1] To those who are advocating material abundance Gandhi said: "If by abundance you mean everyone having plenty to eat and drink and to clothe himself with, enough to keep his mind trained and educated, I should be satisfied. But, I should not like to pack more stuffs in my belly than I can digest and more things than I can usefully use. But neither do I want poverty, penury, misery, dirt and dust in India."[2]

Gandhi disilludes those who conceive of modernity and progress in terms of high standard of living measured by conspicuous consumption. He defined true civilization as: "Civilization, in the real sense of the term, consists not in the multiplication but in deliberate and voluntary reduction of wants."[3] Gandhi with his deep insight into human nature saw that material abundance did not lead to contentment and happiness. Gandhi argued that, "even if the paradise of material satisfactions which they envisage as their final goal were realized on earth, it would not bring mankind either contentment or peace."[4] He was of the opinion that more we indulge in our passions the more unbridled they become.

Another reason why Gandhi insisted on the limitation of wants was that it was inseparably related to the achievement of the goal of *sarvodaya,* the welfare of all. What Gandhi aimed at was the total eradication of poverty. Though in the paradigm of the multiplication of wants, the greatest good of the greatest number is promised, what has been really fulfilled at best is "the greatest good" of the blessed and crafty few. While a few become fabulously rich, the vast majority are doomed to perish in abject poverty. He believed that limitation of wants was an indispensable condition for the realization of his objective.

Gandhiji was thus of the view that man could attain real happiness only through the limitation of wants and the acceptance of voluntary simplicity. The greatest good or welfare visualized in *sarvodaya* is not the material abundance or affluence as promised in economic ideologies. He knew well that it was impossible to raise the standard of living of the rest of the world population to the level of affluence of the Western developed societies simply because the earth did not have enough natural resources to achieve this. Thus, Gandhiji promoted sustainable consumption as important element to achieve long-term economic growth that is consistent with environmental and social needs. As Gandhi said, "earth has enough to satisfy everyone's legitimate needs but nor anyone's greed". Given the finite nature of earth's resource, any attempt to go on artificially multiplying human wants is doomed to failure. Thus, the limitation of wants becomes a *sine qua non* for sustaining the earth's ecosystem. A key issue in such a scenario will not be just reducing the volume of goods and services consumed, but also the extent to which improvement in environmental quality can be achieved through the substitution of more efficient and less polluting goods and services.

Gandhi advocated simplicity and limitation of wants not only for individuals, but also for society as a whole. Just as Gandhi visualized for the individual a simple but ennobled life that lent contentment and happiness, in the case of society he visualized not an affluent society wading and wallowing in material abundance like the Western industrial-urban society, but a self-sufficient, no-poverty, prosperous society based on non-violence and voluntary co-operation ensuring a dignified and peaceful existence for all.

It is now being universally realised by all that the rich tend to exploit the nature substantially, their actions have to be governed. The exploitation of nature by rich in unbridled fashion needs to be restricted. The taste and preferences of a rich consumer will have to be reformed and limits to his wants will have to be introduced in the society in order to contain the perpetually increasing consumption of material goods and services. It is difficult to achieve environmental governance in the absence of regulation of human wants to its basic minimum. The utility maximisation approach in mainstream economics is based on the assumption of unlimited and ever-increasing wants of the consumer. To curtail the perpetually rising consumption on the part of the consumer, his tastes and preferences need to be changed in such a manner that he not only limits his demand for material goods, but also limited goods in limited quantity and gets maximum satisfaction. In fact, the quantity and quality basket of individual consumption should be made more restrictive. In this era of science and technology, the scope for luxury expansion is enormous. But this scope needs to be guided first towards satisfying basic needs of the world poor rather than creating spurious demand for the rich. The aspiration to reach the living standards of rich of the developed nations by world population is impossible task, as the world has a limited stock of natural resources. Thus, there is an urgent need for every individual to discipline himself regarding his wants.

Village Life

A major component of his vision of *sarvodaya* is preservation of the villages. The cities and towns did not find a place in Gandhi's *Swaraj*. According to him, the city people may be getting big profits and good wages, but all that has become possible by sucking the blood of villagers. The poor villagers are exploited by the foreign governments and also by their own countrymen—the city dwellers. They produce the food and go hungry. The half a dozen modern cities are an excrescent and serve at the present moment the evil purpose of draining the life-blood of the villages. The cities with their insolent torts are a constant menace to the life and liberty of the villages. Gandhi regarded the growth of cities as an evil thing, unfortunate for mankind and the world. He held that the growth of the cities is only a symptom of the malady.

According to Gandhiji, village life based on minimum wants ensured happiness. If the villages perish, India will perish too. The revival of the villages is possible only when they are no longer exploited. Industrialization on a mass scale will necessarily lead to passive or active exploitation of the villagers as the problems of competition and marketing came in. Therefore, we have to concentrate on the village being self-contained economically capable of defending itself against the whole world; manufacturing mainly for use. All facilities for worthwhile living should be available in every village. Provided this character of the village industry is maintained, there would be no objection to villagers using even the modern machines and tools that they can make and afford to use. Only they should not be sued as a means of exploitation of others.[5] He told Nehru: "We realize truth and non-violence only in the simplicity of village life. The essence of what I have said is that man should rest content with his real needs and become self-sufficient."[6]

Swadeshi is that spirit in us which resists us to the use and service of our immediate surroundings to the exclusion of the more remote. The *Swadeshi* doctrine would enable every village in India to be almost self-supporting and self-contained unit, exchanging only such necessary commodities with other villages, which are not locally producible. Gandhi was drawn by his vision of a rural civilization where men and women in small groups would, by their activity, be self-sufficient in meeting their elemental needs and yet interdependent for many others in which dependence is necessary. As far as possible every activity will be conducted on a cooperative basis and this cooperation should be based on non-violence.

Gandhiji wanted Independent India to be a union of such self-sufficient, but interdependent village republics. It was this rural civilization whose economic organization was a happy and balanced blend of subsistence farming and sustainable industries that Gandhi admired and projected as a model. What Gandhi visualized was not a revival of the ancient village system as such, but a modified form of it that will serve the needs and aspirations of the rural people of India. He could visualize that the only way to save the impoverished rural people who constituted more than eighty per cent of the total population was to refurbish and regenerate the system of village economy. His conception of an ideal village was a comprehensive one encompassing the economic, political, social and educational dimensions. Gandhi's conception of village was not anchored on the modern (urban industrial) notion of development, but on the post-modern perspective of quality of life. His main emphasis was on the quality of life.

Swaraj generally means self-governance or 'home rule'. It lays stress on governance not by a hierarchical government, but self-governance through individuals and community building. The focus is on decentralization. Gandhi insisted on decentralization of production and encouragement of cottage industries so long as there was available human and animal power. He observed: "*Khadi* mentality means decentralization of the production and distribution of the necessaries of life. Therefore, the formula, so far evolved, is that every village is to produce all the necessaries and a certain percentage in addition for the requirements of the cities. Heavy industries will need to be centralized and nationalized. But they will occupy the least part of the vast national activity which will mainly be in the villages."[7]

Behind Gandhi's insistence on village economy was his grand design of the new civilization based on sustainable development in the real sense of the term. He wanted the human intrusion into the functioning of the biosphere to be minimized by closing man dominated systems such as cities, agricultural and industrial activities to the point where their net effects on the biosphere approximated those of the natural systems they have replaced. No other system of human settlement can achieve this except the village in the form of an Urban Centre.

The task before every lover of the country is how to prevent the decay of the villages or how to reconstruct the villages of India so that it may be as easy for anyone to live in them as it is supposed to be in the cities. The village movement is as much an education of the city people as of the villagers. Workers drawn from the cities have to develop village mentality and learn the art of living from the villagers. It is only when the cities realize the duty of making an adequate return to the villages for the strength and sustenance, which they derive from them, instead of selfishly exploiting them. Therefore, we have to make a choice between India of the villages, that are ancient and India of the cities, which are a creation of foreign dominance. Exploitation of villages is itself organized violence. If we want *swaraj* to be built on non-violence, we have to get the villages their proper place. Therefore, there is a need to reconstruct the villages and establish village *swaraj*.

Industrialization

Gandhi gave his qualified support to the use of machine for production. His opposition to it was on the ground that it should not replace human labour which in India is available abundantly. What Gandhi objected to was the craze for machinery, not machinery as such. The craze for what is called labour saving machinery. Gandhiji rightly recognized that we cannot do away with machinery. But machinery should not throw people out of jobs and rob humans of the dignity of labour without which human beings cease to be human beings. This is what Gandhi calls necessary human labour. That use of machinery is lawful which subserves the interest of all.

He thought that if the craze for machinery grew in India it would become an unhappy land. According to him such machinery helps a few to ride on the backs of millions. The impetus behind it all is not the philanthropy to save labour, but greed. Gandhi also thought that machinery was repugnant to decent living; it only complicates life, which should be simple. He stressed high thinking was inconsistent with complicated material life based on high speed imposed on people by Mammon worship, and all the graces of life were possible only when people learnt the art of living nobly.

Gandhi felt the machines killed cooperation and promoted competition. He opined that the future of industrialism was dark. Machines led to the concentration of wealth in the hands of a few. They made the rich richer and the poor poorer. He wanted the concentration of wealth not in the hands of a few, but in the hands of all. He desired all to become co-sharers of the wealth produced. Their mass production necessitated a system of distraction, which thrived on fraud and speculation. He warned that as mass production invariably led to overproduction, it would bring imperialism in its train. While securing foreign markets, the industrially strong nation dominates eventually over the markets; the industrially strong nation dominates eventually over the weak nation politically also. Gandhi, nonetheless, thought machines were inevitable. He welcomed machinery, which did not deprive masses of men of the opportunity to labour, but which helped the individual and added to his efficiency and which a man could handle at will without being its slave. The use of machinery becomes unlawful when it is solely meant for increasing the profit to the owner of the machinery at any cost. Gandhi would reject anything that does not fit into his scheme of *Sarvodaya.* He said "he would favour the use of the most elaborate machinery if thereby Indian's pauperism and resulting idleness could be avoided."[8]

What Gandhi said in respect of industrialism is turning out to be true in twenty-first century. Industrialism has not banished poverty. Millions of people go to bed hungry and live in conditions incompatible with human dignity. Even the very life-sustaining eco-systems have become fragile due to excessive and thoughtless modes of industrialization. Such industrialization can be termed a curse for humanity. Industrialism at present pace could reach the height of darkness unless priorities are rearranged. Gandhi was by no means anti-technological. He opposed the indiscriminate multiplication of technology, an obsession of the modern person, the technocrat, and the citizen of a technopolis, what Gandhi referred as craze for machinery. Gandhi was absolutely right in saying that machinery helps a few to ride on the backs of millions. Today multinational corporations ride on the backs of millions of consumers and befool them with substandard products. He was against the machinery as it led to concentration of production and distribution in hands of few, which is the current scenario leading to the exploitation of not only labour but also the consumers.

A lot of people are dissatisfied with the technology and are moving towards alternative technology which is very much in keeping with the spirit of Gandhian philosophy. Alternative technology is also known as appropriate, careful, frugal participatory technology giving a radical challenge to contemporary technological practice. It is based on small group initiative rather than societal mobilization. They cover cooperative organizations for medicine, farming, food delivery, marketing, financial credit, communications, insurance, banking. Alternative technology groups emphasize a re-emergence of neighbourhood identity by tapping the artisan skills of various members of the community through "sweat equity" exchanges of services. The alternative technology is based on two norms: sustainability and democratic patterns of organization. The concept of sustainability is leading to selection of only practice that can be continued into the indefinite future. It is in light of the fact that some existing industrial practices are interfering with the regenerative capacities of the earth's life-sustaining process leading to depletion of the natural resources, which provide air, water, fertile land and a stable climate. Such industrial practices will have to be drastically modified so that sustainability can be achieved. There is an emphasis on conservation, on curtailing the flow of materials from manufacture to consumption. Democratic management of technological enterprises calls for decentralization of productive facilities into small, relatively autonomous units, which could be the only way to realization of democratic self-management. Through alternative technology, human sanity and ecological balance can be preserved. Large-scale industries and consumerism may eventually create a sick world. Therefore, the merits of alternative technology deserve serious reflection.[9]

Revolution in Values and Ethics

Gandhiji's approach to individual behaviour was based on the ethical premises. Gandhi did not recognize the separation of economics from ethics and what he wanted to achieve in the economic field was the ethical ordering of the economic life of society. The science of economics as Gandhi found it in the beginning of the twentieth century was "free from all values except those of the marker"; it was viewed as "an autonomous logical system unconcerned with human beings except as workers and capitalists."[10] Gandhi believed that certain moral ends are so important they must be treated like non-negotiable and cannot be compromised. Mahatma Gandhi thought and introduced the idea of regulating the human action by influencing human nature at the beginning of the development process itself.

Gandhi had no difficulty in identifying this divorce of economics from ethics as the root cause of the general degradation to Western civilization. Thus, he wanted to reinstate the human element and the value factor into economics and thereby achieve the integration of moral sentiments and the science of economics, which is considered to be a felt need of the times. The economic philosophy that has been gaining ascendancy in the present world is based on value premises of which the central core is materialism defined in terms of raising the standard of living or maximizing consumption and thereby optimizing the pattern of production.

For Gandhi, without a revolution in values, humans will be ill prepared to handle technology. The main reason why Gandhi denounced modern economics was the fact that it ignored and disregarded moral values and promoted instead acquisitiveness and vulgar consumerism. The perception that "the unlimited character of human want is the sole determinant of economics activity and its unrestricted satisfaction is the index of human progress" was totally unacceptable to Gandhi. He said that "Economics that hurts moral well-being of any individual or nation is immoral and therefore, sinful." An economics that inculcates Mammon worship, and enables the strong to amass wealth at the expense of the weak is a false and dismal science. It spells death. True economics, on the other hand, stands for social justice; it promotes the good of all equally including the weakest and is indispensable for a decent life."[11] Gandhi foresaw that perverted notion of human nature and progress in which humanity finds itself today will be the root cause of the crisis and therefore, denounced this notion of economic progress.

The distinction between need and want is also important in Gandhian approach. The satisfaction of need is a necessary condition for a human being to be alive and to perform to their *dharma*, but it is not sufficient. These needs are very few and limited in range and number. They require categories of goods and not specific products. These needs are basic wants. The wants, other than the basic wants, are not essential for human well-being and they tend to change with time and are conspicuous in nature. Gandhian moral human being, besides the need to survive, i.e. food and shelter; also has a need to exercise her capacity to care for others. The ultimate goal of man in Gandhian thought is quest for Truth that Gandhi called the God. His idea of human nature consists of "need to perfect oneself through love and social action" (Lutz, 1985). The by-product of which would not be self-interest, but self-suffering. The two central pillars of Gandhian thought, *viz.* Truth and *Ahimsa* determine the nature of human. The truly rational human being, armed with Truth and *Ahimsa*, would not be guided by the purely economic considerations, but by the conscience or inner voice. This is the key to moral growth and self-actualisation.

Gandhian doctrine of non-possession also helps one to understand individual self-discipline. Gandhiji has said, "Just as one does not deceive, so one must not possess anything which one does not really need. ... In observing this principle, one is led to progressive simplification of one's life." As against the economists who believe in insatiable propensity for conspicuous consumption as a prerequisite of economic growth, Gandhi believed that possession of goods beyond the limits to need, is a form of theft and, hence, immoral. Instead of maximization of wants, his economic thought was minimizing of wants and consumption. Thus, he advocated voluntary reduction in wants and not by coercion. It implies that individual should limit her needs and spend the rest for the welfare of others. Gandhiji suggested a consumption pattern and behaviour for the affording classes that was to be moderated by ascetic and paternalistic values.

Gandhiji believed in the formulation of individual preference not in the term of the goods, but in term of the characteristics of the goods in question. Hence, when one talks about food, what are more important than the taste and packaging are the nutritive content, its digestibility and ease of cooking. He preferred *gur* to sugar, brown rice to white rice etc. He believed that with education, individual tastes and preferences could be changed in the right direction.

Gandhi believed that as man does not have control over the future consequences of his actions, he should control his actions in present. He rediscovered and devised a set of individual action that he called *Yam-niyam. Yam-niyam*, in Indian culture, is a set of rules that an individual should pursue for the betterment of present life and *moksha.* Gandhi renames them as *Ekadash Vrats*, i.e. eleven vows. They are: Truth, Non-violence, Chastity, Control of the Palate, Non-stealing, Non-possession, Fearlessness, Removal of Untouchability, Bread Labour, Respect to all Religions and *Swadeshi.* These vows regulate individual behaviour, making him disciplined and thereby helping immensely in individual self-improvement. In the context of environmental governance, these help in limiting individual desire for using more and more goods and services, thereby restricting the demand for consumption and saving the scarce natural resources. A self-disciplined individual in a society would lead to sustainable development path more effectively than the society imposing discipline on the individuals.

One of the major problems of humanity is that there is a wide gap between our scientific progress and our moral progress. We have become materially richer, but morally and spiritually poorer. The modern world demands re-establishment of the moral ends in personal character and social justice; otherwise it is possible that the self-centred, consumerist society may collapse prematurely. Materialism is engulfing humanity today. Overemphasis on materialism in the form of a consumer culture weakens the moral and spiritual fabric of humans. The consequences of this economic growth divorced from morality are clearly visible today. There are problems like depletion of resources, energy crisis, eco-degradation, environmental hazards, cut-throat competition for appropriation of all the resources and for monopoly over market. This is giving rise to local, regional and international conflicts resulting in arms race and war. An integrated value system ought to be given its rightful place in our society. There is a tremendous sense of urgency for humanity to choose between non-violent co-existence and violent co-annihilation before it is too late.

A conception which regards human being as lord and nature as the mere stuff upon which to exercise human will implies a challenging, dominating attitude towards nature. Such an attitude leads not only to the ecological disruptions, but also to a truncation of human experience. Affirmation of the primacy of the moral leads to the recognition that human beings are primarily moral beings and as a moral being s/he is not the master of the world. It requires humility on the part of humans. Multinational corporations, power-mongers, chauvinists and racists pose a threat to the world, both physical and human. The moral person ought to make a choice to save the world from the irrational and the immoral. This choice implies suffering and sacrifice. The moral person has to protect beings from technological predators. Leaders of movements for environmental protection and for a safer and cleaner world have to be eternally vigilant against the enemies of nature and money-mongers. Non-violent resistance must be adopted for such protests, vigilance and pressure without fear or favour. The moral person perceives the contemporary technological threat as rooted in and originating from violence. Apart from this, the moral person understands that violence has crept into the world—violence in our thinking, violence in our attitude towards the other and in our interpersonal relations and finally, towards nature resulting in ecological catastrophes. The moral person has the tremendous task of transforming everything on the basis of non-violent, universal, unselfish love which alone can guarantee not only the survival of the world and the species but also, more basically, a joyful, meaningful and rich experience of life for humans.

Our technology is rooted in violence, as there is abuse of technology by rich and mighty. Thus, we need a powerful means to achieve a just, rational and human use of technology. To counter the violent technological process, further violence cannot be employed. Therefore, we have only one strategy to adopt, that is, the strategy of non-violent resistance. One of the great virtues of non-violent resistance is that it reduces hostilities to a minimum. It maintains moral, rational and cooperative attitudes amidst conflict and thus increases the moral forces instead of destroying them. Non-violence can be employed to resolve all conflict situations. Non-violence is not merely a tactic, but a moral imperative and a way of life. Non-violence seeks to restore the wholeness of a community. It reconciles the oppressor with the oppressed.

Only in a non-violent culture can technology be at the service of humans. In such a culture, technological enterprise has to recognize the fundamental human rights and has to respect the dignity of the human person. Absolute preference should be given to the alleviation of human suffering, to the eradication of hunger and disease, to the fight against social injustice and to the struggle for lasting peace. In a loveless society, technology can become a monster. Gandhiji with his commonsense approach to technology can be relied upon as a sure guide with regard to our technological enterprises in the forthcoming millennium.

Conclusion

Gandhi's philosophy offers a practical way to a peaceful social revolution to improve the quality of life. What he preached was not only for the Indian masses, but for the entire deprived people of the world. His message was not for a particular time, but for the future of the mankind, especially his theory of non-violence and peaceful co-existence. But his immediate concern was the Indian masses, especially in the countryside. Gandhiji was of the view that the Indian problem was not merely political or economic but many-sided. In fact people needed courage and sense of self-respect to enable themselves to come out of the slavish mentality developed over centuries of bondage. In his view, if these conditions were to be changed, politics, education, social reform, economy, and technology had to suit the genius of the society. Gandhiji with his commonsense approach to technology, production and consumption can surely be relied upon as guide with regard to sustainable production and consumption. Environmental protection found place of importance in his scheme. According to him, society has to limit its wants. Greed will destroy the world and in this way he focused on sustainable consumption.

Notes

1. *Hind Swaraj*, p. 43.
2. *Harijan*, February 12, 1938, p. 2.
3. *Hind Swaraj*, pp. 44-45.
4. Pyarelal, *Mahatma Gandhi: 1958, The Last Phase,* Vol. II, Ahmedabad, p. 139.

5. M.K. Gandhi, *Sarvodaya*, 1984, Navajivan Publishing House, Ahmedabad.
6. Quoted by U. N. Dhebar in *Lectures on Gandhian Philosophy*, Annamalai University, p. 40.
7. *Constructive Programme*, Navajivan Publishing House, Ahmedabad, p. 12.
8. *Young India*, 3.11.1921.
9. See Kuruvilla Panadikattu, (Ed.), *The Meaning of Mahatma for the Millennium*, Maadhyam Book Services, pp. 148-151.
10. Ramesh Diwan and Mark Lutz (ed.), *Essays in Gandhian Economics*, G.P.F., New Delhi, p. XIII.
11. *Harijan*, October 9, 1937, p. 292.

References

Ashu Pasricha, (2011) (Ed.). *Gandhi in Twenty-First Century*, Delhi: Deep and Deep Publications Pvt. Ltd.

Glyn Richards, (1982). *The Philosophy of Gandhi—A Study of His Basic Ideas*, Curzon Press.

Kuruvilla Pandikattu (2000). (Ed.), *The Meaning of the Mahatma for the Millennium*, Maadhyam Book Services.

M.P. Mathai, (2000). *Mahatma Gandhi's World-View*, Delhi: Gandhi Peace Foundation.

N. Radhakrishnan, (2003). *The Paradoxes in Present-day Life Style: A Gandhian Perspective*, in K.V. Sundaram, M. Moni, (Ed.,) *Reshaping Our Earth View-Creative Thoughts and Alternative Futures*, New Delhi: Tata McGraw-Hill Publishing Co. Ltd.

Nimisha Shukla, "*Self-discipline as a Regulatory Instrument for Environmental Governance and Gandhian Approach*", *www.ecoinsee.org/fbconf/Sub%20Theme%20I/Nimisha.pdf*

R.S. Narayan, (1982). *Gandhi's Contribution to Political Thought*, Prasaranga, University of Mysore.

V.K. Natraj, Kamlesh Misra and Neeru Kapoor, (2005) (Ed.), *Gandhian Alternatives—Economics Where People Matter*, Vol. 4, New Delhi: Gandhi Smriti and Darshan Samiti.

3

Challenges of Sustainable Consumption

Indian Context

Sheetal Kapoor

Introduction

In 1987, the United Nations' World Commission on Environment and Development often referred as the Brundtland Report brought the concept of sustainable development to mainstream attention, and made it clear that our pre-existing approach to economic development, our systems of production and our systems of consumption are unsustainable. Sustainable Development means meeting our needs without jeopardizing the ability of future generations to meet their needs.[1] By 1992, around 70 different definitions of sustainable development had been noted and the proliferation of them continued.[2]

Further, the issue of sustainable consumption has been of growing interest after the conclusion of the Earth Summit at Rio de Janeiro in 1992.[3] This Earth Summit Treaty signed by 143 nations provided international recognition to sustainable consumption and production by adopting the Agenda 21 action plan. In that Summit, sustainable consumption was fully supported and the major causes of continued deterioration of environment were discussed. Environmental disasters in Alaska, Bhopal and Chernobyl in the early 1990s led to the growth of a consumer segment concerned with the preservation of the environment. Green marketing, also known as ecological marketing and environmental marketing is not a recent phenomenon, but it became a worldwide phenomenon during the nineties.[4] Eco-foot printing seeks to calculate the level of resources we consume as an individual, organizations, cities, regions and nations and compares this with the resources nature can provide and sustain in terms of land, water, energy and resources. The first global footprint on humanity was published by WWF in 1998. It clearly showed that human beings are exceeding the physical capacity of the planet to support its numbers, activities and lifestyles.[5]

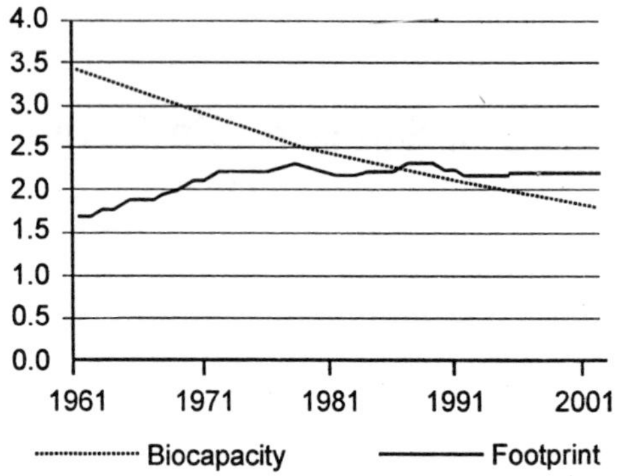

Source: *WWF Our Living Planet, Geneva, 1998, www.footprintnetwork.org*
Fig. 3.1: Ecological Footprint vs Global Bio-capacity.

In 2002, humanity's demand on the biosphere, its global Ecological Footprint, was 13.7 billion global hectares, or 2.2 global hectares per person. Thus in 2002, humanity's Ecological Footprint exceeded global bio-capacity by 0.4 global hectares per person, or 23 per cent. This finding indicates that the human economy is in ecological overshoot: the planet's ecological stocks are being depleted faster than nature can regenerate them. Thus, we are eroding the future supply of ecological resources and operating at the risk of environmental collapse.

In 1992 Rio Summit, 2001 Kyoto Summit, and 2009 Copenhagen Summit have continued the dialogue, leading to international agreements, and national laws. In the past, the focus was on population control, on environmental degradation and pollution. Today and for the next few decades, the sustainable development debate will centre on "Climate Change and carbon accumulation" in the earth's atmosphere. Energy use is at the heart of this process and global corporations are at the centre of this debate. They are now a major influence on the global carbon cycle.

United Nations has also framed Global Compact (UNGC) Programme based on the world's largest corporate citizenship initiative aiming for a more sustainable and inclusive world economy. It is supported by over 4000 participants in over 100 countries. It includes many of the world's most influential companies, such as Coca Cola, Levi Strauss, Nestlé, Microsoft and many more. Companies from all-over the world report their progress on implementing the 10 Global Compact principles. United Nations Secretary-General Kofi Annan first proposed the Global Compact in an address to the World Economic Forum on 31 January, 1999. The Global Compact's operational phase was launched at UN Headquarters in New York on 26 July, 2000. The Secretary-General invited business leaders to join an international initiative—the Global Compact—that would bring companies together with UN agencies, labour and civil society to advance universal, social and environmental principles.

Challenges of Implementing Sustainable Consumption in India

India is a country not only rich in spiritual values, it is now increasingly been seen as a powerhouse of human talent and technology and an emerging political and economic force to be reckoned with. With the opening up of our markets in 1991 for foreign competition and with market-oriented economic reforms, India continues to move forward with a stable GDP of 9 per cent and a very young population (average age 25 years). Reforms such as, liberal foreign investment and exchange regimes, industrial decontrol, reductions in tariffs and other trade barriers, opening and modernization of the financial sector, significant adjustments in government monetary and fiscal policies, and more safeguards for intellectual property rights have made India second largest economy in Asia. A study by the McKinsey Global Institute (MGI) suggests that if India continues its recent growth, average household incomes will triple over the next two decades and it will become the world's fifth largest consumer economy by 2025, up from 12th now.[6] Indians, frugal in their spending for many years, are buying commodities like never before with their newly found wealth.

Consumption can be considered as the reason why things are made in a market economy. There is a causal relationship between consumption, natural resource use and degradation of the environment. Some other challenges for the implementation of sustainable consumption are rapid population growth, technological changes and growing affluence as seen in the rise of the middle class in India. This can be expressed through (Impact = Population + Affluence + Technology) formula.[7]

1. *Population*: Population is the total number of people living on earth. The vast population of the World lives in Asia, especially in China and India. On 11 May, 2000 India had a population of 1 billion[8] (100 crore) people, i.e. 16 per cent of the world's population on 2.4 per cent of the globe's land area. If current trends continue, India would overtake

China in 2045, to become the most populous country in the world. While global population has increased threefold during this century, from, 2 billion to 6 billion, the population of India has increased nearly five times from 238 million (23 crores) to 1 billion in the same period. India's current annual increase in population of 15.5 million is large enough to neutralize efforts to conserve the resource endowment and environment. Table 3.1 shows India's population in 1991 and its projections to 2016.

Table 3.1: Population Projections for India (million)[3]

March 1991	*March 2001*	*March 2011*	*March 2016*
846.3	1012.4	1178.9	1263.5

Source: Technical Group on Population Projections, Planning Commission.

2. *Affluence*: In India, lifestyles were regulated by traditional practices. But with the increasing purchasing power, wasteful consumption-market-driven consumerism is stressing the resource base of India.[9] The break-up of the joint family system is also posing a challenge to India as our cultural practices were easily transferred from one generation to another. The rapidly growing software sector is boosting service exports and modernizing India's economy. Software exports crossed $35 billion in FY 2009, while business process outsourcing (BPO) revenues hit $14.8 billion in 2009. Personal computer penetration is 14 per 1,000 persons. The number of mobile users is expected to rise to nearly 1 billion by 2020. At the end of June 2016, 616 million unique users have subscribed to mobile services.

Around 300 million consumers in India enjoy a level of affluence. NCAER study in 2005 titled "The Great Indian Market" found a rapid rise in incomes leading to an even faster increase in demand for consumer durables and expendables. As a result, the ownership of goods is going up significantly.

Table 3.2: Demand of Consumer Durables

(*Figures in '000*)

	1995-96	*2001-02*	*2005-06*	*2009-10*
Cars	276	788	1,560	3,466
Motorcycles	760	2,599	4,663	8,369
CTV Regular	1,785	4,580	6,295	9,957
Refrigerators	1,850	3,006	4,335	6,774
White Goods	3,437	6,024	8,727	13,149

Source: NCAER 2005 "The Great Indian Market".

India's middle class has been defined by Asian Development Bank as those who are able to spend between $ 2 and $ 20 a day-measured in international dollars, i.e. adjusted for purchasing power parity. The ADB does add further nuance by splitting the middle class into three sub-sections: lower middle class ($2-$4), middle middle ($4-$10) and upper middle ($10-$20). Indian middle class has expanded to about 420 million, according to an ADB report on Asia's middle class.[10] Further, the Report by the Asian Development Bank (ADB) mentions that India's middle class population, will exceed 600 million by 2030, will be a major driving force in global consumption next only to China. McKinsey, another research firm has predicted that Indian middle class will grow up from 5 per cent to 40 per cent in 2025. Table 3.3 shows the growth of middle class and projections in future.

Table 3.3: McKinsey's Study on the Growth of Indian Middle Class

(Figures in %)

Year	*Middle Class*	*Lower Class*	*Poor*
2005	5	40	55
2015	20	45	35
2025	40	35	20

Source: Mckinsey & Co. Study.

Mckinsey & Co. published "The Bird of Gold: The Rise of India's Consumer Market", forecasting that there would be more than 570 million middle class Indians by 2025 and over 290 million people would move from desperate poverty to a more sustainable life. What's more, India would become the world's fifth-biggest consumer market, seven places up since the mid-2000s. NCAER has predicted that more than half of the population in top 20 cities would become truly middle class by 2016. These cities are home to less than 10 per cent of India's population, but between them generate more than 30 per cent of its income.[11]

With sufficient incomes, Indian consumers are spending huge money on refrigerators, air conditioners, television sets and DVD players. Further, they are buying cars in large numbers as can be seen from Table 3.4.

Changing lifestyle is also showing a change in the food consumption. Although 20 per cent of the Indian population is strictly vegetarian, but the younger generation is changing their food habits to non-vegetarian and other processed foods. With rising income levels, domestic meat consumption is on the rise in India. The data provided by Earth Trends Food and Agricultural Organisation of United Nations FAO reveals that in 2002, per capita consumption of meat in India per person was

Table 3.4: Share and Usage Pattern of Top 67 Cities in 2001-02 (Ownership in per '000 households; share of stock in per cent)

Durables	*Usage Pattern*		*Stock (% Share)*
	Top 67 Cities	*All India*	
Scooter	243.2	78.6	44
Motorcycle	138.0	70.8	27
CTV Regular	486.7	145.6	47
Cars/Jeeps	145.8	30.0	68
Refrigerators	492.5	134.0	52
Washing Machines	316.4	72.4	61

Source: NCAER 2005, "The Great Indian Market".

5.2 per kg.[12] NSSO survey also indicates that Indian food consumption patterns are slowly shifting from cereals and pulses to high value fruits, vegetables, processed foods and meat and meat products.[13]

Table 3.5: Meat Consumption: Top Ten Countries and Worldwide (1998-2002) (Meat in this Table means livestock and poultry only)

(Millions of metric tonnes)

Country	*1998*	*1999*	*2000*	*2001*	*2002*
China	59	60	64	65	68
United States	33	35	35	35	36
Brazil	12	13	14	14	15
Germany	7	7	7	7	7
Russian Federation	7	6	6	7	7
France	6	6	6	6	6
Japan	5	6	6	6	6
Mexico	5	5	6	6	6
India	5	5	5	5	6
Italy	5	5	5	5	5
World	**224**	**228**	**234**	**238**	**247**

Source: Based on statistics collected by the Food and Agriculture Organization of the United Nations (FAO), FAOSTAT on-line statistical service (FAO: Rome, 2005). Earth Trends, World Resources Institute, displays FAO statistics online as the *Agriculture and Food Searchable Database*.

These three consumption activities have sizeable environmental impacts. First, the household appliances usually run on electricity generated by fossil fuels—with all that implies for build-up of carbon dioxide and other greenhouse gases in the global atmosphere, thus bringing on climate change. Secondly, by possessing cars more consumers are contributing to CO_2 emissions. At least one-seventh of CO_2 emissions worldwide come from passenger cars. In India, there are an estimated five million premature deaths each year because of air pollution, up to 70 per cent of which is due to motor vehicles. Some 40 million people suffer the effects of asthma. Fortunately, there have been major efforts to improve air quality in New Delhi, by the usage of CNG buses and making it mandatory for every vehicle to have a pollution check certificate.

Moreover, meat is increasingly raised in major measure on grain, thus putting pressure on limited irrigation water and international grain supplies. Several countries import large amounts of grain for the primary purpose of feeding livestock rather than people, even though most of those countries feature many millions of malnourished people.

3. *Technology*: In modern societies technology is present everywhere. Technology includes skills, processes, technical methods, tools and raw-materials. On one hand, technology has a positive effect, such as cars help us to move around and transport goods. On the other hand, the negative impact is its effect on the environment. Most technologies were designed first for economic effect without considering the ecological environment. In future, the ecology and the post-purchase use and disposal of products would become an important tool in the design of new technologies such as fuel-efficient cars, low energy houses, energy efficient houses etc.[14]

All these three factors mentioned above, i.e. population, affluence and technology are having an impact on the environment.

Environmental Impact

The outcome of the three factors in the IPAT equation is the Environmental impact leading to Global Climate Change. Global Climate Change is not just a research question, or a topic, or an area, it is a whole "Science" with 80,000 scientists, journals and conferences, studying it for over 40 years. The best scientific consensus is in the IPCC Reports, which offer a comprehensive view of scientific findings.[15] The natural Carbon Cycle of the earth is being changed by Anthropogenic or human activities. Carbon is the most fundamental element on earth and earth's atmosphere and productivity rests on a balanced carbon cycle.

For 6,50,000 years, Carbon has remained between 170 ppm and 280 ppm. Since, the mid-1800s it has started rising, and expected to go on rising as Carbon accumulation is growing at 2.3 ppm per year. Now, it has reached 380-400 ppm. IPCC reports indicate it will reach 970 ppm.

change, further locally and seasonal products should be preferred, and greater composting of biodegradable food waste.

2. ***Sustainable Housing Consumption Choices***: Emphasis on purchasing homes using sustainable materials and choosing and creating homes with high level of insulation and energy efficiency.
3. ***Sustainable Travel Behaviour***: This may involve reducing the amount of travel undertaken by doing work from home or teleconferencing services. Car pool or finding alternative transport means such as cycling wherever possible.

This would involve a movement by consumers towards ethical consumption, role of business in sustainable marketing and initiatives by the government and society in promoting sustainable consumption.

Role of Consumers in Ethical Consumption[19]

Consumers can play an important role towards sustainable consumption by making purchasing decisions, lifestyle choices and peer-to-peer influencing. Ethical consumption stresses the role of the consumer in preventing labour exploitation, environmental degradation and adherence to basic labour and human rights while buying products. When a consumer goes beyond the brand name and label information and tries to find out about the business, which produces and sells the product, s/he walks into the realm of ethical issues in consumption. By consuming consciously and ethically, consumers can realistically create change. Before buying anything s/he should ask: Who makes it? Who needs it? And who profits from it?

The effects of constantly buying things, while discarding old, but often functioning things, are increasing demands on the world's resources for this consumption, managing more waste, exploiting other people to labour over this, and so on. And all this while many still go hungry and poor because their lands are being used to export food and other resources for producing products to be consumed elsewhere. As a responsible consumer, we should consume products consciously.

Ethical consumption is a way to help us feel that we have power as consumers that we can vote with our rupees. By using this consumer power, we can have impact on the larger economy and help create a world where the economy benefits all people in equal ways. Some suggestions regarding ethical consumption are:

1. Consumption should be need-based and we should not be swayed by marketing-forces.
2. Using products, which are energy efficient, and also reduce consumption of fossil fuel.
3. Making a point to ask about the people who make the things we buy.
4. Considering the environment cost of producing the product. One should avoid buying a product whose manufacturer is polluting rivers, land or air.
5. Thinking about how we would dispose of the product once we finish with it.
6. Supporting fair trade by checking that the manufacturer pays a remunerative price to farmers.
7. Reusing things and fixing things that are broken.
8. Not getting swayed by advertisements and sales promotion devices.
9. Investing money ethically into socially responsible corporations.
10. Boycotting companies that exploit workers, deceive or cheat consumers, harm the environment or display any form of socially irresponsible behaviour.

Radically restructuring the usage of the environment can be achieved by discipline and selflessness. Instead of throwing something away, one should take time to fix it or take it to a trade-person to fix it. The cost may be cheaper than buying a new one and we would be reducing waste.

Role of Business in Sustainable Marketing

Sustainable marketing accepts the limitations of marketing concept and is a macro-marketing concept. It embraces the idea of sustainable development, which requires a change in the behaviour of virtually everyone, including both producers and consumers. Sustainable marketing emphasizes on triple bottom line of ecological, social and economic issues.[20] Thus, sustainable marketing is defined as building and maintaining sustainable relationships with customers, the social environment and the natural environment. Moreover, sustainability marketing is related to Corporate Social Responsibility (CSR). CSR is a concept whereby companies integrate social and environmental concerns in their business operations and their interaction with stakeholders on a voluntary basis.[21] Systematic approaches to integrating environmental responsibilities include environmental systems such as, EMAS and ISO 14000, which are voluntary in nature. Many companies such as, Philips through its energy efficient lighting, Henkel's by introducing phosphate free detergents, Adidas's green footwear and apparel, Nokia's energy efficient products are some of the approaches adopted by companies towards sustainable marketing. A recent global consumer survey carried out by Nokia showed that 44 per cent of unused phones by people are simply kept at home. Responding to the survey, Nokia established 5,000 collection points for unwanted mobile devices in 85 countries, the largest voluntary scheme in the mobile industry, and is developing a series of campaigns and activities to give people more information on why, how and where to recycle their old and unwanted devices, chargers and mobile accessories. Nokia estimated that if all Nokia users unplugged their chargers when their phones were fully charged, enough energy would be saved to power 1,00,000 average-sized European homes. Marketing has a vital role to play in decoupling material consumption from consumer value. It has the ability to facilitate both innovation and choice influencing for sustainable consumption, because it allows products and information to flow between producers and consumers. Figure 3.2 shows a Sustainable Enterprise Framework, which includes organizations, environment and the eco-system in a sustainable manner.

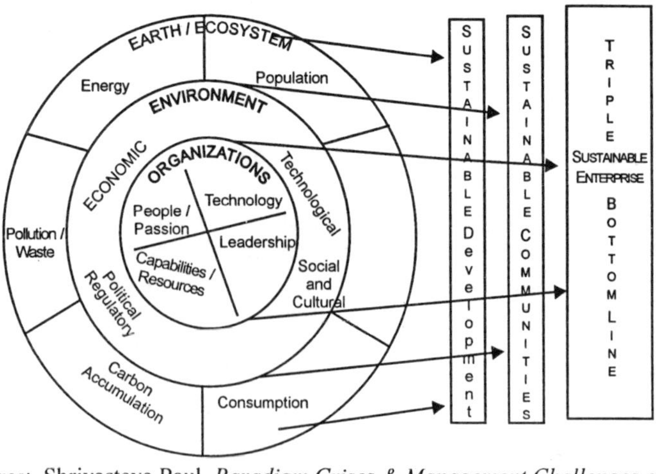

Source: Shrivastava Paul, *Paradigm Crises & Management Challenges of the 21st Century*, Working Paper delivered at University of Delhi on 14th January, 2010.

Fig. 3.2: Sustainable Enterprise Framework.

Role of Government and NGOs in Sustainable Consumption

It is important to promote sustainable consumption through environmental education and public awareness campaigns sponsored by the Central and State Governments and advocacy groups. In several areas, desirable limits and standards for consumption need to be established and applied through appropriate mechanisms including education, incentives and legislation. Development decisions regarding technology and infrastructure are a major determinant of consumption patterns. In India, we have the Bureau of Energy Efficiency, which was set-up in March 2002 under the provisions of Energy Conservation Act, 2001 to provide a legal framework for the government's energy efficiency initiatives in the country. Energy consumption in residential buildings is 116 billion units *vis-à-vis* in commercial buildings it is 33 billion units.

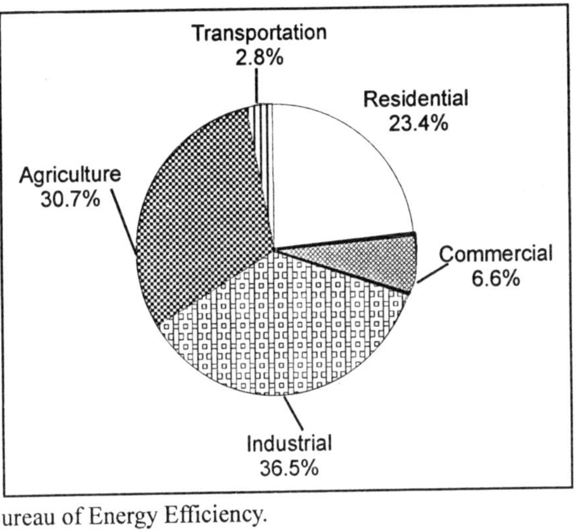

Source: Bureau of Energy Efficiency.

Fig. 3.3: Sector-wise Energy Efficiency.

It is, therefore, important to evaluate and make development decisions, which structurally lead to a more sustainable society.

Conclusion

Sustainable consumption is a systemic challenge. Businesses, governments, civil society and consumers all have the power to affect change, sometimes in ways that are not traditionally perceived to be their role. Consumers may feel a moral responsibility to live sustainably; however, they cannot do so without effective support from governments, NGOs and the businesses with which they interact. Businesses, governments and civil society must be aligned with these values since, they depend on the spending and votes of individuals. There should be certain value shifts within society to allow a more sustainable society and economy including:

From	*To*
Egocentric (me first)	Altruistic (Others First)
Conservative	Open to change
Indulgent	Frugal
Materialist	Post-materialist
Techno-centric (Technology knows best)	Eco-centric (nature knows best)
Anthropocentric (human centred)	Bio-centric (all species matter)

As the Nobel Laureate Mother Teresa said that "We ourselves feel that what we are doing is just a drop in the ocean, but the ocean would be less because of the missing drop."

Notes

1. World Commission on Environment and Development (WCED), 1988, p.8.
2. Kirkby J. O'Keefe and Timberlake, L., (1995) *The Earthscan Reader in Sustainable Development, Earthscan*, London.
3. Clapp Jennifer and Peter Dauvergne: (2008) *Path to a Green World: The Political Economy of the Global Environment*, New Delhi: Academic Foundation.
4. Jain, Sanjay K. and Gurmeet Kaur, (2003) *Review of Commerce Studies*, Delhi School of Economics, University of Delhi, Vol. 22 (January-June 2003).
5. WWF Our Living Planet, Geneva, 1998.
6. *The Bird of Gold: The Rise of India's Consumer Market*, 2007. Report by McKinsey.
7. Ehrlich, P.R. and Ehrlich, A.H. (1990) *The Population Explosion*, New York: Simon and Schuster, pp. 58-59.
8. *Source*: Technical Group on Population Projections, Planning Commission.

9. Subhashini Kaul and Abhishek, (2007) Consumerism and Mindless Consumption Sustaining the New Age Urban Indian's Identity. *International Marketing Conference on Marketing & Society*, 8-10 April, IIMK.
10. Indianmiddleclasstoshineworldwidehttp://indiatoday.intoday.in/site/Story/109758
11. Shukla, Rajesh, (2010) Consumption and Consumerism, *The Economic Times*, 5th July, 2010.
12. http://earthtrends.wri.org
13. Protein-hungry India switches to beef: Study Published: 2008, 23:29 IST Agency: PTI http://www.dnaindia.com
14. Belz, Frank-Martin and Ken Peattie, (2009) Sustainability Marketing: A Global Perspective (Wiley).
15. IPCC 4th Assessment Report 2007, http://www.ipcc.ch/ipccreports/ar4-wg1.htm
16. K.K. Khullar, (2005) "Globalisation and India", *Employment News*, January 29-4 February.
17. WBCSD, (2008) Future Leaders Team Business Role Workstream – Dialogue on Sustainable Consumption in India.
18. Tukker, A. Huppes, G., Guinee, J., *et al.* (2005) *Environmental Impact of Products* (*EIPRO*), European Commission Joint Research Centre.
19. Kapoor Sheetal, (2004) "Ethical Consumption", *Consumer Voice*, March-April.
20. Van Dam, Y.K. and Apeldoorn, P.A.C. (1995) "Sustainable Marketing", *Journal of Macro-Marketing*, No. 15 (3), pp. 55-56.
21. Commission of the European Communities (2002) *CSR: A Business Contribution to Sustainable Development*, Brussels, Commission of the European Communities, p. 5.

4

Consumption: Need *vs.* Greed

A Gandhian Alternative

Indramohan Jha

Seven Sins for Gandhi

- Politics without principles
- Wealth without work
- Commerce without morality
- Education without character
- Pleasure without conscience
- Science without humanity
- Worship without sacrifice

In strict sense of the term, every living being—humans, animals and plants, is a consumer. Humans are the most highly evolved and enlightened among species. They have all the three levels of intelligence—sub-conscious, conscious and super-conscious. Animals and plants are governed by only one fully developed intelligence, i.e. sub-conscious, which is far below that of humans.[1] Animals and plants consume as per their physical needs. Humans, on the other hand, formed the habit of conspicuous consumption influenced by their insatiable greed. As a result, they have become mere consumers deriving satisfaction or pleasure from the utilization of a commodity. In the process, the commodity gets used up or even destroyed. Thus, destruction becomes inherent in the consumption habit of mankind. This resulted in the culture of consumerism—the hallmark of modernity—which is destroying humanity as a whole thereby reducing it to a conglomerate of living and non-living machines. Such a worldview perceives the whole universe as a machine, which can be repaired and even replaced. However, it is a well-known fact that the universe is not a machine. This is more apposite in the case of biological systems. Human body may be compared with a machine, but it is not merely an assemblage of organs, tissues and cells. There is a higher level of integration and interdependence exhibiting a unique symbiosis guided by emotion and intelligence simultaneously. Its parts cannot function independently of the whole. Machines are run by the energy supplied from outside whereas energy is generated within a living being itself. Therefore, neither human body nor the social system can be treated as a machine for conspicuous consumption and mass production through large-scale industrialization. This whole process is rooted in greed and exploitation of man-and-nature. Therefore, Gandhi predicted that industrialism was going to be a curse of mankind. Unfortunately, the bane of madness for machine has had been the fundamental characteristic of the Western civilization and got replicated in other parts of the world as well. All this has brought the world on the brink of a cataclysm in the very first decade of the twenty-first century, which began with a bang celebrating the victory of the so-called free world (Capitalism/democracy) and science and technology.

This is obvious and explicit from some of the recent findings and revelations. Even in the most crucial area for survival, such as food, the situation is alarming. Already, the combination of global food crisis and economic recession has pushed the number of hungry people beyond the one billion mark in 2009. Every year about 2.2 million children die of hunger related conditions and most of them are in the poorer countries. More than 90 per cent stunted children are in Africa and Asia. India might take pride in its growing economic and military prowess but ironically, it is home to 42 per cent of world's underweight children.[2] This is bound to become worse in years to come due to rising population and climate change. Earlier food insecurity was a curse of poorer countries, has now assumed worrisome proportions even in the USA—the most powerful country in the world. The US Department of Agriculture in a scathing report—*Household Food Security in the US, 2009*—revealed that 14.7 per cent of American households faced food insecurity some time during 2009, including 5.7 per cent with very low food security. This is the highest record level since 1995, when the first food survey was conducted.[3] Moreover, there is a warning, "Agricultural production will need to increase by 70 per cent in the world and double in the developing countries to feed a global population expected to reach 9.1 billion by 2050. All this will have to occur in the face of chaotic climate conditions and scarce natural resources."[4] Fallacious nature of modern economic growth was exposed by the global recession (2007-09). Unemployment increased by more than 30 million since 2007, taking the global figure to 210 million. Nevertheless, the human costs of the downturn will have a debilitating impact on the succeeding generation as well due to lower lifetime earnings, health impairment of the workforce, and diminished educational attainments of children.[5] The Living Planet Report reveals some alarming facts related to the extent to which modern Western lifestyles are plundering natural resources at record levels. Overall, the earth's population is consuming the resources equivalent of 1.5 planet's worth of natural resources; that is, it takes one-and-half years to replenish the resources used in one year. Even with modest projections for population growth, consumption and climate change, by the year 2030 humanity will need the capacity of Two Earths to absorb CO_2 waste and keep up with natural consumption. Mostly the developing tropical countries have to bear the brunt. This part witnessed the decline of about 60 per cent of species—different mammal, bird, reptile, amphibian and fish species. The nature of global trade, commerce and production has become so discriminatory that it is adversely affecting the ability of the poor people to develop, feed, and industrialize as the developed ones are taking away their natural capital, and only a small number of people in those countries benefit.[6] In this sequence, British Consultancy Maplecroft recently revealed that poorer/developing countries are most at risk from climate change. Bangladesh is at the top to be followed by India at the second position. They may face the loss of a large part of their coastal landmass to rising waters. Maldives is already at the top of the list of islands likely to disappear under water.[7] These glaring facts speak volumes of rich man's greed to destroy the earth for a life of leisure and pleasure. Undoubtedly, Gandhi proved prophetic when he said, "Earth has enough resources to satisfy everybody's need, but not their greed." Besides ecological and economic challenges, health is a major victim of modernity. Gandhi rightly pointed out that the system of modern medicine is responsible for spread of most of the diseases. He explained in *Hind Swaraj*:

> How do these diseases arise? Surely by our negligence or indulgence. The doctor helps to indulge by medicines. Body feels more at ease but mind becomes weak. A continuance of a course of medicine must, therefore, result in loss of control over the mind. Had the doctor not intervened, nature would have done its work, and I would have acquired mastery over myself, would

> have been freed from vice...Hospitals are institutions for propagating sin. Men take less care of their bodies and immorality increases. We wantonly indulge in what we like. Doctors induce us to indulge, and the result is that we have become deprived of self-control and have become effeminate."[8]

Clearly, modern medicines spread diseases instead of cure; and at times treatment proves more fatal than the disease. Even modern medical science has come to the conclusion that most of the diseases can be prevented by changing the lifestyle from hedonism to austerity. We have landed-up in a situation that attempts are being made to counter one disease by another. Malaysia is releasing genetically modified mosquitoes to combat the Aedes Aegypti mosquitoes, which spread dengue. However, environmentalists are sceptical about its results and are afraid of its unintended consequences.[9] This is one such example demonstrating that this age uses poison to kill poison and in this process, our globe is becoming unsuitable for sustaining any lives. Nevertheless, there is a growing concern about the horrendous impact of modern lifestyle and attempts are being made to rectify the glaring blunders of the twentieth century. UAE, one of the largest producers of oil is emerging as a world leader in renewable energy. It is building a city called Masdar. It will be self-contained "carbon-neutral". Cars would be banned. Waste and water would be recycled. It is also exploring a range of clean energy-sources for the city.[10] As a visionary, Gandhi denounced the modern-machine age/ Western civilization as self-destructive about a century ago and called it Satanic and Black Age. It is contextual to note that his reference to Western civilization was moral and philosophical, and not mere geographical. He would have presented similar scathing criticism of growing urban centres or slums in India echoing the vices of modern-machine age imbued with a culture of crime—consumerism and sex. Gandhi condemned it on the following grounds:

1. It equates human body with machine consisting of inter-connected limbs, tissues and cells. Life emerged as a matter of chance and has no other significance. It has firm faith in Darwin's theory of evolution of species and does not brook any intervention by any supra-natural power in the functioning of the universe.
2. It makes body welfare (material development) the object of life and neglects moral progress. It is obsessed with better houses to live, clothes to wear, weapons to fight, faster means of

transportation to move around and improved mechanical devices to dispense with manual work.

3. It is irreligious because it is devoid of morality and universal human values.
4. Its claim of being democratic is false and illusory. In a democracy people are free to make choices, they are fearless and know their rights and duties. Modern civilization is based on inequality and divides people on the basis of wealth, religion, race and gender.
5. Money is the God and sex is the Goddess of modern civilization. It is totally geared to make more money and derive sexual pleasure at any cost. Both are poisons as they destroy body, mind and soul.
6. It promotes violence. Conflict is the essence of modern civilization.
7. It is competitive, not cooperative. Its functioning is such that man is pitched against nature, man against man, and man against himself.
8. Modern society is hierarchical as a pyramid with wide base and narrow at the top. A few at the top command maximum power with minimum duty. Such a system based on inequality with biased command and control is inherently violent. There is little care for the welfare of marginal ones.
9. Its truth is derived from scientific research and reason. However, science and reason have their limitations. In order that science can uncover the secrets of the material world does not take man astray, it must be tempered with spirituality.
10. The so-called modern welfare institutions have proved counter-productive. Hospitals spread diseases, courts promote litigation; and educational institutions impart only with information to earn more money instead of wisdom.[11]

For all these reasons Gandhi was highly critical of modern civilization which only promoted unlimited indulgence leading to moral degeneration of man and society as a whole. In this regard, the examples of Rome and Greece are significant.

Gandhian Alternative

Therefore, every Gandhian endeavour was to achieve high moral ground and strength. This was possible only by self-control and renunciation;

because true improvement in life in its qualitative terms lies in human conscience, which is beyond the reach of external conditions. Rightly so, he explained *Swaraj* in terms of self-rule or control over senses. This called for the fulfilment of moral duties based on the doctrine of love. Gandhi explained true civilization in terms of good moral conduct: "Civilization is that mode of conduct which points out to man the path of duty. Performance of duty and observance of morality are convertible terms. To observe morality is to attain mastery over mind and passions. So doing we know ourselves."[12] Hence, a true civilization contributes towards self-realization of human beings which was possible only by means of control of desire by subjugating animal instincts. Gandhi explains:

> The mind is a restless bird; the more it gets the more it wants, and still remains unsatisfied. The more we indulge our passions the more unbridled they become...therefore, set a limit to our indulgences...happiness was largely a mental condition. A man is not necessarily happy because he is rich, or unhappy because he is poor. Observing all this, our ancestors dissuaded us from luxuries and pleasures.[13]

Likewise, he wrote in *Young India* (1927), "I do not believe in the multiplication of wants and machinery contrived to supply them...I whole-heartedly detest this mad desire to destroy distance and time, to increase animal appetites and go to the ends of the earth in search of their satisfaction. If modern civilization stands for all this, I call it satanic."[14] Setting heart after pleasurable material things makes man slaves of his animal instincts and leads a life without any moral fibre. There was no need to produce more by machine than what can be with hands and feet for fulfilment of essential needs. More than that meant grabbing the rightful share of others. This was the source of real health and happiness. Gandhi explained this through the principle of "Bread Labour" by insisting that every individual should do physical labour equal to that needed for his own consumption. This will meet the needs of all and enhance the dignity of labour. This was all the more required for a country like India with huge workforce. Naturally, Gandhi gave priority to "production by the masses" over "mass production by machine". Besides giving livelihood to all, this would prevent concentration of wealth in the hands of the few. He cautioned in *Harijan* (1935).

Dead machinery must not be pitted against the millions of living machines represented by the villagers of India. Machinery to be well used has to help and ease human effort. The present use of machinery tends more and more to concentrate wealth in the hands of the few in total disregard of millions of men and women whose bread is snatched by it out of their mouths.

In simple terms he prescribed that human body must be fully worked and utilized. That is, the need of the body must be supplied by the body itself. This has become all the more significant today. This Gandhian approach of sustainable consumption is highly valued by the champions of sustainable development. Control of consumption by the rich is sought to prevent overexploitation of nature and to save the natural resources for the future. At a macro-level, Gandhi argues for an India of self-reliant, self-sufficient villages pursuing the path of *Swadeshi*, which presupposes fulfilment of needs by locally produced goods. He explained, "*Swadeshi* is an observance. There are many things that we cannot get in India, we must try to do without them. We have to do without many things, which we may consider necessary, but when you are in that frame of mind, you will find a great burden taken off your shoulders. You will feel freer man than you are now, immediately you adopt *Swadeshi*."[15] This would save societies from the bane of industrialism for the reason that when production and consumption both become localized, the temptation to speed-up production would automatically disappear.

The Gandhian village is small in size wherein people have face to face communication. Everybody knows one another. There is a feeling of cooperation instead competition. It will be in harmony with nature. In a sense, it has all the characteristics of *Swaraj* at grassroots level. Gandhi's village *Swaraj* is a complete republic, independent of its neighbours for its own vital wants, and yet, interdependent for many others in which dependence is necessary. Every village will grow its own food crops and cotton for its clothes. It should have a reserve for its cattle, recreation and playground for children. Cash crop should be grown in rest of the land. It should also have clean water supply. It will maintain a village theatre, school, and public hall. Education will be compulsory up to the final basic course.[16] The village is an ideal place for the growth of a well-groomed citizens imbued with fraternal feeling of care and share instead of being in competition with his neighbours. Explaining this social structure, he formulated the concept of "an ever increasing oceanic circle". That is, when one throws a stone in water, a series of circular ripples are formed. The ocean refers to a vast human society formed of innumerable drops of water or human beings. Its centre will be individual; growing as family, village, community of villages to the outer most circle which is the global society. This formation is built on maximum autonomy with maximum inter-dependence. For functional purposes, none is superior or inferior unlike the hierarchical pyramidal structure of the West. The individual will be always ready to sacrifice for the villages, the latter to perish for the circle of villages, till at last the whole becomes one life composed of individuals, never aggressive in their arrogance, but ever humble, sharing the majesty of the oceanic circle of which they are integral units. The outermost circumference will not wield power to crush the inner circle but will give power to all within and derive its own strength from it.[17] All contribute towards collective societal goals in best of their capacity and their needs are looked after by the society. Therefore, Gandhi's vision of society aimed at welfare of all in every dimension of life. He criticized Western democracy's claim for freedom being false and socialism's equality as limited and narrow only to be achieved by violent means. Man had no freedom or equality in its true spirit. As opposed to this Gandhi wanted every individual to be a fully developed member of the society. He called it *Sarvodaya* (the welfare of all) under the influence of John Ruskin's *Unto This Last* which is said to have transformed his life. The book emphasized three basic principles:

(1) The good of the individual is contained in the good of all.
(2) The lawyer's work has the same value as the barber's, inas-much-as all have the same right of earning their livelihood from their work.
(3) A life of labour, i.e. the life of the tiller of the soil and the handicrafts-man is the life worth living.[18]

Sarvodaya emphasized the importance, equality and dignity of labour along with a dialectical relationship between individual and social welfare. Such a relation can flourish only when the unit and whole both are generous enough to contribute more for collective welfare by eschewing personal pride and greed. It is possible that someone might be richer or may have more wealth than his needs due to better physical competence, talent or inheritance. That is, one may have more possessions. It is not possible to shed all possessions. However, it is required that men must get rid of possessiveness, which is at the root of most of the evils. Tolstoy's ideal of non-possession and renunciation was developed by Gandhi into his Trusteeship doctrine to tackle the tendency among people to indulge and accumulate wealth. This was based on the simple logic that, "Everything belonged to God and was from God. Therefore, it was for his people as a whole, not for a particular individual. When an individual had more than his proportionate portion he became trustee for that portion for God's people."[19] For Gandhi the only way to get rid of recurring inequalities and residual ownership of their evil was to regard all possessions not ours in the absolute sense, but a trust from God to be used in his service, in other words, in the service of society.[20] It was a mean to transform the present capitalist order into an egalitarian one and provide the owning class an opportunity to reform itself. This whole argument is based on the faith that human nature is never beyond redemption if there is a sincere desire for that.

Humanity, today, faces a serious question starkly—Can society produce a *satyagrahi* (follower of truth) to fight out the seven sins enumerated by Gandhi? His answer was yes in unequivocal terms because he was a firm believer in inherent goodness of man to reach perfection by means of truthful pursuit of spirituality. In this regard he was deeply influenced by Tolstoy who is referred to as the founder of Gandhism. Besides Tolstoy's writings, his exemplary life—his passion for truth and ceaseless striving after perfection made Gandhi his avid follower. In him, he found a kindred spirit—a seeker after truth; an aristocrat turned peasant and a shoemaker in pursuit of the meaning of life who dedicated his life talent and genius to the service of humanity while he himself strove to live by his body labour. Gandhi found in him a pioneer of the science of the spirit, which Gandhi made his own and put to use with striking success.[21] He exhorted one and all to follow the path of truth in every walk of life—politics, economy or religion. He strived to gain spiritual power to sway his politics, struggled valiantly to control his senses (internal) to influence his outer environs.[22] Unique means, methods and goals bestowed on him a rare charismatic persona to be envied by anyone who thought and worked to bring respite to the suffering humanity.

Conclusion

Gandhi, a firm believer in the Ruskinian simplicity of wants described greed as the root cause of all the ills of humanity. His severe condemnation of machine-based modern civilization is for the reason that it serves only outwardly desires and does not care to fulfil even basic daily needs. It is instructive to note that he was not opposed to a machine necessary for human well-being. He despised only the craze for machine geared to more and more production for hoarding and making profit to be amassed by a few at the cost of hungry labourers. Such a mindless production process is based on the principle that an ever-increasing consumption is good for economy. This, in turn, is sustained by a new modernist value system emphasizing the unlimited desires of human beings and their overweening ambitions to achieve rare goals. Self-aggrandizement is the supreme value in this material-machine age having no spiritual orientation at all. Every human action is directed towards attaining physical pleasure, power or strong positions to dominate. Such a social culture produced a large-scale industrialization and also led to the mushrooming of urban slums as centres of vices. This in turn has caused irreparable ecological imbalances. The twenty-first century witnessed the culmination of machine and modernity. However, it has its horrendous pitfalls as well. Cyber-crimes and easy access to weird pornography etc. are some ugly offshoots of the culture of violent power and hedonism. Existence-threatening environmental crises are already there. Billions are spent on leisure and pleasure while millions die of hunger and disease. In the year 2010, 1.8 billion people use internet, but one billion people still have no access to adequate supply of fresh water.[23] What a paradox of development! Thus, a modern man lives under the brutal tyranny of artificial wants and scarcity. This has alienated him from the self and society as well.

Certain new initiatives, such as education of values and ethical consumerism are being taken to salvage the situation. Undoubtedly, there is a growing concern for ethical consumerism attaching economic values to concerns for human rights, animal rights and the environment. Ethical consumer market has grown as people are opting for green house, cars, organic foods, local shopping, energy-efficient boilers and bulbs, ethical cosmetics etc.[24] However, they have made little impact towards addressing the problem; and has nothing to do with the maladies of modernity. Instead, they are used as non-tariff trade barriers by developed countries to the disadvantage of the poor ones. At best they have some palliative value or they are yet another means to cater to the greed of the rich.

Follies of Capitalism-Communism have brought Gandhism to the fore as a beacon of hope for suffering humanity. Other 'isms' rely upon external-institutional control whereas Gandhi preached and practised internal-spiritual limits. This demanded enormous individual strivings to achieve perfection. Obviously, he explained True Civilization in terms of performance of duty and observance of morality; that is to attain mastery over mind and passions for physical pleasure. Therefore, Gandhi emphasized the values of non-possession, non-stealing, detachment, contentment etc. for people living in small village communities having self-sufficient economy to fulfil their basic needs. He institutionalized and experimented them in the Phoenix settlement and other *ashrams* celebrating the virtues of simplicity of wants and dignity of labour. His own experiments in the vow of *Brahmacharya* (celibacy or lust control) gradually grew into asceticism. He explained *Brahmacharya* in terms of conduct adapted to the search of *Brahma*, i.e. Truth. That is control of all senses. That calls for the practice of simultaneous self-control in all directions. He realized that observance of celibacy becomes easier if one has mastery over the palate. Food has to be taken as we take medicine, that is, without thinking whether it is palatable or otherwise, and only in quantities limited to the needs of the body.[25] Rightly so, he declared renunciation as the highest form of religion; that he applied in his political life for public welfare. For he made no distinction between public and private, internal and external, religion and politics; as they all are meant to pave the way for a perfectly pure life. Thus, Gandhi exemplified a life of meaningful balance of right and duty as a societal goal instead of individual pursuit.

At the moment it seems utopian in a world pervaded with greed. He set moral standards at such a high pedestal that even an ardent Gandhian found it difficult to emulate. However, as a humanist he had immense faith in the innate goodness of human nature. He rightly averred, "*Atman* is the same in every one of us. All souls possess equal potentialities; only some have developed their powers, while others have them in a dormant condition. The latter too will have a like experience, if only they try."[26] It is required to realize the benefits of limiting one's desire only for need based consumption. This would enable him to do away with the evils of greed and society would become free from the curse of unbridled industrialism. A common man must face teething troubles to attain the Gandhian goal; but prescription is to embark on this path as there is no other alternative if humanity seeks to survive happily.

Notes

1. R.P. Misra (ed.) (2007), *Rediscovering Gandhi* [New Delhi: Concept Publishing Co. (P) Ltd.], p. 33.
2. See *Global Hunger Index 2010*, (Washington, IFPRI, October 2010).
3. *Hindu* (Delhi), November 17, 2010.
4. This was informed by the FAO's Director-General Jacques Diouf at the 36th Session of the Inter-governmental Committee on Food Security (CFS) in Rome on October 13, 2010, *Hindu*, October 16, 2010.
5. *Hindu*, September 10, 2010.

6. *WWF Living Planet Report 2010*, and *Hindu*, October 14, 2010.
7. See info@maplecroft.com
8. *Hind Swaraj*, (Ahmedabad: Navjivan, 2006, Reprint), pp. 51-52.
9. *Hindu*, 11 October, 2010.
10. *Hindu*, 12 October, 2010.
11. See *Hind Swaraj*, *op. cit.*; 8 and R.P. Misra, *op. cit.*, pp. 27-29.
12. *Hind Swaraj*, p. 53.
13. *Ibid.*
14. *Young India*, 17 March, 1927, p. 85.
15. *Ashram Observances in Action* (Ahmedabad: Navjivan, 1959), pp. 137-39.
16. *Harijan*, 26 July, 1942, p. 238.
17. *Harijan*, 28 July, 1946, p. 236.
18. M.K. Gandhi, (1984) (ed). *An Autobiography* Or *The Story of My Experiments with Truth* (Ahmedabad: Navjivan), p. 250.
19. *Harijan*, 23 February 1947, p. 39.
20. Pyarelal, (1965) *Mahatma—The Early Phase* (Ahmedabad: Navjivan), p. 708.
21. *Ibid.*, p. 628.
22. See S.H. Rudolph and L.I. Rudolph, (1987), *Gandhi: The Traditional Roots of Charisma* (Delhi: Orient Longman).
23. *Living Planet Report, 2010.*
24. See *Ethical Consumerism Report 2007* www.co-operativebank.co.uk/ethicalconsumerismreport
25. Sriman Narayan, (1968), *The Selected Works of Mahatma Gandhi*, Vol. IV, (Ahmedabad: Navjivan), p. 223.
26. *Navajivan*, 25 May, 1924, p. 306.

5

Cultural Dimensions of Sustainability

Roopa Vajpeyi

"There is enough for everybody's need, but not enough for anybody's greed." —*Mahatma Gandhi*

Introduction

Indians have been rated as the greenest and the most sustainability conscious consumers in a recent global survey. Therefore, the relevance of sustainability in the context of Indian consumers can be questioned or considered redundant. "*Greendex 2014: Consumer Choice and the Environment—A Worldwide Tracking Survey*" is a comprehensive measure of consumer behaviour in 65 areas relating to housing, transportation, food and consumer goods. Greendex 2014 surveyed 18,000 consumers in 18 countries and ranked the countries based on sustainability and measured the way consumer patterns are responding to environmental concerns. The countries examined included Australia, India, China, the United States, the United Kingdom, Brazil, South Korea, Argentina, Hungary, Russia, Mexico, Sweden, Spain, South Africa, Germany, France, Japan and Canada. India came in first, pulling in a Greendex score of 61.4. China was the second-most sustainable according to the index. On the other end of the list are the United States and Canada.[1]

However, even though we seem to know how to be sustainable consumers and many of us may choose to continue to make sustainable choices, yet the pressures of urbanization are such that even while knowing better, most of us are likely to be pushed to make unsustainable choices. The reasons for this could be many and the most likely amongst these are lack of time and the lure of the convenience. The changing family patterns and the emergence of nuclear and single households, increasing number of women working away from home, aggressive advertising, marketing and proliferating super-markets, all have a role to play. Market dependence, in urban areas, is on an increase, because it is supportive of lifestyles where 'ready for use' and disposability are top priorities.

Greendex 2014 Overall Scores

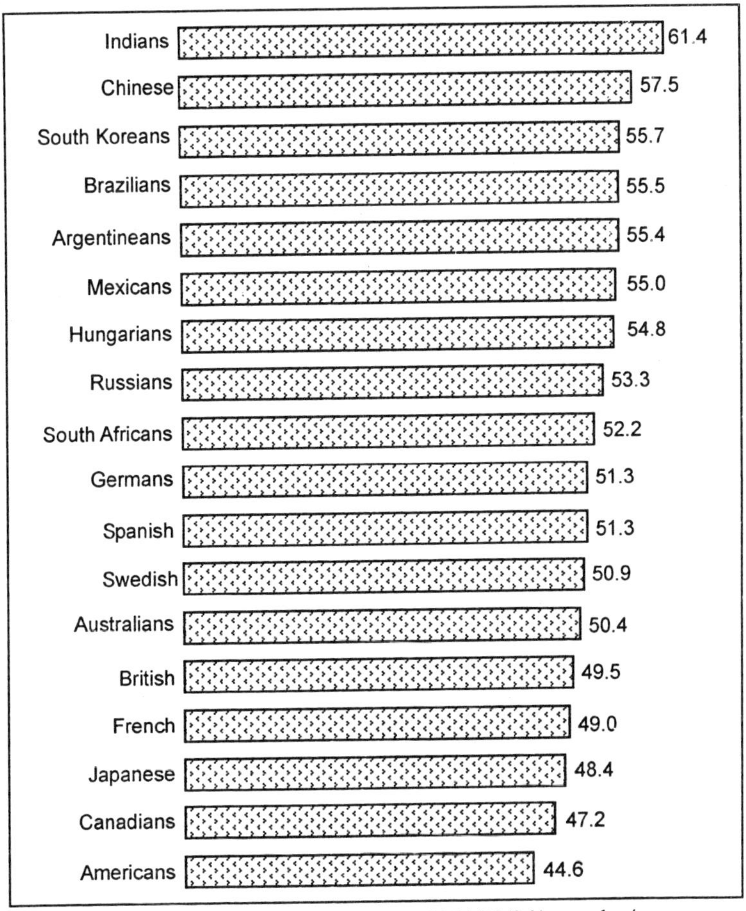

Source: http://press.nationalgeographic.com/2014/09/26/greendex/

Consumers need to be guided to support intelligent handling of market strategies so that consumers can be the kings that they are meant to be and not hapless victims, as they are likely to become, if they are not alert or aware as consumers. It is, therefore, in the consumers' interest to learn to walk the tight rope and create a balance through informed choices for better health for the family and the environment. Choosing fair trade practices, organic and green products and a socially viable approach to consumption need to be prioritized, but in the Indian context, such advice might prove redundant because, neither such products nor their certification is in place.

Indians have the advantage of a vast storehouse of traditional knowledge along with access to the world's best technologies and scientific knowledge and it is thus not too difficult to make a mix and match strategy for sustainable consumption. Good practices circulating regionally and nationally can be consciously adapted to suit individual needs and preferences, as is indeed already being done.

Sustainability in the Indian Context

Any discussion about or reference to sustainable practices in the Indian context, must take into consideration the ancient Indian sciences, philosophies, cultural and traditional practices (call them what you will), like:

1. ***Vaastu***—The science, practice and philosophy of human habitat, which ultimately is about energy conservation as well as optimal use of natural resources.
2. ***Ayurveda***—The science and practice of a way of life, health, disease prevention and management, including food intake.
3. ***Yoga***—The science, philosophy and practice of physical, mental and spiritual management.

Most Indians continue to follow principles and practices, advocated in these approaches for enhancing the quality of day-to-day life of individuals, and society as a whole. All this has continued simultaneous to the development and progress within the structure of everyday life of the people, until it has all acquired a status as an alternate track for dealing with life and its problems on a daily basis. Solutions offered by these approaches are within the reach of the people, cost nothing, unless you want to spend money on the peripherals invented by the market, or access these knowledge systems in their commercialized formats.

Currently in imminent danger of being commercialized, or rather in the process of being commercialized these knowledge systems are freely available to any and everybody. Continuous use over centuries has built in flexibility and adapted them to individual and community needs. These methodologies are time-tested in the lab of life and have proven validity through experience. These are self-sustaining, free of cost, 'do it yourself' strategies catering to sustainable options. Consulting a *'Guru'*, *'Acharya'* or a *'Vaidya'* is sometimes recommended, but most people have a self-help approach to these. The knowledge has been freely circulating in communities and society in general. According to Indian philosophy, *'gyan'* or 'knowledge' cannot be dated as it is *'shashwat'* or eternal and autonomous truth which is relayed through oral narratives, rituals and even in art forms and folk literature in different parts of India. When daily practice is ritualized or knowledge structures pass into the daily lives of people they transcend formalized avenues of dissemination and become part of cultural practices. These knowledge formats pass into public domain and get absorbed into living patterns. Sustainable practices are the norm, have been the norm in Indian life in all its segments and are in need of support so that they can continue to be a part of the daily life of Indians.

Strategies have to be worked out to help urban consumers shop with a conscience, for a healthy and environmentally supportive lifestyle, without stressing their budgets too much. If Indian consumers continue to use their traditional good practices to balance the benefits of modern markets, there is no reason that they should not continue to lead as the greenest consumers in the world. Comparative testing, certifications, proper labelling etc. have to be in place for urban consumers, re-connecting them to sustainable good practices and must be actively made available to people, who are perforce moving away from the traditional knowledge base.

Sustainability Redefined in the Urban Indian Context

1. To use what you have within reach and from local sources and resources.
2. To modulate consumption to seasonal variations so that market dependability is minimized.
3. To creatively use and re-use what you choose to bring home, to share it within the family, and to pass it on to others less privileged.
4. A basic tenet of sustainability is to share what you have with others, another is to re-use and recycle.
5. Yet another to eschew waste, because waste and our cavalier approach towards it is what leaves behind an unmanageable carbon footprint.

6. Sustainability is also to be less self-centred and to attune consumption to an extended time frame embracing as many people as possible. Thus, it is to be aware of where what comes from, and where it goes, and at what cost, and for whom?

There is nothing personal about consumption as any consumption choice involves production and disposal processes and those are not in individual hands. It is time now for us to re-examine consumer rights and to re-define them from the sustainability angle. Consumers are not stand-alone entities and they need to be responsible, not only to their own needs, but also to those of the entire planet and those of the future generations. If we had all been aware of our responsibilities as we were taught to be of our rights, we would not be talking so urgently about sustainability today.

To Which Problems does Sustainability Try to Give an Answer?

First problem that a sustainable mindset addresses is the problem of market dependability. Consumers have increasingly taken to looking at the market to define their needs for them, and for it to provide everything in the 'use and dispose' mode. Everyone knows how this fosters dependability. We all cry ourselves hoarse when it is a question of making our future generation self-reliant. We advise and caution each other not to molly-coddle them or to make it too easy for them. We fear that this would make them unappreciative of the true cost of things. However, we as consumers, are nothing better than spoilt, bratty children, who are self-centred, greedy and wasteful. In their case, the true cost spells parental resources. For consumers, the earth is a kind of a mother figure and we as consumers feel we not only have a right to all its resources, but also have the prerogative to wilful waste and squandering of those resources. This is the root cause of all our problems today.

Indian children are taught to be responsible to their parents, just as parents are responsible towards them. That is a good equation and needs to be nurtured, because this basic relationship is, believe it or not, the basis of all give and take in life. Mutuality is the keyword in sustainable options. You give as much, if not more than what you take, or be ready to face problems. Life moves in circles and what goes round, comes round.

The Triple Bottom-line

We all live in social dimensions, which have, of necessity, a frame. The frame consists of mutual dependence and the fact that everything has a cost. The first of these costs has an economic dimension. The first, because in urban societies most transactions are purchased or paid for in money and sustainability as an issue has arisen as an antidote from the consumption choices of these societies.

Most consumers feel that higher price is a guarantee of quality, but that is not always true. For checking the true value of any product, reference to published comparative tests is a reliable gauge. There are at least two independent Indian consumer organizations, currently carrying out comparative test programmes on a wide variety of products. Subscribing to their information can help consumers make informed choices. Another approach, which can be adopted by consumers for sustainable preferences, is to opt for fresh produce in the local markets, wherever possible, or tap the unorganized markets for both quality and economy, with the social angle built in. The unorganized sector in India is huge and most of the population from rich to poor purchases various items of consumption and everyday use from the unorganized sector. Very few people can afford the branded products across all segments. Further, most consumers in India are very price sensitive and not really brand conscious, therefore, the unorganized sector plays a very crucial role in the nation's domestic trade and consumption segments. The unorganized retail is a source from where food items and other everyday necessities of millions of Indians are accessed on a daily basis. It is also a major link between rural and urban societies, offering right products at the right time at the right place. In a country with a huge population, and high levels of poverty, this model of retail democracy is the most appropriate.

Next is the human resource cost, which reflects the involvement of people around us, or in our immediate vicinity, as also those not visible but yet contributing significantly to our needs, like farmers, industrial workers etc. This constitutes the social dimension and nobody understands better than us Indians, how important social units are. Modalities may change but equations remain the same. In our lifestyle, whether of urban or rural dimensions, mutual dependence is extensive and as consumers, we need to put a value or cost on each component. It is the only way to a fair and equitable society. Beyond, encompassing all this, are the environmental costs. The planet and its resources are the basic supply-line of our consumption needs. Tremendous growth in population and its needs is burdening the environment. Above all, it is the greed and waste that has taken a toll.

Sometimes we are so pre-occupied with the immediate and the visible that we become oblivious of the larger context of our needs and requirements. This is when we tend to become unsustainable because we link ourselves only to the markets and fail to see what sustains the markets, the people and the natural resources. Thus, when the links come alive for us, we begin to think of sustainability.

In which Way can the Individual Play a Role?

However, at the centre of all this is the individual. Ultimately, we all make our own choices from whatever choices exist around us and must learn to take responsibility for the choices we make, as our choices are not as individual as we might like to think. The choices are made available to us through very complex social and environmental processes.

Indian consumers have a distinct advantage. We have access to what the world's markets have to offer consumers, along with all the scientific and technologically supported choices. We also have a long tradition of consumption and production which is healthy and sustainable and which is backed by experiential knowledge about natural resources. Thus, if we so choose, our market dependency, in this day and time too, can continue to be minimal, when compared to the rest of the developed world. We have time honoured honed, tried and tested strategies and methodologies in most areas of consumption and production, ranging from food, clothing, travel, recycling and re-use, which involves, beside humans, other life forms as well. Thus, sustainability is about to co-existence.

It is good to remember that consumer is the ultimate king; if and when consumers decide to use their power to lobby for change, it happens. If consumers lobby to boycott an unsustainable product, the product has to be recalled or withdrawn. For doing that, the consumer needs to be informed. To become an aware consumer one needs to be in a networking mode with other consumers. These days it should be the easiest thing to do through social networking sites. Exchange of information can be transcontinental and globalization should no longer pose a threat to consumer interests. Making sustainable choices is also about using consumer power to steer manufacturers and producers to make sustainable choices available in the market. Consumer power can also be used to influence government policy, which in its turn promulgates rules, regulations, standards and their implementation. An awareness of these strategies can equip urban consumers to strengthen their sustainable mode of consumption.

This can also be used for our and for the planet's advantage. We can mix and match and create a new set of survival strategies, combining technology and tradition. We can continue with our 'do-it-yourself' approach and eschew waste as we have always done. As individuals again, no Indian has ever been taught to think only of himself or to think he or she is the centre of the universe. We have learnt to regard the world as our family and that is what a sustainable approach is asking us to do. Should that be difficult?

What is in it for the Consumer-Health? Money? Ethical Satisfaction?

It might not be difficult but a consumer well might ask: why should I even try? Or you might want to know if you stand to benefit in anyway. The answers by now should be self-evident. The 'do-it-yourself' approach, combined with considered and informed consumption definitely saves you money and also is a healthier option for you if you bring your cultural and traditional wisdom into active use. After all what does it take to pull a healthy sustainable meal together?

A Pocket full of Money and a Nearby Super-Store?

Well that is certainly the most convenient choice as long as money is no consideration, but since in most cases that remains an important consideration, the next best option would be the local vendor with the added advantage of freshness and seasonality, minus the burdensome packaging, the additives and the processing. Burdens for consumers come in many *avatars* these days! Nobody doubts the satisfaction one derives from time and money well spent and with a clear conscience of not having harmed or burdened anyone. Above all, this consumption pattern allows each one of us to take personal control of our own and our family's health.

Are Sustainable Options more Expensive?

Depends on how one calculates costs. If time is at a premium, you should go for the ready to consume. If your health is important and you can balance the time, mix and match self-help with technological support. Sustainability is costly because it functions within smaller frames. For example, what is grown organically is manageable only in smaller farms. However, the basis of trade is larger the number, cheaper the commodity, because it can then be mechanically and industrially managed (e.g. the meat and the poultry industry). Therefore, traditionally, sustainability has worked well in small communities. The Indian mind-set has not changed. Even in modern urban spaces, the localities function like self-contained/ sustained communities, with the unorganized sector as their main supply line.

Consumers work with the understanding that consumers need to be local and supplement their needs with self-help strategies and not everything needs to be bought, and we do not always really need what we end up buying. Optimizing usage and curtailing needs can be done to remain sustainable. Human help (since that is easily available to us Indians) rather than mechanical help is a more socially sustainable choice. The essential challenge of Sustainable Consumption and Production is how to dissociate economic development from environmental degradation, in order to operate within the limits of the planet's ecosystems. Meeting this challenge will also require technological innovation, rethinking current business models and political determination.

With increasing purchasing power, wasteful consumption linked to market driven consumerism is stressing the resource base of developing countries further. It is important to counter this through education and public awareness. In several areas, desirable limits and standards for consumption need to be established and applied through appropriate mechanisms.

Several traditional practices that are sustainable and environment friendly continue to be a regular part of the lives of people in developing countries like India. These need to be encouraged rather than replaced by more 'modern', but unsustainable practices and technologies, which are difficult to disseminate, despite people-friendly media formats, as people are not only poor but also illiterate.

Often subsidized resource accessibility is seen as an answer, but subsidies often lead to wasteful and unsustainable consumption by distorting the value of a resource. All pricing mechanisms need to be evaluated from a sustainable point of view.

Sustainable production and consumption deals not only with the problem of over-consumption, but also under-consumption and poverty. The social dimension gains weight in times of increasing imbalance in the material wealth between north and south/east and west even within countries. A very wide income gap between the wealthy and the poor exists in India, with only a very small minority of the population reaping the benefits of India's economic growth and some living below the poverty line.

In 1992, a plan for achieving sustainable development in the twenty-first century "Agenda 21" was adopted during the First Earth Summit. Agenda 21 is a comprehensive plan of action to be taken globally, nationally and locally by government, organizations and major groups in every area in which humans affect the environment. It includes issues like combating poverty and handling population and demographic dynamics.

With nearly 1.1 billion people in India and a projected growth up to 1.6 billion in the year 2050, the population pressure will become a serious task for India's future social, environmental and economic development. Combating poverty and hunger besides dealing with environmental problems is also part of the United Nations development targets called the Millennium Development Goals (MDG) (2000). The MDG address issues concerning the UN's future development strategies until 2015.

Purchasing decisions usually reconcile short-term costs with relatively short-term benefits for a given product or service. A growing number of consumers need to talk beyond these considerations to the impact their spending has on people and the planet around them. The products we buy have a history and a future beyond their immediate use. Whenever money is spent, a tacit endorsement is made for the full life cycle of impacts associated with that product. Conscientious consumption is an ethic that acknowledges the power of consumer activism in the movement towards sustainability. When consumers neglect to consider where their products come from; how and by whom they are made; what they require and do when in use; and where they go when obsolete; manufacturers, in the absence of effective legislation, are effectively given permission to exploit people and the environment. Conscientious consumption requires satisfactory answers to three simple questions in regard to consumption choices:

1. Where does any product in use, come from?
2. How is it used?
3. Where and how will it end-up?

How Do We Get Started: Find a Balance?

Sustainable consumption demands a change in our attitude towards nature. Nature is not just a material resource for human consumption. Man is also part of nature and this view is neither new nor unfamiliar to Indians, as like indigenous people anywhere Indians believe in the presence of the divine in Nature.

Sustainability in consumption is not the business of the government and private companies alone. It is the business of the people in general. It is a process which has to be initiated at each and every level of human endeavour and life. It involves individuals, families, communities, corporate bodies, nations and global society. It has to be a movement, because it involves paradigmatic change, which is difficult to bring about unless great many people get involved.

Following are some of the factors, which can support transformation:

1. Build awareness of sustainable consumption and production issues;
2. Build understanding of current practice in sustainability focused approaches to new product development; and
3. Re-enforce, reinvent and revive the connectivity of people to their cultural and sustainable practices in their daily lives. If they are made aware of these as choices and options that work in their favour and in favour of the planet earth, people should have no difficulty in accepting these facts as they already play a role in their lives.

Note

1. https://www.onyalife.com/environmental-news/greendex-ranks-18-countries-based-on-sustainability/

References

Aaron Smith, (2009),*The Internet's Role in Campaign 2008* (Washington, DC: Pew Internet and American Life Project, April 2009).

American Academy of Pediaetrics, "News Briefs", 3 October, 2005; Brian L. Wilcox *et al.*, *Report of the APA Task Force on Advertising and Children* (Washington, DC: APA, 20 February, 2004).

C. Torgan, "Childhood Obesity on the Rise," *Word on Health: Consumer Health Information Based on Research from the National Institute of Health*, at www.nih.gov/news/Wordon Health/jun2002/childhoodobesity.htm.

Capitalism from Allen Kanner, "Globalization and the Commercialization of Childhood", *Tikkun*, September/October 2005, pp. 49-51.

Christopher Morgan, "Archbishop Warns of Dysfunctional Infant Adults," *Sunday Times* (London), 17 September, 2006; Zoe Williams, *The Commercialisation of Childhood* (London: Compass, December 2006).

Deepa Srikantaiah, "Education: Building on Indigenous Knowledge," *IK Notes* (World Bank), No. 85, 2005; Pat Pridmore and David Stephens, *Children as Partners for Health: A Critical Review of the Child-tc-Child Approach* (London: Zed Books, 2000), p. 127; G. Mishra, "When Child Becomes a Teacher—The Child to Child Programme," *Indian Journal of Community Medicine*, October-December 2006, pp. 277-78. For information on the Grandmother Project, see www.grandmotherproject.org.

Eco-footprint and Figure 1 from Global Footprint Network, *The Ecological Footprint Atlas 2008*, (Oakland, CA: rev. ed., 16 December, 2008).

For more on systems thinking, see David W. Orr, *Earth in Mind* (Washington, DC: Island Press, rev. 2004), and Fritjof Capra, "Ecoliteracy: The Challenge for Education in the Next Century", Liverpool Schumacher Lectures, Centre for Ecoliteracy, Berkeley, CA, 20 March, 1999.

G. Ananthapadmanabhan, K. Srinivas, and Vinuta Gopal, 2007, *Hiding Behind the Poor* (Bangalore: Greenpeace India Society, October).

Gaia Education, at www.gaiaeducation.org

Grandmother Project field notes, Koulikoro, Mali, June 2004; maternal and child health programmes from Judi Aubel, "Participatory Communication Unlocks a Powerful Cultural Resource: Grandmother Networks Promote Maternal and Child Health," *Communication for Development and Social Change*, Vol. 2, No. 1 (2008), pp. 7-30.

International Workshop, "The Role of Early Childhood Education for a Sustainable Society," Gothenburg, Sweden, 2-4 May, 2007; Centre for Environment and Sustainability, *The Gothenburg Recommendations on Education for Sustainable Development* (Gothenburg, Sweden: Chalmers University of Technology and University of Gothenburg, 2008), p. 28.

K. Morgan and R. Sonnino, (2008) *The School Food Revolution: Public Food and the Challenge of Sustainable Development*, (London: Earthscan.

Lisa J. Graumlich, and Will L. Steffen, (eds.) (2007) *Sustainability or Collapse? An Integrated History and Future of People on Earth*, Cambridge, MA: The MIT Press.

"McDonald's to Expand in India", *Wall Street Journal*, 30 June, 2009; Anurag Sharma, "Cartoons—Animators Look at Licensing, Business Deals", *The Press Trust of India Limited*, 10 May, 2009.

Paul Ekins, (1991) "The Sustainable Consumer Society: A Contradiction in Terms?" *International Environmental Affairs*, Fall, pp. 243-58. Box.

Population projection for 2050 from United Nations Population Division, *op. cit.*, note 12.

Positive experiences from Sustainable Development Commission, "Outdoor Experiences, No Child Left Inside Coalition, "About the No Child Left Inside Act", at www.cbf.org.

S. Clayton and S. Opotow, (2003) (eds.) *Identity and the Natural Environment: The Psychological Significance of Nature* (Cambridge, MA: The MIT Press).

Sarvodaya Empowerment Programmes, at www.sarvodaya.org/about/empowerment-programmes.

Sustainable behaviour from Tim Kasser, "Frugality, Generosity, and Materialism in Children and Adolescents", in Kristin Anderson Moore and Laura H. Lippman, (eds.) (2005) *What Do Children Need to Flourish? Conceptualizing and Measuring Indicators of Positive Development*, New York: Springer, pp. 357-74.

T. Herbert, "Eco-intelligent Education for a Sustainable Future Life", in Pramling Samuelsson and Kaga, *op. cit.*, note 4, pp. 63-67.

The Ladakh Project, International Society for Ecology and Culture, at www.isec.org.uk/pages/ladakh.html#womensallianceofladakh.

United Nations, *World Youth Report 2005* (New York, 2005), p. 76; Cara Heaven and Matthew Tubridy, "Global Youth Culture and Youth Identity", in Oxfam, *Highly Affected, Rarely Considered* (Oxford, 2008), pp. 149-60, with quote on p. 154.

Wilderness traditions from L. Cook, "The 1944 Education Act and Outdoor Education: From Policy to Practice".

Y. Kaga, "The Role of Early Childhood Education in a Sustainable World", in Pramling Samuelsson and Kaga, *op. cit.*, note 4, pp. 9-18.

22 November, 2006; $17 billion from Juliet Schor, *Born to Buy: The Commercialized Child and the New Consumer Culture* (New York: Scribner, 2004), p. 21; Roisin Burke, "Food Giants Serve Up a 1.2bn Dish to Children," *The Sunday Independent* (Ireland).

6

Towards Ethical Consumption

Mamta Pathania

Introduction

Sustainable consumption is a controversial concept: politically, socially and intellectually. Consumption drives our economies and defines our lives; making it sustainable is an enormous and essential challenge. Consumption and lifestyles in the world's richest countries are a significant cause of global environmental problems. The global consequences of environmental problems, particularly climate change, affect both political agendas and people's everyday life. While there is a wide consensus that environmental challenges require shared responsibilities, how and to what extent consumers can bear these responsibilities is a debated issue (Jacobsen & Dulsrud, 2007). Consumerism is increasingly recognized as a major drain on global resources and the search for sustainable consumption is emerging as a key policy issue.

The World Summit on Sustainable Development in 2002 set in place a 10-year programme for national governments to develop strategies for sustainable consumption and production. The opinion-formers and policy-makers are facing a problem due to the changing consumer behaviour and making the lives more sustainable continues to be a challenge for them. The concept of sustainability and sustainable development has taken hold throughout the world as a new guiding principle of economic development. Sustainability involves "meeting the real needs of the present without harming the biosphere so that future generations will be able to meet their own needs."

The increased levels of consumption that have accompanied our consumer-oriented culture have also given rise to some consumers questioning their individual consumption choices, with many opting for greater consumption simplicity. This link between consideration of actual consumption levels and consumer choices is evident among a group of consumers known as ethical consumers. Ethical consumers consider a range of ethical issues in their consumer behavioural choices. Particularly prevalent is voluntary simplification due to concerns for the extent and nature of consumption.

The definition of sustainable consumption as proposed by the 1994 Oslo Symposium on Sustainable Consumption is "…. the use of services and related products which respond to basic needs and bring a better quality of life while minimizing the use of natural resources and toxic materials as well as emissions of waste and pollutants over the life cycle of the service or product so as not to jeopardise the needs of future generations."[1]

Thus, sustainable consumption can be defined in the following way:

Sustainable consumption integrates a range of social, economic and political practices at the individual, household, community, business and government levels that support and encourage:[2]

- reducing the direct environmental burden of producing, using and disposing goods and services;
- meeting basic needs for key consumption goods and services, such as food, water, health, education and shelter;
- maximizing opportunities for sustainable livelihoods in the South;
- consuming goods and services that contribute positively to the health and well-being of women and children;
- increasing the development and adoption of energy and water efficient appliances, public transport and other demand-side measures;
- the production and sale of new goods and services adapted to global environmental constraints; and
- lifestyles that place greater value on social cohesion, local traditions and non-material values.

The IUCN Conference on Conservation and Development held in Ottawa, Canada in 1986 made the following contributions towards defining sustainable development. Sustainable development attempts to address five main challenges:

- Integration of conservation and development;
- Meeting basic human needs;

- Achievement of equity and social justice;
- Promotion of social self-determination and cultural diversity; and
- Maintenance of ecological integrity.

Looking at definitional part it seems that there is a dire need to analyse the issues of social, economic and ecological sustainability raised by consumerism, ways in which the impacts of consumption can be reduced, and ways in which issues such as these can be integrated across the curriculum. Therefore, to meet the challenge of sustainable development, businesses can help to foster more sustainable levels and patterns of consumption. There is a significant opportunity for business to help consumers choose and use their goods and services sustainably. In order to do so, business must create sustainable value for consumers by supplying products and services that meet their functional and emotional needs—now and for future generations—while respecting environmental limits and the common values.

However, consumerism touches all aspects of daily life in the modern world and might be seen as a core value in the North and, increasingly, throughout the South as well. Indeed, mass consumption is now entrenched as one of the key defining processes of economic and social life around the world in contrast with the values of sustainability that are characteristic of indigenous communities.

Chapter 4 of Agenda 21 identified unsustainable patterns of production and consumption, especially in industrialized countries, as "the major cause of the continued deterioration of the global environment". Agenda 21 goes on to say that this is "a matter of grave concern" because "the basic consumer needs of a large section of humanity are not being met" and "the excessive demands and unsustainable lifestyles among the richer segments ... place immense stress on the environment."[3]

Accordingly, Agenda 21 encourages governments in the North to take a leading role in promoting sustainable patterns of consumption through policies that: encourage efficiency in production patterns; reduce wasteful consumption in the process of economic growth and encourage a shift to more sustainable patterns of production and consumption, taking into account the development needs of developing countries. In this way, Agenda 21 heralded a new approach to consumer education, aligning it with health, citizenship and environmental education as part of the reorientation of education towards sustainability.

Thus, in order to march towards ethical sustainable consumption one needs to analyse patterns, causes and impacts of global and personal patterns of consumption and appreciate the ethical dimension of reducing the social and ecological impacts of consumption.

Consumer Behaviour and Sustainability

Consumerism is being used by some stakeholders as a basis for social change, based on the theory that companies make decisions about their offerings as a result of consumer demand. Recent changes in consumer behaviour, and the advent of constructs such as 'green marketing' (Arnould *et al.*, 2004) and 'sustainable consumption' (Jackson, 2005) have led to many studies that were designed to understand how to motivate and encourage consumers to adopt ethical behaviours (Jackson, 2005). In addition, it has been recognized that there is a need for better understanding of the environmental impact of goods and services (Schaefer, 2005). This has come about as today's consumers demand environment friendly goods and services, and are willing to pay more for products that are 'emotionally satisfying' in terms of the perceived quality, performance, brand image, and the stature they provide (Marshman-Goldblatt, 2008). This includes 'green products', thus providing an incentive for marketers to offer such products (Schaefer, 2005). The likelihood of adopting sustainable behaviour depends on the amount of behaviour modification required (Byrne and Polonsky, 2001), which requires an understanding of the attitudes, demographics, values and behaviours of consumers.

Dimensions of Sustainability

As advocated by the World Commission on Environment and Development (1987) on the description of sustainable development: "Sustainable development is development that meets the needs of the present without compromising [or, impairing] the ability of future generations to meet their own needs [or, to enjoy similar, if not better, quality of life and opportunity as ours". Sustainable development is generally perceived as an overlapping of dimensions or components, namely environment, society, and economy (UNESCO, 2005).

Elaborating the individual dimensions, the environmental dimension encompasses natural resources, climate change, rural transformation, sustainable urbanization, and disaster prevention and mitigation, while societal dimension embraces human rights, peace and human security, gender equality, cultural diversity and intercultural understanding, health, HIV/AIDS and governance. The economic dimension, by contrast, includes poverty reduction, corporate responsibility and accountability, and market economy. These three dimensions are thought to operate as three overlapping same-sized circles with the overlapping area being perceived as the human well-being. For higher levels of human well-being, the three dimensions need to be more aligned and this would lead to higher area of overlapping hence replicated as higher level of human well-being. This means that a balanced, harmonious and interdependent, consideration of environmental, societal and economic dimensions is needed in our pursuit of development and enhanced quality of life.

Further, it is indisputable that sustainability is addressed through the provision of quality education. As such, quality teaching and learning will produce quality teachers who, in turn, help churn out quality citizens that contribute to quality society in which we and our future generations live in. As such, quality teaching requires quality training, constant upgrading of one's skills and knowledge in pertinent areas, undertaking of research that informs development in one's areas of expertise, and furthermore highlighting and stressing on the aspect of consumption patterns and sustainable lifestyles to be adopted and helping the future generations to also march on the same path.

Environmental Concerns

The United Nations Conference on the Human Environment, otherwise known as the Stockholm Conference which took place in Sweden in June 1972 was the first UN Conference to focus the debate on international environmental issues. The representatives of 113 countries attended the Conference. The Conference was effective in drawing attention to environmental problems on a global scale and as a result of increased awareness generated by the conference, many governments created specific government agencies dedicated to meeting the environmental challenges. It was also important in encouraging international cooperation on tackling global issues.

The Declaration of this Conference—the *Declaration of the United Nations Conference on the Human Environment* laid out a set of fundamental principles that recognized the right to a healthy environment and the need for international action to uphold this right. The conference laid the foundations for creation of the *United Nations Environment Programme*, a division of the United Nations established in 1972, which is committed to: "providing leadership and encouraging partnership in caring for the environment by inspiring, informing, and enabling nations and peoples to improve their quality of life without compromising that of future generations."

In 1987, the Brundtland Commission produced its report entitled *'Our Common Future'* (often referred to as *The Brundtland Report*). This report represents a key milestone in the development of the arguments and ideas that have shaped the field of Sustainable Development during more than two decades. It presents coherent and comprehensive perspectives on the global environmental, social and economic threats facing humanity, their interrelations, and the common challenges we face. The Report calls for cooperative action by governments, voluntary organizations, citizens, businesses, institutes and others to address the pressing problems and challenges described in the document. The idea of sustainable development is an attractive one, where a system is organized so future generations can continue in the same way for the foreseeable future. Taken by itself this idea seems perfectly logical, why should we destroy the resources given to us? Who are we to use these things and not leave anything for those that come after us? However, mankind has not travelled this path for many (may be legitimate) reasons such as prioritizing short-term survival over long-term planning and lack of knowledge. Humans have now organized a highly complex system, increasingly globalized in nature. An important question is how sustainable is this system? For how long will the fundamentals needed for the continuation of humanity exist? Threats to the planet and the current system are many: these threats include the high rate of use of non-renewable energy sources, the number and size of violent conflicts, poverty traps, the changing climate of our planet, population growth and the degradation of our land and sea resources. A look at economic aspects of sustainable development raises important questions which need to be considered:

- Economic growth is used as a marker for the health of the economy, but can economic growth continue without end?
- The health of the economy can have a dramatic effect on ecology: when a person is not sure whether they will have enough to eat in the short-term, any considerations of long-term consequences will be thrown out the window. Are there ways to either minimize the impact of bad economic times, or prevent the duration and frequency of such economic times?

- To what extent should the ecological impact of a business have on the measurement of economic success? Should pollution be counted as an economic cost?
- The costs of moving from a current system to a system of greater sustainability could be large, such as the conversion of equipment to renewable energy systems. In which case and how should these costs be managed?
- Climate change, the rise in the Earth's temperature and its potential to wreak havoc on the agricultural, geographic and other systems is a very serious issue. Pressing questions abound such as how much and what can mankind do to prevent or mitigate this threat? What consequences of any change to our climate could there be? If sea levels rise how could the ensuing catastrophes be managed? What economic, health, or socio-political effects could there be and what could or should be done now to plan to manage these issues?

Thus for the world to be truly sustainable, we will have to cease our reliance on fossil fuels. Transport issues could be solved by renewable energy sources, but also by reducing the need for transport. The issue of food miles has become popular. However, is the issue more complicated than simply the less food miles the better? Should the impact of the agricultural practices and fossil fuel use during production and the actual need for the type of good produced also be considered? Renewable energy such as solar, or wind may be able to solve the transport and agricultural needs, but it is unclear how the plastic problem will be solved. Although using biological materials as a substitute may be possible, this may cause major problems by taking away resources from food production ethanol effect. As was seen recently, the use of agricultural resources to produce ethanol caused inflation in food prices and subsequent poor nutrition and starvation. The need for fresh clean water is of utmost importance, it is necessary for life itself. Poor agricultural practices can devastate water systems, causing salinity, pollution and other problems. Any alteration in weather patterns can affect the river, rainfall and lake systems, causing rivers to stop flowing or floods causing sanitation concerns. Water for general sanitation and health, irrigation and industrial uses causes conflicts and the viability of human habitation.

The question remains, do we have enough freshwater in the world to meet the demands of food production and industry? How can we ensure that water systems are managed sustainably and that all mankind has access to clean water? Similarly the endangered species list is growing fast which is also an aspect to be thought of. The consumption patterns are such that one is not satisfied with the existing resources one has. Everybody wants the latest thing may it be mobile, a car or any other thing which would be just dumped in for getting new ones, leading to e-waste which is quite unethical in itself.

The Way Out

The problems are numerous but solutions can also be thought of the only thing required is a positive attitude and a will both at individual and collective level to adopt sustainable patterns in our lifestyles. For that one has to identify the availability and proximity of resources for both the urban and non-urban areas including: energy, renewable energy, water/ recycled water, telecommunications, public transport, develop key sustainability performance indicators for both residential and commercial development. Efforts should be made in minimizing total potable water consumption (water delivery targets, water recycling targets) minimizing greenhouse gas (GHG) emissions per household, minimizing energy consumption, minimizing waste generation and disposal, maximizing recycling, minimizing total land cost delivery, minimizing annual household costs, minimizing the dependence on private vehicle ownership and use maximizing the level of public transport.

The UN "Earth Summit" in Rio (1992) referred to social development, economic development, and environmental protection, as the three "interdependent and mutually reinforcing pillars" of sustainable development. The challenge for early educators is, therefore, to develop educational systems, curriculum and pedagogic practices that promote sustainable actions with respect to each of these pillars. The Three Pillars of Sustainable Development Education for Sustainable Development provides a vision of education that seeks to balance human and economic well-being with cultural traditions and respect for the environment.

Sustainability and Consumption

Sustainability was defined in terms of its impact on the environment and the systems in place in society that aim to ensure that the community's actions do not threaten the planet's long-term viability. Getting consumers to adopt a sustainable lifestyle is a gradual process that is part of a holistic move towards a new lifestyle (Gilg *et al.,* 2005).

Consumption is defined in the terms of several different disciplines, such as economics, physics, ecology or sociology. It is the human transformation of materials and energy. Consumption is of concern to the extent that it makes the transformed materials or energy less available for future use, or negatively impacts biophysical systems in such a way as to threaten human health, welfare or other things people value. Consumption involves producers and distributors as well as "consumers". We need to understand consumption in the context of sustainability—that is, whether our present actions sacrifice the ability of future generations to meet their needs. The rate of transformation of energy and materials that is sustainable depends on: the rate of natural regeneration of resources; the capacity of the environment to assimilate effluents without substantial negative impact on human health and the biosphere; and the rate at which more abundant alternatives or substitutes can replace energy sources and materials of limited availability. At the same time, societies need to examine their values and consider how goals can be met with the least damaging consumption. Scientists can help to understand the causes and dynamics of consumptive behaviour. They can also develop indicators that track environmental impacts and link them to consumption activities, build understanding of how environmental and social systems respond to stress, and analyze the effectiveness of different strategies for making and implementing policy choices in the presence of uncertainty.

In the words of Professor Jeffrey Sachs, economist, "Our challenge, our generation's unique challenge, is learning to live peacefully and sustainably in an extraordinarily crowded world. Our planet is crowded to an unprecedented degree. It is bursting at the seams. It's bursting at the seams in human terms, in economic terms, and in ecological terms."[4]

Conclusion

It is quite imperative that as we move into the era of Education for Sustainable Development, educational institutions should play their respective roles in addressing sustainability. Sustainable consumption is not easy to attain, but it is also not a pipe dream. As we enter an era where global food production will need to double in the face of escalating environmental challenges, food systems must minimize their ecological footprint; interdisciplinary, multi-scale approaches offer the most promises and for that, commitment from consumers, farmers, industry and government is required. Challenges are numerous but efforts are required to made from every nook and corner to combat with these unethical consumption patterns leading to environmental imbalances. One needs to be optimistic that we can reach the goal of sustainability. Today we are seeing a mainstreaming of ethical concerns around consumption that reflects an increasing anxiety with—and accompanying sense of responsibility for—the risks and excesses of contemporary lifestyles around the globe.

There has been much discussion about environmental, sustainable and ethical consumption. Raising consumers' awareness of ethical concerns is needed to achieve a degree of concern for the environment as well as sustainable and ethical consumption in the community. Environmental ethics occur when natural resources are treated not just as commodities but also as segments of the whole ecology (Shaw *et al.*, 2005b), and an awareness of environmental ethics can lead to environmental consumerism. This is also referred to as 'environmentally responsible consumption' and 'green consumption'. The sustainable and/ or ethical consumption in the marketplace cannot be achieved unless the target market's ethical concerns are addressed.

Notes

1. [Norwegian Ministry of the Environment (1994)], Oslo Roundtable on Sustainable Production and_Consumption, http://www.unesco.org/education/tlsf/TLSF/theme_b/mod09/uncom09t06.html
2. Robins, N. and Roberts, S. (1998) *Consumption in a Sustainable World*, Workbook prepared for the OECD Workshop on Consumption in a Sustainable World, Kabelvaag, Norway, 2-4 June.
3. United Nations (1992), *Agenda 21,* United Nations Conference on Environment & Development (3-14 June, 1992), Rio de Janeiro, Brazil: United Nations.
4. Jeffrey Sachs, "http://festivalofthinkers.hct.ac.ae/Themes/Sustainable%20 Development.pdf
   Future Resources: Envisioning Sustainable Development, Reith Lecture, 11 April, 2007.

References

http://www.327matters.org/Docs/ESD%20Book%20Master.pdf
http://www.iea.org/textbase/nppdf/free/2007/key_stats_2007.pdf
http://www.livingearth.org.uk/LEF_Sustainable_Development_Primer.pdf

http://www.resourcesmart.vic.gov.au/documents/Guidelines_for_Future_Developments_Final.pdf!

http://www.unescoapceiu.org/bbs/files/doc/2002/esd/TLSF/theme_b/mod09/uncom09bod.htm

Towards Sustainable Consumption: A joint statement by the Royal Society and the United States National Academy of Sciences.

United Nations (1992), *Agenda 21,* United Nations Conference on Environment and Development (3-14 June, 1992), Rio de Janeiro, Brazil: United Nations.

World Commission on Environment and Development (1987) *Our Common Future*, Oxford: Oxford University Press.

7

Consumers and Sustainable Consumption

Towards a Sustainable Global Society

Jayashree Pillai

"A principle is a principle... and in no case can it be watered down, because of our incapacity to live it in practice. We have to strive to achieve it, and the striving should be conscious, deliberate and hard." —*Mahatma Gandhi,* 1939

Introduction

The last few decades have seen dramatic changes on a global scale due to political developments, changing consumption patterns and rapid progress in information and communication technology. Globalization has emerged as a key word leading to the emergence of a global village and community. In the wake of consumerism, we are witnessing unforeseen social, environmental and cultural changes. On the one hand, the developed nations are trying to lead other countries with manufactured goods, while on the other, the developing nations are struggling to cope with the emerging market changes. In our incessant effort to buy and accumulate things, consumers today have neglected concern for health or environment. This process has grown into threats for the very existence of the human race. The so-called progress is adding to the environmental degradation the world has been facing. The consumers today have to induce significant changes.

I would like to invite your attention to the present issues facing the society in the context of consumerism. The lure of consumption is leading us to a never before scenario of wastage and pollution, at the cost of several traditional values. The proliferation of technology and the ease of manufacturing goods should also show responsibility towards the future of the planet. Sustainable consumption should be the preferred option. Development in harmony with nature and sustainable consumption only will lead to a better future, not reckless shopping for unnecessary things just to have the satisfaction of something fashionable or to fulfil our insatiable lust for accumulation.

Sustainable Production and Consumption

A key issue in the 1992 United Nations Conference on Environment and Development in Rio de Janeiro was sustainable production and consumption. Ten years later, at the World Summit on Sustainable Development in Johannesburg, the international community was called upon to improve global living conditions and to "encourage and promote the development of a framework of programmes on sustainable consumption and production (SCP) in support of regional and national initiatives to accelerate the shift towards SCP."[1]

The United Nations Commission on Sustainable Development (UNCSD) Symposium on Sustainable Consumption, Oslo, 1994 defined sustainable consumption as "the use of goods and services that respond to basic needs and bring a better quality of life, while minimizing the use of natural resources, toxic materials and emissions of waste and pollutants over the life cycle, so as not to jeopardize the needs of future generations."[2]

The United Nations Development Programme (UNDP) describes conspicuous consumption as places where there is heavy societal pressure to maintain high consumption patterns and where competitive spending and display of wealth are encouraged by society.

Consumerism and Affluence: A Way of Life

'More, more, and more' is the maxim of consumerism, which has been spreading from the wealthy societies to the developing world. The trendsetters are the rich and super rich whose income and numbers have exploded in the last three decades. As a result of globalization, people in various parts of the globe have begun to share the same wish-lists, and the same brands are available now for whosoever can afford them. While privileged few over-consume, the consumption options of millions are so limited that they are confined to a hand to mouth existence.

Rich societies and relatively wealthy consumers account for by far the greatest per capita share of consumption and environmental footprint. According to estimates by World Wildlife Fund (WWF), three planets would be required if the rest of the world were to adopt the consumption patterns and lifestyles of the average citizen from the United Kingdom. Similarly, five planets would be required if they were to follow the lifestyle of the average North American.[3]

Impact of Consumption Patterns on Environment

The modern consumption pattern has completely devastated the environment. The real issue is not consumption itself, but its patterns and effects—inequalities in consumption are stark. Globally, the 20 per cent of the world's richest population account for 86 per cent of total private consumption, the poorest 20 per cent of humanity a miniscule 1.3 per cent. More specifically, the richest 20 per cent consume 45 per cent of all meat and fish, the poorest consume 5 per cent, the richest fifth consume 58 per cent of total energy, the poorest fifth less than 4 per cent, the richest fifth consume 84 per cent of all chapter, the poorest fifth 1.1 per cent, the richest fifth own 87 per cent of the world's vehicle fleet, the poorest fifth less than 1 per cent. Runaway growth in consumption in the past 50 years is putting a never before strain on the environment.[4]

Towards a Sustainable Global Society

Awareness of the environment of the earth, of its species and of the place of humanity in that environment, goes back a very long way in time. To some, the watershed of modern day environmental concern was the first Earth Day celebrated in the US in 1970. The benchmark of world environmental concern for many others was the 1972 UN sponsored World Environment Conference in Stockholm, Sweden. But the idea of harmonious co-existence with nature has deep roots in the ancient culture of India. The *Vedas* and *Upanishads*, dating back to several thousand years before the present calendar, have talked about environment. They have expounded rules for the protection of nature, which were required by the civil society to follow. The following references from the *Vedas* and *Upanishads* give just an indication of the reverence our ancestors had cultivated:

> "Let the handsome peasants harness the ploughs extend the yokes and scatter the seeds on the manure, prepared soils; May the

bunch of crops be bountiful, May the sickles draw the ripened crops even closer." —*Atharva Veda* 3/17/2

May the plants and crops, the sun and stars
And the water be as sweet as honey;
Let the firmament be sweet to us;
To us let the farmers be sweet
May the footsteps of these farmers
Be unhindered... —*Atharva Veda* 20/143/8

I invoke the splendorous earth endowed with fragrance
Providing perpetual nutrients
Which have been well manured
And the controller of all elements. —*Taittiriya Upanishad*

Every human activity must lead to growth with certain environmental responsibility and development integrated with nature. Any sustainable agenda must be concerned with intergenerational equity, ensuring that future generations have the same capability to develop as the present generation. There is a need for evolving an environmental policy on a global scale to prevent ecological degeneration and to encourage sustainable methods of development, inclusive of consumption patterns.

Issues and Challenges

The environment of developing countries in particular and the globe as a whole is facing deteriorating conditions that may lead to a catastrophe in the near future. While the human race has acted in haste to accelerate this process, the onus of the rapid exploitation of natural resources falls squarely on the shoulders of the modern 'leaders' of the race—the developed nations.

Currently, 80 per cent of the world's natural resources are being consumed by about 25 per cent of the world's population. They also produce most of the pollutants. Tons of dangerous chemicals and harmful bye-products are emitted in our atmosphere, which have made holes in the ozone layer. Some of the dreaded reducing agents that lead to the formation of the holes in the ozone layer in the upper atmosphere are: Chlorofluorocarbons (CFCs) used in refrigerators and air-conditioners, Methyl chloroform (CH_3CCl_3) used in cleaning solvents and aerosols, Carbon tetrachloride (CCl_4) used in bleaching and dry-cleaning, and Halons used in fire fighting equipments.

It may not require statistics to prove that the per capita consumption of energy—whether it is food or any other form—in a developed society like the one the USA has always exceeded the average worldwide consumption and is many times that of any country in the Third World. According to published data, one US citizen is responsible for producing as much greenhouse gas (GHG) as 19 Indians, 30 Pakistanis, or 269 Nepalese. In other words, over-consumption and unchecked damage of the environment and ecology have been rampant in the First World, and as a result of globalization of issues and a concern for the future of the planet, the developing nations are being forced to carry the cross.

Sustainable consumption and protection of environment should have found priority in the national and international agenda of planned development. Though certain changes are irreversible, it's time developing nations and developed nations formulate a common agenda, whatever be the divisions of accountability and responsibility, for the welfare of the planet, its bio-diversity, ecology, and the future of mankind.

While the issues related to environment is of particular importance, there are other spheres in which globalization casts its long shadow. Several countries of the world are facing an identity crisis and split personality. The growth of consumerism across the world is cutting into the fabric of indigenous production and traditional trade of local goods. The cultural diversity of the planet is under pressure from the commercial propagation of big multinational business. Societies are being passively seduced by different means to accept the world-view of corporate conglomerates. Small economies are held to ransom by the mighty power of the rich countries.

The Dilemma of Development

In its effort to catch up with the developed countries, the developing nations are recklessly following them in every area. The agricultural growth, especially in an agrarian society like India, has raised some questions of environmental costs. High yielding varieties are rapidly replacing the numerous locally adapted varieties, making crops more vulnerable to disease. Soil health problems, such as deficiency of micronutrients and organic matter, incidence of soil salinity and damage to the physical structure of soil, have arisen in the intensively cultivated areas. The challenge is not only to sustain and increase agricultural growth, but to do so without damaging the environment. On both counts, the desired objectives still remain far from being met.

Polluted Land, Rivers and Sky

The insatiable thirst for progress has forced developing countries to ruthlessly tap all available resources for food, energy and shelter. In the process, our atmosphere and water resources have been left polluted with dangerous consequence for the flora and fauna. Developing countries are facing a number of catastrophes leading to many geological and climatic changes. In the same way, the explosive growth of population in the developing countries has vigorously accelerated the slow process of natural changes.

To satisfy the ever-increasing needs large tracts of green cover over the earth have been denuded. Million years old strata of oil and coal deep inside the womb of mother earth have been extracted and all this has triggered the mechanism of geological change. The polluted air that we all breathe in, the polluted water that flows down our rivers or the chemical fog often seen over our cities all point towards a deteriorating environment around us.

According to one estimate, the tropical forests are vanishing at the rate of 50 hectares (124 acres) per minute, of which a major portion falls in the developing countries. With the increase in population, more and more land areas are being encroached upon to cater to the needs of food and shelter. In the process, natural resources and habitats are being disturbed and destroyed. This is one of the prime reasons for extinction of certain animal species.

Global Drivers of Consumption

Current global consumption patterns are unsustainable. Based on facts and trends, it is becoming apparent that efficiency gains and technological advances alone will not be sufficient to bring global consumption to a sustainable level; changes will also be required to consumer lifestyles, including the ways in which consumers choose and use products and services.

- Global consumption levels and patterns are driven at the most fundamental level by: Rapid global population growth—Population of 9 billion expected by 2050.
- The rise in global affluence and associated consumption—Global middle class expected to triple by 2030.
- A culture of "consumerism" among higher income groups, who account for the greatest per capita share of global consumption.[5]

Global Consumption Patterns and Impacts

Global consumption is putting unsustainable and increasing stress on:

- *The Earth's ecosystems*—60 per cent of the Earth's ecosystem services have been degraded in the past 50 years.
- *The supply of energy and material resources needed for industrial growth*—Natural resource consumption is expected to rise up to 170 per cent of the Earth's bio-capacity by 2040.
- *Human social systems and well-being*—Human well-being does not necessarily rely on high levels of consumption.

The Role of the Consumer

Consumer attitudes and behaviours play a critical role in ensuring sustainable consumption patterns. Consumers need to be increasingly concerned about environmental, social and economic issues, and increasingly willing to act on those concerns. Consumer willingness often does not translate into sustainable consumer behaviour because of a variety of factors—such as availability, affordability, convenience, product performance, conflicting priorities, scepticism and force of habit.

The role of producers and the role of consumers are intrinsically linked in terms of the sustainable use of products. Consumers choose to buy a product for many personal reasons. One of the important reasons will always remain excellent performance at an adequate price. In the future, performance that is both based on sustainability and recognized as added value will become increasingly important for consumer choices. This offers great potential as a driver for innovative products—not merely in the sense of 'green' products, but in the sense of offering smarter consumer-relevant solutions that link product quality to the shared responsibility of producers and consumers.

To be able to lead sustainable lifestyles based on informed purchasing decisions and changes in behaviour, consumers need the support of all actors: business, government and civil society. Business houses must have dialogue with stakeholders (such as consumers, retailers, marketers, policy-makers, NGOs) and between businesses to define sustainable products and lifestyles and to formulate actionable responses.

An Agenda for a Sustainable World

One drastic fall out of globalization trends that can be seen in many developing societies is that it diverts local people from their survival needs to succumbing to the limitless appetite of the global market.

"Sustainable development is the situation which has paths of human progress so that it meets the needs and aspirations of the present generation without compromising the ability of future generations to meet their own needs."[6] Whether we like it or not, there are clear indications and patterns in the horizon, which compel us to examine whether consumption and sustainability can go hand in hand. Sustainable consumption should be able to satisfy our needs and aspirations and we must develop habits based on long-term environmental, social and cultural goals.

Basic needs of the larger masses, like food, clothing, shelter, education and medical care should not be the leftovers of the rich nations and rich people. The responsibility of reversing the damage done and preserving the planet lies more with the societies who have consumed its resources most. The developed and developing nations must jointly face the issues and challenges of a sustainable global society, with the first and foremost objective of putting an end to reckless wastage and irresponsible consumption.

The need of the hour is to understand and abide by the fact that wealth and possessions are not the prime motivators of happiness and dignity. As it has been believed from ancient times in our country, true satisfaction and happiness evolve not from pursuing wanton desires, but curbing such desires. Only this can lead to peace of mind, and without peace of mind how can there be happiness.

Every stakeholder, be it the government, business, or consumer, must focus on the long term impact of our actions, and should not be misled by the glitz and glamour of a consumerist society, which as we can see, is not a sustainable way of life.

Notes

1. WBCSD (1997) Sustainable Production and Consumption from a Business Perspective.
2. United Nations Commission on Sustainable Development (UNCSD), Symposium on Sustainable Consumption, Oslo, 1994.
3. WWF, Living Planet Report, 2006.
4. Human Development Report 1998 Overview, UNDP.
5. WBCSD (1997) Sustainable Production and Consumption from a Business Perspective.
6. As defined by Brundtland, in his report of the World Commission on Environment and Development (WECD).

References

AMBIO—A Journal of the Human Environment, Vol. XXIX, No. 3, May 2000 (The Royal Swedish Academy of Sciences).

Ashby, Eric (1978) *Reconciling Man with the Environment,* Stanford, California: Standard University Press.

Biswas, A.K., and Qu-Gepin, (Ed.,) *Environmental Impact Assessment for Developing Countries* (London: Tycooly International Publishers).

Chandra Pal, *Environmental Pollution and Development, Environmental Law, Policy and Role of Judiciary.*

Global Environmental Outlook 2000, (UNEP's Millennium Report on Environment).

Hardin, Garrett, (1980) "*What is a Global Problem?", Bios 51*, September, pp. 136-37.

Hirnawi Essam and Hashmi Manzur-Ul-Haque, (Ed.) (1982) *Global Environmental Issue: United Nations Environment Programme,* Dublin; Tycooly International Publishers.

Maurya, S.D. (1989) *Urbanisation and Environmental Problems,* Allahabad: Chugh.

Millar Marian, A.L., (1985) *The Third World in Global Environmental Politics,* Open University Press.

Mohan, I., (1989) *Environment and Habitat,* New Delhi: Ashish.

Mohan, I., (1988) *Environmental Awareness and Urban Law,* New Delhi: Ashish.

Narayanan, L.R.A., (1983) "The Eye in the Sky", *The Hindu*, New Delhi, November 7.

Thomas, Keith (1982) *Man and Nature: A History of the Modern Sensibility,* New York: Pantheon.

V.I. Vernadsky, "The Biosphere and the Noosphere", *American Scientist* 33—January 1945: 4.

Weiss, Edith Brown, (1989) *In Fairness to Future Generations: International Law, Common Patrimony and Intergenerational Equity,* New York: Transnational Publishers.

8

Transforming Unsustainable Lifestyles

Key to Sustainable Consumption

Shruti Mittal and *Suresh Prasad Singh*

Introduction

Survival and sustenance of mankind is critically dependent on survival and sustenance of nature as it provides resources which are used for all development purposes, which in turn sustain human lives and livelihood. Nature[1] and its resources are used to satisfy simplest as well as the most complex needs. It is also no aberration to argue that nature has been and will remain the actual base for all human development and prosperity, human efforts have achieved or will achieve in future.

Future development of mankind, therefore, requires a balance and sustainability in use and preservation of nature and its resources. However, our recent experience over the last few decades clearly shows that nature and its resources are increasingly being used in an unsustainable manner. This phenomenon is impacting mankind in two different ways: increased carbon footprints leading to increased pollution of air and water, and exhaustion of available natural resources. This undoubtedly poses a potential threat to lives and livelihood of both current and future generations. Some of the most important factors responsible for this unsustainable pattern are: increase in population; increase in purchasing power; and unsustainable consumer lifestyles. While the first one is relatively more difficult to control and is subject of state policy, the second one is an important offshoot of development initiatives and is perhaps needcd to uplift millions of people above the poverty line. In the existing circumstances, bringing a change in the third one and its transformation could thus be an effective tool to minimise carbon footprints from consumption and thus making the environment sustainable for the present and future generations.

Human needs and utility obtained are the primary forces driving consumption. Ever-growing needs have made consumer lifestyles environmentally unsustainable, thus making it imperative to ingrain the idea of sustainability in both consumption and production processes. Consumer lifestyles represent consumption patterns, habits and purchasing decisions of consumers. These reflect consumer behaviour, which is influenced by values and surrounding environment. Presently, consumer lifestyles involve overconsumption and wastage of goods (food as well as consumer goods). Such lifestyles are environmentally unsustainable due to limited availability of natural resources, which are used to produce goods, and limited assimilating power of the nature.

Consumer lifestyles appear to be the most powerful factor that has shaped unsustainable consumption in the current periods. Therefore, any effort to amicably address the issue calls for an improvement/transformation in the existing consumption pattern. Consumer lifestyle can be improved by reduction in overall consumption and waste generation; and secondly, consumption of goods, which have lower environmental impact, i.e. green goods.[2] Rising purchasing power and multiplying human population make the first method practically difficult to follow. The second method is, thus, more feasible and might have a higher probability of success.

The objective of this chapter is to find out ways through which consumer ecological footprint can be minimized. This can be achieved by increasing the consumption of green goods. But there is an obstacle that their cost of production is higher than non-green variants. This can be tackled with a two-pronged approach—reduction in cost of production and increasing consumer willingness to pay a premium for environment friendly goods. Production cost can be reduced by government subsidies and development of relevant technology. Simultaneously, consumers, whose consumption decisions are driven by utility gains, can be educated about the value addition from green consumption such as better physical health and quality of life, lower stress, simplicity in consumption patterns, along with long term economic and environmental benefits, i.e. lower pollution and cleaner atmosphere. These could encourage consumers to pay an environmental premium, i.e. the price differential between green and non-green products. It can be expected that with these initial initiatives, eventually with economies of scale, the differential will shrink and larger masses will have access to these goods.

A holistic approach with active involvement of various stakeholders—the Government, producers, CSOs, media, and the people at large—will be essential. This chapter analyses how the movement towards sustainable consumption could be strengthened. It is divided into four sections: Section I highlights the importance of sustainable consumption in the emerging world order. However, there are economic, socio-cultural and political obstacles in the promotion of idea of sustainable lifestyles. Section II analyses major hurdles to sustainable consumption, which include economic, social and cultural factors. To overcome these hurdles, all the stakeholders need to play their respective roles. Section III maps the role of various players and outlines the approach that India needs to pursue, and lessons drawn from other countries. It focuses on the role-mapping of different stakeholders in ushering in an era of sustainable consumption in India. Section IV gives the way forward and concludes.

I

IMPORTANCE OF SUSTAINABLE CONSUMPTION IN THE EMERGING WORLD ORDER: THEORY AND PRACTICE

Sustainability in Theory

The approach to promotion of sustainability differs under different schools of economic thought. The Neo-classical school of economic thought emphasises on the interaction of demand and supply forces of commodities (and services) in the market, with minimum government interference. The Keynesian school propagates the role of the government as a regulator and controller of activities. This approach, when followed in the present context, implies high environmental regulations to check production processes, consumption decisions and waste generation/disposal by the government.

If the neo-classical approach for sustainability is followed, then in order to promote environmental sustainability, under uncontrolled market conditions, the main emphasis needs to be on creation of favourable conditions for interaction of demand and supply forces of eco-friendly goods (and practices). Out of these, emphasis on promotion of consumer demand for green goods is the weaker link which needs detailed analysis and action.

The neo-classical idea of consumption demand is based on three broad principles, viz. rationality of preferences, maximisation of utility and profits, and independent actions based on full and relevant information. In the case of promotion of consumption of green goods (or sustainable consumption), these assumptions lay ground for three essential action points:

1. Creation of higher utility for consumers of green goods, as compared to utility derived from non-green variants which are characterised by high environmental impact.
2. Maximisation of profits for the producers as an incentive from sustainable production, i.e. production of green goods and production of goods in general with lower emissions and wastes.
3. Creation of awareness among consumers about available green products and the incentives from sustainable consumption.

Free interaction of demand and supply side forces is expected to create a self-sustainable system for green goods. However, as per Keynesian school which applies well to a democratic system, the role of the state is also essential to ensure welfare in the society. Thus, the government uses regulations and incentives to encourage interaction of demand and supply forces responsible for sustainable lifestyles. Hence, we deduce that a synthesis of neo-classical and Keynesian school of thought would be best fit for promotion of sustainable consumer lifestyles in present-day market economies.

Emerging World Order and Need for Sustainability

A large number of economies of the world have been still reeling under the adverse impacts of financial crisis, which originated in the largest economy (USA) of the world, for past two years. The financial crisis has exposed the unsustainable systems and practices in the affected economies. However, initiatives taken to overcome the crisis, more often than not, have paved the way for a possible transformation from unsustainable to sustainable consumption.

The current crises has led to alteration in the existing global economic system and raised curtain to an emerging World Order. The new world order, which is still in its infancy, has developing economies or the erstwhile Third World at the focal point. Brazil, Russia, India, China and Souoth Africa (BRICS nations) form the spine of the changing world economic system since they have achieved high rates of economic growth, investment and employment, and growing consumer markets. These emerging economies were relatively less affected by recessionary trends due to relatively larger demand in domestic market and, therefore, would have a greater role to play in creating an era of sustainable consumption and production.

The idea behind Environmental Sustainability is to use resources and goods in a manner that the stock of these goods over the long run remains unaltered, i.e. extracting and using the amount of resources which can be replenished by nature. This concept refers to available stock of natural resources and assimilating capacity of the nature.

Maintenance of high growth rate as well as reduction of environmental impact of growth in economies needs a two-pronged approach. Firstly, countries must resort to unconventional, replenishable resources, which will keep the growth rate steady despite decline in dependence on conventional, exhaustive resources. Also, as far as possible, people also need to save and contribute to replenishment of natural assets such as forests, land nutrients etc. Secondly, emission of pollutants, other effluents and waste generation must also be brought down significantly. This reduces the pressure on the assimilation capacity of nature.

A new model of development of the economies needs to be formulated, based on the above approach. The basic tenets of this growth model are sustainable production and consumption. Both facets of sustainability involve practices which cause least harm to the environment. Also, they are interdependent in the manner that the magnitude of the latter is the driving factor for the former. In the following sections, we discuss the main factors responsible for low level of sustainability in present consumption and production patterns.

II

MAJOR HURDLES TO SUSTAINABLE CONSUMPTION IN INDIA

Sustainable consumption, as explained above, is a significant aspect for promotion of overall sustainability. These practices not only reduce direct environmental harm inflicted by unsustainable consumption but indirectly as well, since, they provide incentives to producers through increased revenue from production of green goods. However, this is also a fact that sustainable consumption is not being practiced as widely as is required to bring about the transformation in unsustainable consumption.

In India, the consumer spending has risen significantly in the past few years. Reports indicate that India is one of the fastest growing consumer markets and consumer confidence in Indian markets is the highest among the world markets.[3] This growing market has been fuelled by multiple factors such as rapid growth in Gross Domestic Product, growth conducive change in demographics—higher number of people under 30 years of age and rising middle class, changing consumption habits of people, increasing urbanisation as well as higher purchasing power in urban and rural areas, due to planned expenditure in developmental activities.[4]

Despite the new developments as indicated above and which indicate India's march towards higher consumption, studies demonstrate that Indian consumers' lifestyle is one of the most sustainable lifestyles in the world.[5] This is, however, yet to translate into a substantial market for green goods, which even now remains at a significantly low level. There are multiple challenges in the path of sustainable consumption. These could be broadly categorised into economic, socio-cultural and political challenges.

Economic Challenges

Production and consumption of environmentally friendly goods[6] in India is constrained due to various factors which impede sustainability of these products in market places. Production of green goods requires (a) raw-materials which are organic, locally produced/obtained or environmentally friendly; (b) green-energy-based technology; and (c) waste treatment plant. Even though there are indications that impressive changes are taking place, the outlined factors are yet to be embedded fully with the production processes in India. These create two main challenges: firstly, the problem of availability and acquisition of green raw material and technology, which is a critical challenge for the producers in developing countries like India given the lower level of research and development (R&D) and issues arising from transfer of technology from other nations.

Second and a more important challenge is the high cost of production of green goods since the inputs (raw material and technology) invariably cost higher than the ones used for non-green variants. This cost differential between green and non-green goods is called Environmental Premium. Higher the cost, greater will be the premium involved and higher will be the producer's risk.

The consumers also face certain constraints which are decisive in their choice of green goods. It is to be noted that these obstacles are interlinked. First challenge is the environmental premium (higher price of green goods). Given the income constraint, consumers prefer to purchase goods which give them highest utility at the lowest price.

Evaluation of utility from physical consumption of environmental goods at present is at a disadvantage to satisfy this condition, since the price is higher than non-green variant which provide equivalent utility.

Consumers' preference for consumption of green goods suffers due to two basic drawbacks:

(a) Lack of awareness about the need for environmental protection and impact of individual's consumption pattern on environment. Uninformed consumers attach a lower utility to environmental goods.
(b) Consumers give more value to the present utility derived from the products. In the case of consumption of green products, utility could be derived by both the present and future generations. This is not accounted for by the consumers while making purchase decisions.

As a result of these factors, the demand remains low, which becomes a disincentive for the producers of green goods.

Socio-cultural Factors

Consumption behaviour is based on socio-cultural factors like reference group, social status, religion, beliefs, education, laws, and infrastructure among others. Combined effects of these factors pose limitations to sustainable consumption in India. With the rising middle class, the scope of factors like social status and reference group has widened. The reference group for an Indian middle class is now middle class families in developed countries like USA or Europe. This has led to a demonstration effect across the country. This has also led to a rise in the preference for international brands. This poses a serious challenge for sustainable consumption.

Education has significant influence on the consumption behaviour of individuals and households. Literate and educated consumers better understand the linkages between human consumption and environment. With higher the level of education, it is easier to propagate sustainable consumption through development of an understanding of the environmental impacts of current patterns of consumption. The adult literacy rate in India for 2001-2004 is 61 per cent.[7] But the statistic lowers drastically with only about 52 per cent of the population receiving secondary education and a mere 11.9 per cent going for tertiary education.[8] Low literacy rate in India has become a major factor inhibiting sustainable consumption in the country.

Another important aspect is the legal framework for promotion of sustainable consumption. India, like most other countries of the world, does not have laws to address sustainability on the demand side. However, there are only few, mostly voluntary, regulations which regulate the production processes and supply chains of goods to ensure least possible harm to the environment. Along with this, the infrastructure required to ensure access to consumers of goods promoting sustainable consumption are lacking.

Religious beliefs and culture are also significant drivers of consumption decisions. From the view of sustainable consumption, traditions and values prevalent in India have a mixed impact on sustainability. On the one hand, vegetarianism is widespread here due to religious sentiments, on the other hand, the practice of bursting large number of crackers during festivals causes excessive pollution and is against the idea of sustainable consumption.

Political Factors

Political factors are one of the most important determinants of economic and social policies of the government, which in turn shape consumption and production patterns in the country. Usually in a democratic country like India with a significant segment of the population below the poverty line, political decisions are based on ground level realities, which often work against the sustainability approach. India has, since the launch of economic reforms programmes in 1990s, followed an approach with priority given to economic growth. However, in the recent periods, things have started changing and increased importance is being given to ingrain sustainability in the growth (consumption and production) processes.

Also, international political forces are very important in promotion of sustainability since international negotiations and protocols also regulate national government's efforts for sustainability. But often, nations seek to protect growth agenda of the country at these international negotiations. As a result, promotion of sustainability may not get as positive a response as is required due to attempts to protect domestic interests.

Hurdles, identified above, could be overcome by following well thought-out strategy for various stakeholders who can affect sustainability in the country.

Practice and Approach for the Future

India has made significant strides in addressing the issue of sustainable consumption. Over the past few years, India has taken a more amicable approach. It has agreed to take voluntary measures to reduce carbon emission intensity by 20-25 per cent of 2005 levels. To achieve this objective, the government has introduced certain regulations to check the emissions from industries, encouraged private initiative and investment in production of renewable energy, and has also indulged in government procurement of this form of energy in various states.

However, sustainable consumption has not been promoted through any direct means. Thus, there is hindrance to the creation of an environment favourable to the increase of demand and supply of environmentally friendly goods. Although, government initiative is a necessary condition to encourage sustainable consumption, it is not the sufficient condition to ensure that such patterns actually become popular amongst the various stakeholders.

III

ROLE MAPPING OF STAKEHOLDERS IN THE REVOLUTION FOR SUSTAINABILITY

Consumers are the nucleus for the era of sustainability. In India, the mind-set and consumption decisions of the fast growing middle class need to be targeted for evolution of this era. Main factors driving consumption decisions of this class of consumers, as mentioned earlier in the chapter, are prices of and utility derived from goods upon consumption. A relatively low priced goods, whose consumption maximises utility is the balance which the consumers seek to reach. Although pricing of products primarily concerns producers, but they cannot decide a price in isolation of other players active in a market economy. Prices of green goods are high due to the following two factors:

(i) High cost of inputs such as technology, raw material like organic and environment-friendly inputs.
(ii) Low demand for green goods and lack of willingness to pay environmental premium among consumers, which leads to small production and limited economies of scale.

Stakeholders who have power and capacity to bring in an era of sustainable consumption include government, researchers, product innovators, technology developers, producers, consumers, media, and others. These stakeholders have important roles to play at various stages of consumption cycle, and together they could contribute in sustainable consumption. It is notable that their roles are interlinked and approach of each stakeholder influences others. Also, producers and consumers could be placed at the bottom of this hierarchy since they are highly influenced by other factors and their attitude towards green goods generally develops as a response to the surrounding environment. An elaboration of the role and approach to be followed by each of them, in context of India is given below:

Government

Under *laissez faire*, government interference should be at the minimum. However, the synthesis of this approach with the Keynesian thought is more appropriate for a democratic and planned economy like India. Government could play the role of an agent of economic growth which promotes sustainability in consumption through influencing producers.

Government's role should be to create favourable conditions. The government needs to focus on two broad aspects. First is the reduction of cost of production and increase in access to raw materials and finished green goods. High costs of technology, clean energy and other raw materials for production of green goods can be brought down by government incentives such as reduction of taxes on imported technology, incentivising renewable energy production units and encouraging use of locally available raw materials. It should also contribute to development of human resource through excellent educational and research facilities. If the government encourages high level research and development which results in development of sustainable technology within the country, then cost will reduce substantially and will also help avoid jargons of international cooperation and technology diplomacy.

Secondly, it should raise awareness among consumers, and encourage them to pay environmental premium (or higher price for green goods). These two steps should be taken simultaneously. Government needs to build a network of civil society organizations, consumer organizations and media to generate awareness about the need for environmental protection, benefits of sustainable consumption, to the environment and the consumers themselves.

Researchers/Product Innovators/Technology Developers

"Innovative activity is widely seen as an important influence on a country's international competitiveness in an increasingly globalizing and knowledge-based world economy."[9] Innovation and development of new technology and new products, based on either organic or locally available inputs, is critical for promotion of sustainability. Researchers can develop low cost technologies with higher efficiency, lower emissions (gaseous and particulate), and lower amount of waste generation.

The initiative of a researcher comes from willingness to create and innovate, and royalty earnings from the ownership rights of a technology patented in the name of a scientist/innovator. In order to reduce the cost of production of green goods, the Indian innovators must contribute by creating low cost technologies in the country.

Producers

Key players on the supply side of green goods are the producers. The suppliers of green goods produce at a small scale due to a limited market (demand) for these goods and high costs. Only a small number of consumers buy eco-friendly goods due to 'ethical factors', i.e. social and environmental concerns. Thus, producers need to meet the high utility benchmark for which they need to create value additions for the consumers of green goods. These additions will make green goods superior, in terms of utility, to the non-green variants.

Value additions include factors like quality and durability of product, ease of accessibility, greater emotional and societal value and definitely environmental protection. Also, consumers must be made aware of various personal benefits that can be derived from sustainable consumption (this, however, requires efficient performance of other stakeholders), which are as follows:

(a) ***Health benefits***—Health benefits accrue from the consumption of organic and natural goods, especially food products. Long-term health benefits will accrue from a cleaner, less polluted environment.

(b) ***Other personal benefits***—Consumption of eco-friendly goods add to personal health as well as make life simpler, less complex and closer to nature. Also as indicated above, emotional value attached to locally produced goods can be used to indulge consumers in sustainable lifestyles.

(c) ***Benefits to the future generation***—the USP[10] of green goods is the benefit future generations would derive from present preservation of environment and natural resources.

Producers should also take initiatives for producing eco-labels and energy efficiency labels products on a voluntary basis, which will attract consumers to their 'green factor'. Above mentioned factors will provide a competitive edge to the producers of eco-friendly goods, which otherwise shrinks due to high cost to production.

Producers can also influence cost. On the one hand, they can work to increase efficiency of production, and on the other hand, they can encourage sustainability in supply chains. The first method is common to all the producers, be it green or non-green goods. The second measure is a cost-sharing technique. In this method, once the scale of production increases (for all the supply chains), due to increase in demand, there will be an aggregate reduction in the end cost of production by a multiplied amount, instead of a proportionate reduction in the case of end producer bearing the whole burden.

Consumers

Consumers are at the heart of all initiatives for ushering in an era of sustainability in the country. "Consumers are the key to driving sustainable production and play a central role in sustainable development."[11] Various stakeholders involved in promotion of green goods focus on generation of willingness among consumers to choose green goods over the non-green alternatives. Their choice of goods is driven by their awareness about options available in the market and the utility they can derive from these alternatives. If the consumers get right information about the benefits (personal, health, environmental) and utility (personal and social) which they can derive from green goods and compare the cost-benefit ratios of unconventional and conventional goods, they are most likely to choose the former.

Reuse and recycling are also important aspects of sustainable lifestyles which primarily require consumer initiative. Reuse and recycling of goods increase benefits and utility of a product. Increased utility could act as an incentive for the consumers.

Learning from Other Nations

Many developed nations, with more resources and better technology, have taken initiative to regulate and ingrain sustainability in consumer lifestyles. The OECD countries are at the forefront in addressing the issues of non-sustainability in various dimensions of consumption. These countries are implementing energy-efficiency and labelling schemes.

India and other developing countries are also implementing energy-efficiency labelling schemes. However, in the developed nations, efficiency labelling is compulsory, whereas in India, these are mostly voluntary. Germany has a 'Green Dot' policy which ensures that the producers depict on the product whether they have contributed to recycling of products and packaging material. Under this scheme, the producers need to take care of packages to the end of their life-cycle[12] and bear the cost of collecting, sorting and recycling packages. This regulation follows 'polluters pay' principle and ensures producer's involvement in waste-management. This label aims to promote consumer participation in recycling. Nutritional labelling is mandatory in many countries such as Australia, New Zealand, Canada, and United States. In many OECD countries, compulsory labels of food products showing content of genetically modified organisms (GMOs) is also compulsory (OECD, 2008). India also brought itself in line with mandatory nutritional labels since March 2009[13]; however, it has yet to cover a long distance in making the schemes efficient and more effective.

Taxes on fuels, electricity (household and commercial), water use, waste disposal, packaging and polluting products, *viz.* plastic bags, tyres and batteries, are commonly imposed in Germany, Belgium, Italy, Sweden, Netherlands etc. with the view to reduce their consumption and wastage. These regulatory policies contribute to the 3R policy programme—"reduce, reuse and recycle" (OECD, 2008).

Simultaneously, governments in developed countries also compensate people to encourage the practice of consumption of eco-friendly goods and contribution to reduction of wastes. In 2002, the government in Norway subsidised purchase of each energy efficient cars by EUR1000 each. In cities like Amsterdam, Paris, London, public bicycles are available to commuters at a very low rent. Governmental support and regulations aim to encourage a lifestyle harmonious with the nature.[14]

Apart from regulation, sensitisation of consumers towards the environmental impact of present lifestyles and consumption patterns is one of the key strategies. It is based on the principle of moral persuasion and encourages consumer self-regulation. As has been mentioned earlier in the chapter, education is a prerequisite for consumers to understand environmental problems in a better manner. United Nations (UN) has declared 2005-2014 as the United Nations Decade of Education for Sustainable Development. With UNESCO as the lead agency, this decade has been dedicated to "integration of the principles, values, and practices of sustainable development into all aspects of education and learning, in order to address the social, economic, cultural and environmental problems faced in the twenty-first century."[15] Most advanced implementation of Education for Sustainable Development (ESD) is among the countries in European region. The European nations, US and Canada have made significant progress in development and incorporation of themes for sustainability in formal, informal and non-formal education system.[16] The idea of 'sustainable school' is being supported in Italy ("Schole Futuro") and the United Kingdom, along with some other countries. These schools seek to teach and provide day-to-day practices for sustainable living to young people.[17] 'Eco-schools' are also being developed on a similar pattern.[18]

Advertising is a powerful tool to generate awareness and form a consensus among consumers regarding sustainable lifestyles. Through effective utilisation of this tool, consumers can be convinced to pay an 'environmental premium' for green goods. For more than a decade, producers of many energy and fuel efficient products have attempted to influence consumers' purchase decisions by highlighting environmental benefits of their products in advertisements. For example—automobile producers emphasise on environmental standards (engine, emissions) that their automobiles meet as well as fuel efficiency, which leads to protection of environment and natural resources, along with reduction of fuel expenses for the consumer.

There are some other 'good practices' such as public procurement of eco-friendly goods, creation of institutional structure and legal framework to promote sustainable consumption, creation of a network of NGOs and CSOs and increased number of studies on consumer behaviour which will enhance knowledge of consumer sentiments and expectations, and the ways in which products can be marketed, so there is increase in willingness to pay environmental premium.

IV

WAY FORWARD AND CONCLUSION

Transformation of unsustainable lifestyles holds the key for bringing in an era of sustainable consumption and production. However, there might not be a sudden change in how people perceive their consumption needs and consumption habits. Years of hard work and focused initiatives at various levels are required to bring in the transformation, and all stakeholders—consumers, producers, government, researchers, media, and others—must play their part efficiently and effectively. While some of these stakeholders (Government, CSOs etc.) might have facilitating roles, others such as producers and consumers have multidimensional role in ushering in the new era. This will require strengthening and improving the existing initiatives made by the stakeholders and at the same time raising consumer awareness and generate willingness to purchase green goods for bringing in sustainability in lifestyles. To expedite the transformation, producers must bring in features such as lifestyles, price competitiveness, easy accessibility, health benefits in their products. At the government level, the interlinkages between clean energy and production of green goods should be highlighted and promoted as the benefits of investment in the former reduces the cost in the latter also. This could lead to a multiplier effect of the investments.

To make the sustainability approach successful, India needs to follow the approach of incentivising producers of green goods through preferential allocation of resources (land and raw materials), facilitating development of infrastructure and making the supply chains of resources and technology more efficient and effective. These steps might lead to creation of social and economic overheads for this industry, and channelize government resources towards sustainable development.

The challenge, however, would be to ensure that initiatives to bring in this transformation do not compromise and endanger the lives and livelihood of the present generation, and at the same time promote sustainability.

Notes

1. The forces and processes that produce and control all the phenomena of the material world.
2. For the purpose of this chapter, we define green goods as goods which have lower impact on the environment at any point during their lifecycle. This involves either low impact from production/consumption/disposal, or all three of them. These are also called Environment-friendly or Eco-friendly goods.
3. *Nielsen Global Consumer Confidence Survey*, Report released in May 2010 for latest round conducted between May 10 and May 26, 2010. Available at http://in.nielsen.com/news/20100725.shtml
4. IBS Centre for Management Research (ICMR), A Note on Consumer Spending Patterns in India, http://www.icmrindia.org/casestudies/catalogue/Business%20Reports/BREP047.htm.

5. National Geographic, *GreenDex, 2010* http://environment.national geographic.com/environment /greendex/. The index evaluates environmental impact on the basis of: housing, transportation, food and goods.
6. Environment-friendly is a relative term, i.e. in relation to other goods in the same category, and apart from certain cases has not been defined in absolute terms.
7. UNESCO, *Education for All Global Monitoring Report 2006—Regional Overview*, Available at http://unesdoc.unesco.org/images/0014/001497/ 149783E.pdf. EFA classifies countries into 6 regions. India is a part of South and West Asian region.
8. *Ibid.*
9. *Financial Times*, "Innovation Policy for a Globalizing India, June 7, 2005. Available at http://www.financialexpress.com/news/story/140429/
10. Unique Selling Point
11. OECD, Promoting Sustainable Consumption, 2008, http://www.oecd.org/ dataoecd/1/59/40317373.pdf
12. "Der Grüne Punkt (Green Dot), Germany, http://www.gruener-punkt.de/?L=1
13. These labels show total calories, protein, carbohydrate, fat, sodium, sugars, dietary fibre, vitamins and minerals content in the food product.
14. Guardian Co.UK, http://www.guardian.co.uk/environment/2010/jul/20/ london-bike-hire-scheme-paris-velib
15. UNESCO, *Education of Sustainable Development*, http://www.unesco.org/ en/esd/
16. OECD, Report of the Workshop on Education for Sustainable Development, September 2008, http://www.oecd.org/dataoecd/52/1/41372200.pdf
17. OECD, 2008, Promoting Sustainable Consumption.
18. *Ibid.*

References

A Note on Consumer Spending Patterns in India, IBS Centre for Management Research (ICMR), http://www.icmrindia.org/casestudies/catalogue/Business %20Reports/BREP047.htm

Der Grüne Punkt (Green Dot), Germany, http://www.gruener-punkt.de/?L=1

Financial Times, "Innovation Policy for a Globalizing India", http:// www.financialexpress.com/news/story/140429/

FTC, *Guides for the Use of Environmental Marketing Claims,* http://www.ftc.gov/ bcp/grnrule/guides980427.htm

Guardian.Co.UK, http://www.guardian.co.uk/environment/2010/jul/20/london-bike-hire-scheme-paris-velib

National Geographic, *GreenDex, 2010,* Available at: http://environment.national geographic.com/environment/greendex/.

Nielsen Global Consumer Confidence Survey, http://in.nielsen.com/news/ 20100725.shtml, Released in May 2010

"Nutritional Labels are a must from March", *Hindustan Times* http://www.hindustantimes.com/Nutrition-labels-a-must-from-March/Article1-374899.aspx, February 05, 2009. Accessed on September 25, 2010.

OECD, *Promoting Sustainable Consumption*, 2008, http://www.oecd.org/dataoecd/1/59/40317373.pdf

OECD, *Report of the Workshop on Education for Sustainable Development*, September 2008, http://www.oecd.org/dataoecd/52/1/41372200.pdf

UNESCO, *Education for All (EFA) Global Monitoring Report 2006.* http://www.unesco.org/en/efareport/reports/2006—literacy/

UNESCO, *Education for All Global Monitoring Report 2006-Regional Overview*, Available at http://unesdoc.unesco.org/images/0014/001497/149783E.pdf

UNESCO, *Education of Sustainable Development*, http://www.unesco.org/en/esd/

9

Rethinking Development

People Centred Approach to Sustainable Consumption

Rashmi Tripathi

Introduction

Sustainability is gaining attention and debate across all the forums. The subject ranks high on the legislative agenda of majority of governments; media reporting on this topic has proliferated, and sustainability issues are of increasing concern to ordinary citizens around the world (BCG Report, 2009). The term sustainable consumption emerged as a key issue and a major challenge in 1992 at the United Nations Conference on Environment and Development in Rio de Janeiro, since, then it has become an increasingly important policy element in national sustainable development strategies. Ten years later, at the World Summit on Sustainable Development in Johannesburg, the international community was called upon to improve global living conditions and to "encourage and promote the development of a ten-year framework of programmes on sustainable consumption and production (SCP) in support of regional and national initiatives to accelerate the shift towards SCP."

Presently, there is little consensus in defining sustainable consumption and it is widely recognized to be a contested concept (Seyfang, 2009) which embraces 'competing discourses' (Hobson, 2006). One definition provided by United Nations Commission on Sustainable Development (UNCSD) is "the use of goods and services that respond to basic needs and bring a better quality of life, while minimizing the use of natural resources, toxic materials and emissions of waste and pollutants over the lifecycle, so as not to jeopardize the needs of future generations." While some authorities and individuals offer definitions others draw attention to the intrinsic difficulties in constructing such a definition. A number of definitions of sustainable consumption mirror mainstream definitions of sustainable development. More simply Dahl (2009) suggests that "sustainable consumption refers to the need to stay within the global sustainability of resources."

Jackson (2006) has reviewed and summarized a large number of definitions but notes that these adopt different positions not only on "the extent to which sustainable consumption involves changes in consumer behaviour and lifestyles", but also on whether sustainable consumption implies "consuming more efficiently, consuming more responsibly or quite simply consuming less". Jackson further argues that 'the dominant institutional consensus" is that sustainable consumption "is to be achieved basically through improvements in the efficiency with which resources are converted into economic goods." More generally, a distinction can be made between "weak sustainable consumption" and "strong sustainable consumption". The former has been defined as "choosing products and services that either are less resource consuming, or less burdening for the environment, or less destructive for those people actually producing them" (Jones *et al.*, 2009). While the latter embraces "increases in the (eco-) efficiency of consumption (often *via* more efficient production patterns or an efficiency friendly design) and fundamental changes in consumption patterns and reductions in consumption levels in industrialized countries."

The People Centric Approach

The question of economic and social development has been a central theme of international discussion at different forums since 1950s. But over all these years the idea of universal well-being remains disappointed. In certain aspects, it seems further unachievable. However, despite of numerous mistakes and unsuccessful initiatives in the past, we can see just as many signs of hope and some clear paths to a brighter future. We need to rethink development, building upon what has worked and carefully rejecting failed approaches.

The first lesson we have learnt is that the development must be people centric not only in the traditional sense where people were considered as the engine of change, but also in the less traditional sense of development that puts people first. People are the critical factor in any development process: firstly, in terms of their numbers and the social, health, economic and environmental consequences of their actions; and secondly, in terms of the decisions they make concerning the size of their families and the way they live their lives. People-centred development also means full community participation at both decision-making and implementation levels.

The second important lesson we have learnt is that, the development must be sustainable and environmentally sound. Economic development activities that destroy the natural resource base in the process are self-defeating. The other aspect of sustainable development is population growth; there must be a balance between number of people and resources to sustain them, otherwise the entire system will collapse.

Ensuring Sustainable Consumption in India

India is one of the most populated countries on earth where nearly 15 per cent of the total global population resides. It is also privileged to have a large percentage of natural resources and biodiversity on earth. The ambitions of India to become developed country within the next 10 years, suggests that the trends in India are more geared towards rapid economic growth. Despite cities such as Delhi, Mumbai, Bangalore, Hyderabad being highly congested and populated, want to modernize, be sophisticated, trendy and competitive further provides evidence that India has already embarked on the vision of rapid economic growth as a strategy for the upliftment of their living standards.

The entire world is looking towards India as market of largest consumers on earth, housing one-third of the global poor, holding the ownership to a large percentage of the world's natural resources, does pose a serious challenge towards achieving sustainable consumption not only in India, but also on the entire planet. The question in focus is whether India can meet the challenge and at the same time, whether it is ready to meet it? The present generation may hold the answers as their ambitions, determinations, actions and commitments will have direct impact on the environment and livelihood at large.

While the waves of consumerism are rapidly blowing across the country, a majority of population in our country is still living in villages and city slums and is forced to live low consumption lifestyles. The welfare of these people will depend on a new global socio-economic regime of equitable distribution of resources and opportunities. Although the present national determinations and consumer aspirations show higher consumerist trends, the traditional and cultural background of sustainable livelihood in all-over India still holds a key to the future as well.

The hope of achieving sustainable consumption in India can be based on the knowledge to action partnerships between the intellect and civil society and the pressure placed upon governments to make commitments for industries to behave with responsibility. At present, there is a lack of processes and implementation programmes to promote sustainable consumption in India. Similarly, there is a lack of in-depth understanding among all sectors within the society, including government, industry, civil society and consumers about the conceptual framework of Sustainable Consumption and thus have little expertise to deal with the guidelines, tools and mechanics developed at the international level.

However, it should be noted that at large willingness to accept Sustainable Consumption into National Development Planning and Implementation is prevailing in India. Even though the exact terminology in sustainable consumption may not be used, but the countries do have complimentary legislative instruments that can be traced in their Constitutions, Environmental Acts, Consumer Protection Acts, National Standards, National Policy Statements, National Development Strategies, National Poverty Alleviation Strategies etc.

In India, most of the actions that can lead to Sustainable Consumption are voluntary in nature; be it recycling, certification, product testing, consumer behaviour research or procurement practices within organizations. Most of the projects and programmes are to be carried out voluntarily by the concerned parties mainly due to economic benefits. The Indian government though has taken policy initiatives for providing economic incentives to industrial, business and other promoters of sustainable practices. Government provides economic incentives to sustainable consumption-based action such as recycling programmes, energy efficient products and investment in environmental friendly technological equipments. But, the benefits of these are restricted to upper society due to limited access. In fact, the inadequacies in capacity to conduct monitoring and enforcement becomes a major constrain to achieve desired expectations of legislative mechanisms in our country.

The Indian consumers in general are not well informed, lack understanding of their rights, and are not conscious of their responsibilities. Similarly, rural consumer lacks access to the resources, services and opportunities. The lack of strong consumer protection movement in the country is a major bottleneck for consumers in achieving the right standards of living. The lack of consumer consciousness and commitment is directly related to lack of awareness. In the expansion of consumerism movement the joint forces of industry, business, transnational trade and advertising have the enormous power of capital wealth to invest in promoting brands, products, services to attract and induce consumers. However, in the consumer protection movement both the civil society and government lack such economic capacity and power to invest in promoting sustainable consumption. Not only the individual consumer or community consumer, but the Small and Medium Enterprise (SME) sector in country too are victims of this imbalance of the economies of power.

The Main Challenge in Achieving Sustainable Consumption in Asia

Since the Earth Summit, a number of meetings and discussions have addressed sustainable consumption. The Soria Moria Conference (1994) provided a definition of sustainable consumption. The United Nations Commission on Sustainable Development Adoc Inter-Sessional Working Group on Finance and Changing Consumption and Production Patterns met in March 1996 to identify key issues, conclusions, and possible recommendations and policy options for consideration by the UNCSD at its fourth session.

However, the movement towards sustainable consumption is still in its infancy. There has been little movement from the international forum to the development of national sustainable consumption strategies. The discussion of goals and objectives is underway and a number of programmes and policies already in place, which include reduce, reuse and recycling programmes, education programmes. Some sustainability and social upliftment attempts through corporate social responsibility (CSR) and Social Responsibility Investment (SRI) projects are being made by the large corporate companies in the region. Unfortunately, the main focus of most of these efforts are based on corporate image building and economic benefits rather than actual community or consumer welfare and development objectives, and therefore, fails to deliver the goods to the people. Providing "Better Living Standards" and "Quality Livelihood for All" is the primary challenge in achieving sustainable consumption for people in India (*see* Figure 9.1).

Enabling Required Conditions for Sustainable Consumption Action

Sufficiency in Economy: The first priority for our country is to become a developed economy in next 10 years. Hence, most of the national development policies are geared towards rapid economic growth.

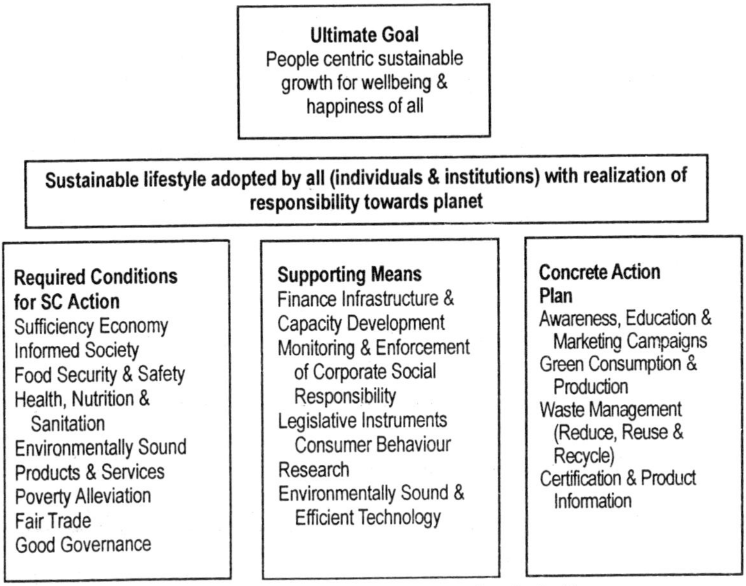

Fig. 9.1: Model to Achieve Sustainable Consumption in India

Although Sustainable Development is used as a term in National Development Policy, the actual focus is on economic and social sustainable development rather than a balance with environmental sustainability.

With all our efforts to achieve a rapid economic growth, we need to learn from the mistakes of West, otherwise we will also end-up loosing our cultural identity and destroy the environment as well. Therefore, the concept of sufficiency in economy is essential to be followed. Sufficient economy has two broad dimensions, i.e. Self-sufficiency and Adequacy. The former means the country attempts to provide for itself with the utilization of available resources. The concept of adequacy is based on the framework of contentment.

Creating an Informed Society: Creating an understanding about harmful consequences of unsustainable consumer behaviour and benefits of positive consumer behaviour can be a strong tool to achieve sustainable consumption goals. While there is a big gap in waste management capacity of our country at the same time, there is a lack of consumer knowledge and discipline to handle the waste. Weak consumer movement, insufficient input in the basic education and lack of adequate financial resources are the major reasons for low level of consumer awareness.

Providing Food Security and Safety: Feeding the large population at least one meal a day remains to be one of the biggest challenges in India. The challenge of food security is both in terms of providing sufficient food supplies and at the same time assuring the health and nutritional standards. The overuse of chemicals in agriculture, genetically modified food production and marketing, inadequate capacity in storage and distribution, lack of sanitation and other health standards observed in food processing, marketing and preparation, and escalating prices due to unfair trade practices are the main threats to food security. There is a need to fast track the organic food movement in India and organic labelling and green marketing should be used to penetrate into mass consumers.

Assuring Health, Nutrition and Sanitation: Sanitation, nutrition and safe drinking water are the unmet needs, which shall be addressed as a priority. Although, health and sanitation is the priority in achieving sustainable consumption, still the country has very low per capita availability of fresh water as compared to developed countries. In 1947, per capita availability of fresh water was 5150 cu mt. and in the year 2000, it was measured to be 2200 cu mt. By 2017, India will be water stressed, per capita availability will be only 1600 cu mt.

The level of public expenditure on health in India is among the lowest in the world. As per the UNDP Human Development Report 2004, India ranks 173 among 177 countries in terms of public expenditure on health. Indian government also needs to address the issue of accessibility and affordability of health services if sustainable and better living standards are to be achieved.

Developing Environmentally Sound Products and Services: A sustainable economy is one dominated and driven by the demand for and supply of environment friendly and environment enhancing products and services, which in turn safeguard and enhance human well-being. A defining indicator of a sustainable economy, accordingly, is the share of environment-friendly and environment-enhancing products and services as a whole in total output and employment. To promote and improve sustainable consumption India needs to develop environmentally sound products and services. The two main service sectors that need prime focus are energy and transport.

Poverty Alleviation: The fruits of economic growth have not benefited everyone uniformly. Some are left behind and some others are not touched by the benefits of economic growth. It is proved globally that the so called trickle down effect does not work in all the societies and India is no exception to this. The country cannot claim economic growth when a section of the people is marginalized to the periphery of the society. The rapid economic growth process should accelerate the access to services like education and health services for all, especially the marginalized citizens.

Fair Trade: "Fair Trade is a win-win for all stakeholders, including corporates, producers and consumers. While corporates get brand respectability, producers get their due return and the consumer has the satisfaction of buying a product which is ethically made and environment-friendly."

India continues to suffer in an unfair trading regime of the world. Labour and services of the region continue to be exploited by multinational corporations and also by interregional trading mechanisms. Unethical subsidy regime and undue pressure remove social protection. Therefore, the issue of subsidies needs greater political debate and control in the country. In addition, low wages for labour and inferior products in the markets continue in large scale and threaten sustainable lifestyles to emerge. Regional trading agreements need to address the issues of fair trade for the benefit of the poor. As much as world is in transition towards finding sustainable consumption lifestyle, India too is striving to find ways and means of regulating unsustainable consumption practices. In these efforts, it is critical that Indian government shows more political will-power and integrity in ensuring fair trade for their citizens.

Good Governance: The high rate of economic growth coupled with comfortable foreign exchange reserves and rising Sensex figures have imparted a growing confidence. The world is also looking at India with respect and considers India and China as ideal economic growth models. India is aiming to have a high growth rate with focus on equity. Although these two objectives are not always contradictory, but the conflict arises when scarce resources are diverted to meet the demands of the growing middle class or business houses by ignoring the needs of the poor. The imperatives of democracy, however, are forcing Indian political leadership to look deeper into the causes of poverty, inequality and suffering of the common man. In this ongoing debate, major shift in national value system has somewhat gone unnoticed and/or underemphasised by academicians, media commentators and India-watchers. While good governance is expected from the national legislative and administrative sectors, it should also be noted that business and civil society too should effectively practice good governance for a society to achieve better living standards as a whole and therefore, sustainable consumption.

Supporting Means to Encourage Sustainable Consumption

Finance Infrastructure and Capacity Development: The willingness and want to achieve both better living standards and sustainable consumption in India is prevailing. Although national policies do not mention sustainable consumption as a national goal, the fact is that sustainable consumption is accepted as a means of achieving better life-styles. However, the main constraint in implementing the concrete action areas identified is lack of financial resources and therefore, infrastructure and capacity to implement. While the first task is making sustainable consumption a stated national priority, the other immediate approach should be to support such policy by enabling finance, infrastructure and capacity building both from internal and external sources.

India has progressed well in legislating laws to promote environmental protection that complements sustainable consumption as well. The weakness in achieving the mandated process is the weakness in monitoring and enforcement. The first reason for weak monitoring and enforcement is attributed to lack of capacity that stems from financial constraints. Although this holds true to a great extent, it should also be noted that corruption, lack of commitment and political interference too are major contributors in this situation.

Monitoring and Enforcement: The Consumer Courts in India is a rare success story in the area of monitoring and enforcement capacity. The unique and decentralised consumer courts system established in India is a positive model that can be adopted by many countries in Asia to provide effective and efficient consumer protection.

The Asia-Pacific region is the most economically dynamic region in the world. In the last decade, growth in industrial production of the region's developing countries outstripped global growth rates. The environmental implications of burgeoning regional economies are more significant in Asia than in any other region. Most developing countries in the region are now afflicted by various environmental problems ranging from land degradation to pollution. These problems have arisen from the process of growth-oriented development that has so often exceeded environmental carrying capacity. Additionally, the phenomenon of market failure has accounted for the aggravation of environmental problems. This failure is largely grounded in the insufficient reflection of environmental resources like water and air as currency values in the decision making process of an economic entity.

The application of economic instruments is one way of promoting more eco-efficient consumption and production patterns. Economic instruments for environmental protection are policy approaches that "encourage behaviour through market signals, rather than through explicit directives regarding pollution control levels or methods." These include property rights, market creation, charges, fiscal instruments, liability systems, and removal of environmentally harmful subsidies. Properly designed and implemented economic instruments can create incentives to minimize resource use, pollution, and waste, and to foster creative approaches for capitalizing on synergies between economic growth and environmental protection.

Corporate Social Responsibility: The traditional social entrepreneurs, viz. TATAs, Birlas, Bangurs, Gonekas were the part of the community hierarchy and voluntarily assumed the role of provider and guardian of the families and community that the enterprise benefits from. These entrepreneurs were responsible for community welfare such as health clinics, schools, road development etc. in the rural villages. Lesson could be learnt from this traditional concept of CSR if the big business and industries truly want to contribute to the well-being of the people and environment. CSR in India is losing its objective and mostly used as a marketing tool rather than a social instrument by the large business enterprises. While some positive cases of CSR can be identified, but mostly it is planned and used wrongly to profit the business rather than to plan for win-win situations. The notable factor is that the new macro-focus on CSR has and is leading towards the diminishing role of the traditional business and industry as social entrepreneur. Government and the society need to seriously rethink and redefine the norms of CSR.

Legislative Instruments: There is no direct legislation in India that mentions sustainable consumption. The leading legislations that promote sustainable consumption are the National Environmental Acts and Consumer Protection Act. However, the Consumer Protection Act lacks the comprehensive understanding of sustainable consumption and rather is restricted to price control and standards setting. The Environment Protection Act, 1986, provides the guidelines for the management of hazardous wastes etc., e.g. safety report, safety audit etc. The other main environmental legislations include regulation of pollution of water, air and soil. The Biological Diversity Act, 2000, has been enacted by the Parliament to secure the conservation, sustainable use of and equitable share in benefits arising out of the use of biological resources and the associated knowledge. In India there are constitutional, legislative and administrative provisions with respect to this right. Among the constitutional provisions, the most important one is the protection of life and personal liberty (Article 21).

The Bureau of Indian Standards Act, 1986 makes ISI certification mandatory for certain products. Despite making it mandatory for certain products to adhere to the Indian Standard Institution (ISI) norms, many products can be found in the markets without ISI specifications/mark. Even the ISI marked products in certain cases are found not to be adhering to the specifications. Majority of the consumers are not aware of the existence of such rules/laws. They are also not aware of their rights and in case of any problem, they are not sure whom they should approach. Besides, rampant corruption in the system makes the laws ineffective in many cases.

From the foregoing discussion, it is evident that in India, it is not that the legislative measures providing the consumer with the mechanism or enabling environment for protecting the various rights are lacking; the challenge is in strengthening of the administrative mechanisms for properly implementing such measures. Further incentives need to be built in for the enforcement officials so that they perform their duties without being influenced or handicapped due to lack of resources.

Consumer Behaviour Research: One of the ignored areas in India is the conduct of appropriate and constant consumer behaviour research. Consumer behaviour in India is taken for granted and consumers are considered as mere followers of Western lifestyles and high consumerist trends. This claim is normally made by using the most urban cities of Asian countries as examples and then making general assumption that the village aspirations to follow-suite. Two realities need to be noted in this review. First, being that the big city mentality along with the high consumerist trends seems to be advancing in Asia. Second reality is that a majority of people continue to live in rural areas where the trends of consumerism have very little opportunity to progress due to lack of infrastructure, facilities and attention. Whatever the situation may be, very little research is being conducted in Asia to ascertain the patterns and changes of consumer behaviour. Most of the consumer research is conducted for market research requirement with clear objectives to identify areas to penetrate and induce the consumer towards more consumption. Although more independent research from government and civil society is required, the lack of finances for such efforts is a continuing constraint.

Environmentally Sound and Efficient Technology: The requirement in India is to encourage environmentally sound and efficient technologies that are affordable and reachable. Projects to promote sustainable consumption in our country essentially need support for their socio-economic plans. Most of the technology used in waste recycling, product testing etc. is mainly small scale and archaic. While advancement of the technology is required, government and civil society are promoting technology that replaces human labour. A region that holds a majority of the earth's population clearly needs to find labour supportive technology that can sustain the consumers' livelihoods.

There are certain crucial issues that need to be focused upon while introducing green technology. For instance, a social awareness about the need for environment-friendly goods and services for production and consumption at a larger scale is required. For this, massive campaigns need to be undertaken.

Designing a Concrete Action Plan

Awareness, Education and Marketing Campaigns: The belief that an informed society acts responsibly towards sustainable consumption requires issue specific and targeted communication and educational programmes. Awareness within critical target groups such as politicians, government officials, NGOs, Business and Industry needs concentrated efforts if consumers are to be ensured with sustainable solutions. The SME sector is in critical need of education on benefits and techniques of sustainable practices to ensure consumer protection, sustainable resource management and environmental conservation.

Waste Management Reduce Reuse Recycle—Effective Way to Go Green Economically: Ways to reduce, reuse, and recycle, whatever possible, is to save money and reduce waste dumped in landfill and other form of pollution. The key to reducing the amount of waste, which is dumped, and to reduce pollution is to make less waste in the first place where possible, or find alternative uses for them and recycle as much as possible so the materials can be used to make something new. Recycle also helps in reducing or saving our precious natural resources.

Certification and Product Information: The main focus under certification and product information has been discussed under standards setting and information and eco-labelling. India has set product quality standards for both consumer products and health products. Though legislation is satisfactory to address the issues of consumer protection, the enforcement capacity needs serious attention. The issue of inferior and sub-standard goods continues to the extent of life threatening levels.

Food production in India needs serious evaluation to ensure a level of sustainable consumption in the region. While malpractices in quantity, quality and standards have become part and parcel of market, the more serious violation of toxic contamination and manipulation not only goes unnoticed, but also is under-dealt by law enforcement.

The second issue of environmental labelling which is seen under the different categories such as eco-label, organic label or even energy efficiency label is far beyond being a successful process. Most of these programmes are an extension of the environmental or organic movement. Such eco-labelled products are more a fashion or prestige item for the upper consumer class that has the purchasing power. The fact that such eco-labelled products are less in quantity, high in price and lack mass accessibility has weakened their potential to be a greater option towards sustainable consumption. India will need to address this issue of producing eco-products for import markets while also promoting eco-products for national consumer's consumption.

Conclusion

In India, as a policy framework or a strategy, sustainable consumption is not present. However, strategies for sustainable consumption are implemented in different legislative and voluntary mechanisms such as national development strategies, environmental laws, national poverty reduction plans as well in numerous socio-economic and environmental programmes. Most importantly sustainable consumption prevails in the forms of simplistic lifestyles still surviving in numerous communities across the region.

In India, people still remain under poverty line, without access to basic human needs such as clean water, adequate food, proper clothing and decent housing. The government should necessarily revamp the entire public distribution system in the country. It should ensure that the poorest, i.e. below the poverty line (BPL) population gets the maximum benefit from the Public Distribution System (PDS) system. In all other basic need issues like health, education etc. the involvement of the community is must. Unless people are empowered or motivated to take part in the development process, the sustainable development programmes are not likely to succeed. One of the most important issues regarding sustainable consumption is the right to consumer education. Though the Department of Consumer Affairs is taking some steps in this direction, the result is not very impressive. A strong consumer movement, which seems to be lacking, is necessary in the country for people centric development. Thinkers from government, academia, civil society, business and all stakeholders and individuals have a tremendous responsibility towards creating a people centric approach for well-being and happiness of all.

References

Dahl, A. (2009) *Sustainable Consumption and True Prosperity*. Available online: http://www.bcca.org/ief/ddahl98c.htm

Hobson, K. (2006) "Competing Discourses of Sustainable Consumption: Does the Rationalisation of Lifestyles' Make Sense". in Jackson, T., (Ed.) *The Earthscan Reader in Sustainable Consumption*, London, UK: Earthscan.

Jackson, T. (2006) "Readings in Sustainable Consumption", in Jackson, T. (Ed.) *The Earthscan Reader in Sustainable Consumption*, London, UK: Earthscan.

Peter Jones, Daphne Comfort and David Hillier (2009) "Marketing Sustainable Consumption within Stores: A Case Study of the UKs Leading Food Retailers", *Sustainability*, 1, 815-826.

Seyfang, G. Local (2009) *Organic Food: The Social Implications of Sustainable Consumption*. Available online: http://www.uea.ac.uk/env/cserge/pub/wp/edm/edm_2004_09.pdf

10

Sustainable Consumption or Sustainable Resource Management

Whose Responsibility?

K. Shailaja Rao

Introduction

It is very difficult to get individuals and families, schools, hospitals, companies and government departments to think critically about the impact of their consumption patterns, especially in these days of inflation, low economic progress and overflowing expenses. However, it has become imperative for government agencies and non-government agencies alike to encourage consumers to think on the lines of changing their consumer activities for sustainable consumption. Change is necessary in their thinking patterns, both 'top-down' and 'bottom-up'.

In the present context, it is very difficult to define sustainable consumption. Is it satisfying basic human needs? Favouring Quality over Quantity? Minimizing wastage and pollution? Thinking about product lifecycle while decision making? Thinking about future generations? To perceive it includes all the above and even more.

It is a matter of grave concern that, because of the inequalities of the advanced countries of the world, their unsustainable consumption practices the planet is getting to a point of no return. On the other hand, in the underdeveloped and developing nations people's basic consumer needs are not being met. These affluent lifestyles and excessive demands place great stress on governments. The governments of the affluent nations therefore, should take a posture towards encouraging efficiency in production patterns, reduce wasteful consumption in the name of economic growth, and encourage sustainable methods of production and consumption, to accommodate developing nations.

The key issues of consumerism have to be brought to the forefront along with health, citizenship, ecological conservation and the need for education in sustainability. Illogical consumerism has become a part of contemporary life, and its effects on social, economic and ecological trends need to be analyzed thoughtfully. If we cannot change consumption patterns, we have to look at other ways of sustaining the resources. This is where efficient waste management plays an important role.

First, as developing countries with large populations, India and China will sooner or later suffer greatly from climate change, more seriously than any other country. Education and awareness in the area of sustainable consumption and waste management is increasingly important from a global perspective of resource management. Here ecological footprinting need to be introduced as an innovative and rigorous way of measuring whether our lifestyles and patterns of consumption are sustainable. How can we leave a safe planet for our children? What can we, as a consumer do to preserve the planet?

Both high consumption and usage of resources, particularly in countries of the West, and population numbers contribute to ill effect on the environment. The impact of all our activities can be linked to an imprint or 'footprint' on Earth. This imprint is referred to as our 'Ecological Footprint'. Just as we say that a computer has a big or small 'footprint', depending on how much space it takes-up on our desktop, we can say that the lifestyle choices we make have a footprint on the Earth. Our Ecological Footprint is a measure of the human impact on nature—it shows how much productive land and water we use to produce all the resources we consume and amount of waste we generate in the process. The term comes from "Our Ecological Footprint: Reducing Human Impact on the Earth" written by Mathis Wackernagel and William Rees in 1996. This book presents calculations which show that the human population requires atleast 20 per cent more biologically productive land than we presently have—and that we would need a total of three planet Earths to support us if all the Earth's inhabitants were to live at the standard as people in the countries such as the United States of America, Australia or Canada live.

For example, the Ecological Footprint of the USA was 9.6 hectares (24 acres) in 1999. This is about the area of 24 football fields. In comparison, the average Canadian lived on a footprint about one quarter smaller (7.2 hectares/18 acres), while the average German required an area less than half the size (4.4 hectares/11 acres). An average area available for one person according to this report is 2.1 hectares. However, humans are not the only inhabitants of the Earth. So, the figure of 2.1 hectares does not allow any space for the 'footprint' needs of other species. If preserving the 10 million other species on Earth requires at least 12 per cent of the biologically productive land on Earth (as recommended by the World Commission on Environment and Development Calculation), the available biologically productive space would shrink from 2.1 to 1.8 hectares per person. In other words, we are consuming more than what nature can regenerate and, therefore, are eating-up the Earth's stock of natural capital. Scientists call this situation 'overshoot' and say that the amount of land 'borrowed' from the future is really an 'ecological deficit'. "We are living on this planet as if we have another one to go to."

Robert Swan the recipient of the Order of the British Empire is the first person in the history to have walked to the South Pole and the North Poles. On his 50-year mission to designate Antarctica as a "Natural reserve for Science and Peace", he says, "It's a mission to save our participation on earth. Today, it comes down to an energy challenge. How we use our energy, how we conserve energy, where our energy comes from—these are our greatest challenges for our survival as a species"? Recently, he was in India with the message that, "The old world messed up. Now, India and China have the opportunity to fast track through all the mistakes we have made. Forget about saving the planet, it is the biggest business opportunity we have."

Former Prime Minister, Dr. Manmohan Singh in his Inaugural Address at the 97th Indian Science Congress on January 3, 2010 at Thiruvananthapuram, Kerala, has said, "We face new challenges of climate change and management of water resources... Last month, world leaders came together at Copenhagen to grapple with the threat that climate change poses to our planet and to our way of life. It is a problem that is challenging the knowledge and wisdom of humankind. We were able to make only very limited progress at the Copenhagen Summit and no one was satisfied with the outcome. And yet, there is no escaping the truth that the nations of the world have to move to a low greenhouse gas (GHG) emissions development path.....All over the world, countries are adapting to such climate change as is inevitable. India must not be behind in these areas."

As per the Census of India Report, India's population is 1.21 billion in 2011. Even if we suppose that less than a quarter of the population disposes of garbage once a day *via* the plastic carrybags, the total number of such bags in the country's garbage would be mind-boggling. And, mind you, this is just the tip of the iceberg. Mindsets should change.

Changing Mindsets

Sustainable consumption asks us to consider issues that go beyond the individual when we shop. These include not only the ecological impacts of what we buy but also the equity, human rights and political dimensions of sustainability in the production and consumption process. These aspects of sustainable consumption provide guidelines on how to reduce the social and ecological impacts of what we consume. For example, the Internet Just Shoppers' Guide in America, suggests criteria to consider while buying daily stuffs such as chocolate, sports shoes, tuna, laundry detergent, soft drinks, chapter, timber, clothing, and so on. Guidelines such as these are not designed to make us feel guilty, but to encourage us to ask questions such as: Do I really need this item? Can I produce it myself? And then, when we have decided to buy something, to think critically about each stage in the 'life-cycle' of a product, i.e. production, transport and retailing, use and disposal. There is a dire need to put your thinking cap on while selecting products for consumption.

Production

Regarding production, the following aspects need to be taken care of— Whether the country is dealing with production of the raw materials or manufacture? What laws does the country of origin have regarding the use of pesticides, safety regulations for workers, wages, and conditions for workers? (Buying locally gives you more knowledge to be able to answer these questions.) What is the brand name? Has the company a good or bad record internationally? How much energy has been used to manufacture the product or its container? What chemicals and processes have been used in the manufacturing or growing of the product or its container that could harm the workers or damage the environment? Are timber products from native rainforest? If the product is from animals are they well cared for? Have animals been used in the testing of the product? etc.

Transport and Retailing

As far as transportation and retailing is concerned, it is essential to know how much fuel has been used to transport the product to the retail outlet. Can one take your own bags and containers with you and buy in bulk rather than pre-packaged? Does the retail outlet have a good employment policy for its workers? How far does one has to travel to reach the retail outlet?

Use

For usage, it is of concern that if the product goes into the drainage system will it eventually harms the waterways? Is the product an energy efficient one? Is the product harmful to you or your family's health?

Disposal

For disposal, it is needed to be taken care of whether the product is over-packaged? Is the product or packaging can be re-used, composted, and recycled? Will the packaging be harmful to animals or the environment if left lying around? However, in today's hectic lifestyles do we have the time to 'stop and stare' let alone think?

Lifestyle Changes

If the question about a sustainability-driven reduction in consumption seems a stretch, think about the lasting impact of the English Raj on the people who lived through it. Despite an overall trend towards the decreasing consumption across hundreds of years, if not thousands, that generation was made to do with less: reduce, reuse, and repair was the motto. "It is less difficult to spend a few minutes to find sustainable products than it is to find a new habitable planet."

What if all of us collectively demand from retailers and manufacturers and emphasis on repair and recycling rather than consumption and disposal? How would that change markets? However, the social, economic and ecological impact of consumerism can be drastically reduced. Why is the degradation of the environment on the increase? Pointing an accusing finger at plastic carry bags is not the answer. The problem lies with the people. Our mindset has been conditioned to follow the herd. We need to think for ourselves, not look askance at others. The onus is on each individual to reduce the usage. A willingness to change one's lifestyle or pattern of consumption is essential, but insufficient in itself to bring about societal change. Similarly, one's action as a citizen, no matter how responsible and far-sighted, is inadequate if one's individual behaviour and lifestyle are wasteful or destructive. Sustainable development requires both individual enlightenment and responsibility and appropriate policies and action by public authorities and the private sector.

If, for example, an individual wishes to use public transportation to reduce urban congestion and pollution, this choice can be effective only if such transport exists and, for most people, will become habitual only if it is both economical and convenient. In short, the move toward sustainable lifestyles is not merely a matter of individual choice; it also requires collective action and responsibility. Agenda 21 of the UN identified unsustainable patterns of production and consumption, especially in industrialized countries, as "the major cause of the continued deterioration of the global environment."

Eco-labels

As consumers and companies become increasingly aware of their environmental impact, a surge of eco-labels has flooded the marketplace. Today, hundreds of eco-labels worldwide compete to tell us which products are best for the planet. These colourful stamps on labels declare products to be "carbon neutral", "forest safe", "fairly traded", or any number of standards of sustainability. But in the self-regulated eco-certification industry, how can consumers and institutional buyers really know what these stamps of approval mean? From environmentally conscious individuals shopping for themselves and their families, to institutional buyers stocking the shelves of multi-billion dollar retailers, purchasers of all sizes need transparent, concise comparisons to decode the eco-labels on the products they are choosing. Improving transparency in the eco-label market place is an important first step to reduce consumer confusion and increase credibility.

What assures Consumers? Project survey, canvassed 2,734 people in the UK and USA in March 2007. Together with an online survey, they conducted interviews with US and UK consumers, and case interviews with businesses, lobbyists, civil society and public sector officials. The study revealed some startling facts that only 10 per cent of consumers trust what companies and government tell them about global warming. Corporate and government efforts to inform consumers on climate change are falling on deaf ears, with barely one in ten people in the UK and US believe what they say on the issue. The research findings show that consumers have little faith in celebrities and the media to provide information on climate change, and would rather seek advice from friends and family, environmental groups and scientists. Many consumers feel unable to change their purchasing habits. The study reveals that 75 per cent of consumers, although concerned about how their consumption effects climate change, feel paralysed to act beyond small changes around the home (such as turning off stand-by modes and converting to energy-efficient light bulbs). The research indicates that this is due to a lack of understanding about what individuals can do, concerns over the financial cost of acting, a perceived lack of availability, and a mistrust of corporate claims about energy efficient products and services.

Tellingly, over half (51.5%) believe governments should be forcing businesses to remove products that are most damaging to global warming, and 70 per cent want claims about climate change by corporations to be independently verified. This would probably be the response in India too. As big themes like "green" and "sustainability" take hold, these same consumers will begin to shop in ways that reflect their collective conversations and sensibilities being shaped now through social media.

Sustainable Development

Sustainable development means meeting the needs of today (food, shelter, employment etc.) without compromising the ability of future generations to meet those needs. We believe in the power of individuals, the private sector, local actors, governments and others to support the United Nations' leadership in conserving the wonders of the natural world towards promoting sustainable development.

Much has been written about recycling plastic and I guess Alexander Parkes, who invented the world's first plastic in 1855, would never have believed even in his wildest dreams that the ubiquitous plastic carry bag or plastic cover as it is known would have environmentalists up in arms. Sustainable consumption alone will not resolve the issue considering our population growth rates and the quantum of waste. Recycling, combined with a reduction in wasteful consumption and plastic usage, will make a positive difference.

Today, we find that even illiterate and semi-literate sections are comfortable with gadgets such as the mobile phones. Such being the case, surely, it is not impossible for us to unlearn habits. Today, the consumer is aware of the problem, but does not know what an individual can do about it. The question arises what needs to be done by the Government, the corporate and the consumer? By working together civil society organisations, governments and corporations can convince and persuade the consumers to adopt habits that they make a positive difference on sustainable development and climate change. Immediate actions should include:

- ***Leading by Example***: National, political, cultural and corporate figures need to act as green role models, to assure consumers they can and should take action.
- ***Strengthening of Standards***: Product labels and indicators about climate change must be clear, comprehensive and independently verified if consumers are to trust the claims being made by businesses.
- ***Reducing Unhelpful Choice***: Choice reduction policies should be developed for all high impact consumer products and services where viable alternatives exist.
- ***Establishing Individual Rights and Responsibilities***: Widespread agreement on what constitutes a sustainable lifestyle must be legislated by 2015. Personal carbon allowances must be considered as a key policy tool for achieving this.

High Awareness of Problem, Low Awareness of Solutions

Awareness and concern about climate change are widespread. People's awareness is built-up by news coverage, what their children learn in school, and their own experience and interpretation of extreme weather. The concern that people express is strong, but it is often beneath the surface. However, big the dangers of climate change are, they are seen to be distant both in time and in mind. Climate change is important, but it is not felt urgent. Despite this distance, people feel inclined to take some responsibility, especially those with children, "because you want to protect them". Some draw an analogy with recycling, which is the dominant way that they "do their bit" today. But in terms of personal actions, they do not know what the analogy would be. "How do you know how to do your bit towards global warming really?"

Positive Reaction to Affordable Solutions

When presented with answers to this question, from low-emission products to carbon offset programmes, many people are ready to consider climate concerns, and would select climate-responsible options if offered, all else being equal. This does not translate into a willingness to pay a big premium. What makes the opportunity real is that people do not have to pay a big premium. For lower-carbon categories, consumers are ready to consider offsets built into the product choice: "Knowing that Sony did that rather than Philips would make me look at Sony TVs first."

Consumers are Concerned, but their Concern is not 'Activated'

Statements like: It is the biggest issue in society. We are starting to see the results of global warming, so, it rather freaks you out. How can you not pay attention? Our kids are going to be severely affected and probably not be able to go outside. It is a bit like poverty, disease and starvation; you can feel very deeply at times, but you cannot go around thinking about disasters all the time because you would go nuts. I do recycling at home and feel I can make a difference; but with global warming, I do not know what I can do. On being told what they can do, all would agree that, it is do-able.

Looking Back at the Past Two Decades

Here I would like to remind our readers about the girl who silenced the UN for 5 minutes. Her name is Severn Cullis-Suzuki, and she has given speech at a UN Assembly in Brazil in 1992, when she was twelve years old. She had raised all the money to travel to the delegation, five thousand miles from her home, herself. Speaking about the hole in the ozone layer, pollution, the devastation of the forests and extinction of so many species, Severn charged that we adults have no idea how to fix these things, in fact cannot fix them, and that we must change our ways. "If you do not know how to fix it, stop breaking it", she pleaded.

Severn continued to say: "I am here to speak for all generations to come. I am here to speak on behalf of starving children around the world whose cries go unheard. I am only a child and I do not have the solutions but neither do you. I am only a child, but I know we are all part of a family five billion strong; in fact, 30 million species strong, and borders and governments will never change that. I am only a child, but I know if all the money spent on war was spent on finding environmental answers, ending poverty, and finding treaties—what a wonderful place this world would be." And here's the amazing thing, this speech was given in 1992, at the Earth Summit in Rio de Janeiro. How much of it is still relevant today? All of it and the more important question is: How much has been changed, accomplished, since Severn spoke that day?

Years later, Severn wrote a piece for *Time magazine* in which she said: "I spoke for six minutes and received a standing ovation. Some of the delegates even cried. I thought that maybe I had reached some of them, that my speech might actually spur action. Now, a decade from Rio, after I have sat through many more conferences, I am not sure what has been accomplished. My confidence in the people in power and in the power of an individual's voice to reach them has been deeply shaken...In the 10 years since Rio, I have learned that addressing our leaders is not enough. As Gandhi said many years ago, 'We must become the change we want to see.' I know change is possible."

Conclusion

National Geographic has partnered with GlobeScan to develop an international research approach to measure and monitor consumer progress towards environmentally sustainable consumption. The key objectives of this unprecedented consumer tracking survey are to provide regular quantitative measures of consumer behaviour and to promote sustainable consumption. This research is a tracking, reporting, and promoting environmentally sustainable consumption and citizen behaviour in different countries.

Greendex 2014, quantitative consumer study of 18,000 consumers in 18 countries (14 in 2008) asked about such behaviour as energy use and conservation, transportation choices, food sources, the relative use of green products *versus* traditional products, attitudes towards the environment and sustainability, and knowledge of environmental issues. The survey indicates that although environmental concerns have widely increased since 2012 and that climate change is presenting an increasingly felt threat to consumers, the pace and scale of uptake of sustainable consumption have remained too little over the past six years. Compared with 2008, consumer habits have improved at least somewhat in all countries surveyed that year, except Brazil. Top-scoring consumers of the 2014 Greendex study are in the developing economies of India and China, in descending order, followed by consumers in South Korea, Brazil, and Argentina. Indian and Chinese consumers also scored highest in 2012. American consumers' behaviour still ranks as the least sustainable of all countries surveyed since the inception of the Greendex study in 2008. An exploration of consumers' intentions to improve their habits, the study also reveals that those in Latin America and India appear to be the most easily influenced to change when informed about their personal impact on the environment. Results also show that consumers who already display behaviour that is relatively sustainable and are told that their behaviour is above average from an environmental point of view are more motivated to improve their behaviour further than are consumers who display less sustainable habits. This suggests that positive reinforcement is likely a powerful tool for enabling behaviour change among consumers.[1]

India is on top may be due to the lack of availability of choices for a majority of the population or lack of economic opportunities whatever maybe the cause, the results proclaim that India is leading in consumer sustainability and environment sustainability. Let us leave it at that and move forward while maintaining this track record in all our future endeavours. Because what we do today, right now will have an accumulated effect on our tomorrow.

Note

1. http://environment.nationalgeographic.com/environment/greendex/

References

Blower, M. and Leon, W. (1999), *The Consumer's Guide to Effective Environmental Choices: Practical Advice from the Union of Concerned Scientists*, New York: Three Rivers Press.

Chambers, N., Simmons, C. and Wackernagel, M. (2000), *Sharing Nature's Interest: Ecological Footprints as an Indicator of Sustainability*, London: Earthscan.

Globescan, (September, 2014), *Greendex 2014: Consumer Choice and the Environment—A Worldwide Tracking Survey,* Highlights Report, http://images.nationalgeographic.com/wpf/media-content/file/NGS_2014_Greendex_Highlights_FINAL-cb1411689730.pdf.

http://www.unesco.org/education/tlsf/TLSF/theme_b/mod09/uncom09.htm

Inaugural address by the Prime Minister on the 97th Indian Science Congress January 3rd, 2010 at Thiruvanathapuram, Kerala.

Mathews, E. (1999) *Critical Consumption Trends and Implications: Degrading Earth's Ecosystems*, Washington DC: World Resources Institute.

Miller, D. (ed.) (1995), *Acknowledging Consumption: A Review of New Studies*, London: Routledge.

Noorman, K. and Uiterkamp, T. (1998) *Green Householders: Domestic Consumers, Environment and Sustainability*, London: Earthscan.

OECD (1997) *Sustainable Consumption and Production*, Paris: OECD.

Shelley Seale, (June 23, 2008), "The Girl who Silenced the U.N. for Five Minutes", *The Weight of Silence: Invisible Children of India.*

Shonali Muthalaly, (2010) "Driven by a romantic journey at his heart", August 16, *The Hindu.*

Vidya Vasudevan (2010) "The carry bag culture", *The Hindu,* 15th August.

Wackernagel, M. and Rees, W. (1996) *Our Ecological Footprint: Reducing Human Impact on the Earth*, New Society Publishers, Gabriola Island, BC, Canada and Philadelphia, PA, USA.

11
Contributory Role of Panchayati Raj in Facilitating Sustainable Economic Development

Joseph Benjamin

Introduction

It is argued that the developed countries comprising roughly 20 per cent of the global population, control about 80 per cent natural resources of the world, and it is they who are the biggest energy consumers and biggest pollutant emitters.[1] The very goal of sustainable development is challenged when one see that one sixth of earth's population enjoys a disproportionate five-sixth of its wealth. For whom do we ask for sustainable development? It seems that sustainable development is a game plan, bogey, nay a conspiracy of developed capitalist nations to stall the development, or at least slow down its pace and keep developing nations on perpetual dependency.

Ever since Independence, India has made a significant progress in various sectors of rural development. The government is continuously striving to bring about rapid and sustainable development and socio-economic transformation in rural India with an integrated approach towards improving the quality of life of rural poor and ensuring equity and effective people's participation. This realization came though belatedly as it was assumed that economic growth would trigger "trickle-down" benefits to poor and marginalized section of the population. This facilitated paradigmatic shift from top-down approach to bottom-up approach to economic growth strategy.

Any strategy for sustainable development must involve the people themselves at all levels. For this, there is a need for revitalizing Panchayati Raj Institutions, which encompasses both administrative and financial devolution of powers. The Panchayati Raj Institutions can be recognized as a catalyst for participative planning and implementation of various development programmes especially sustainable development at grass-roots level. This has a cascading effect if policies are calibrated well.

Panchayats have been the backbone of the Indian villages since the very beginning of history. It is an engine of growth, agent of change and sustainable development. The contribution of Lord George Fredrick Samuel Ripon (1827-1909) in starting local self-government in the year 1881-84 is remarkable. Gandhiji's dream of every village being a republic or Panchayats having powers has been translated into reality after Independence. April 24, 1993 is a landmark in the history of Panchayati Raj in India as on this day the Constitution (73rd Amendment) Act, 1992 came into force to provide Constitutional status to the Panchayati Raj Institutions. The 73rd Amendment Act gives more power to the Gram Sabha.

Sustainable development involves many things. More appropriate technologies, supportive policies, different ethics, and changes in individual behaviour are among the more obvious factors. Sustainable development is a pattern of resource use that aims to meet human needs while preserving the environment so that these needs can be met not only in the present, but also for future generations. Sustainable development can be defined as "the kind of human activity that nourishes and perpetuates the whole community of life on Earth." How the environment can be preserved? How the human needs can be met not only for the present generation, but also for the future? Here the role of Panchayati Raj would be very vital. People's participation and planning in rural areas in sustainable development is very important. Local self-government is important for mobilizing resources and regulating their use with a view to maintain a long-term base for productive activities. At the same time, available resources can be put to their most efficient and sustainable use with location-specific knowledge, which is best, generated and interpreted locally. Sustainable development and environmental security are the functions of the political order in each state and region. For development to be sustainable and the environment to be secure, "patterns of resource control and levels of democracy within the decision-making groups"[2] become important elements of the political order. The necessity of reordering society with decentralization of power, empowerment of local people particularly women, and mass participation in sustainable development, calls for a bottom-up strategy involving people's participation from the lowest level.[3]

The present chapter would focus on the role of Panchayati Raj in sustainable development. People's participation in preserving the environment not only for present, but also for the future generation would be a part of this study. This chapter would highlight the role of Panchayati Raj and at the same time study the various governmental schemes launched in rural areas for preserving the natural resources like water, mountains, riverbeds, soil, land etc. which are to be used by future generations too.

Panchayati Raj and Grassroots Development

The first Prime Minister of Independent India, Pandit Jawaharlal Nehru set in notion Community Development Programme in 1952. But, it was not taken seriously because people were not attuned to this new paradigm. After Balwantrai Mehta it was gradually felt it would be an important agency through which governmental programmes and schemes can be implemented for sustainable development by the people. Government is the largest agency mandated for overall development of people a hangover of "*Maa Baap*" sarkar of the British Raj. Government schemes, thus, are well designed to reach the people especially socially and economically marginalized sections of the society. However, lack of community participation and ownership in such schemes along with poor economic and political inter-sectoral cooperation has restricted the intended impact on sustainable development in rural areas. Panchayats have been the backbone of the Indian villages since the beginning of recorded history. Gandhiji's dream of every village being a republic or Panchayats having powers, has been translated into reality with the introduction of the three-tier Panchayati Raj system to enlist people's participation in rural reconstruction. 24 April, 1993 is a landmark day in the history of Panchayati Raj in India as on this day the Constitution (73rd Amendment) Act, 1992 came into force to provide Constitutional status to the Panchyati Raj Institutions. The salient features of the Act were: (i) to provide three-tier system of Panchayati Raj for all States having population of over 20 lakh; (ii) to hold Panchayat elections regularly every 5 years; (iii) to provide reservation of seats for Scheduled Castes, Scheduled Tribes and women (not less than 33%); (iv) to appoint State Finance Commission to make recommendations regarding financial powers of the Panchayats; and (v) to constitute District Planning Committee to prepare draft development plan for the district as a whole. According to the Constitution, Panchayats shall be given powers and authority to function as institutions of self-government. The powers and responsibilities to be delegated to Panchayats at the appropriate level are: (a) preparation of plan for economic development and social justice; (b) implementation of schemes for economic development and social justice in relation to 29 subjects given in Eleventh Schedule to the Constitution; and (c) to levy, collect and appropriate taxes, duties, tolls and fees. The 73rd Amendment Act gives Constitutional status to the *Gram Sabha*.[4] Under the Act, Gram Sabha has been vested with powers for: ownership of minor forest produce, approval of development plans, selection of beneficiaries under various programmes, consultation on land acquisition, manage minor water bodies, control mineral leases, regulate/prohibit sale of intoxicants, prevent alienation of land and restore unlawfully alienated land of Scheduled Tribes, manage village markets, control money lending to Scheduled Tribes, and control institutions and functionaries in all social sectors.

Local Self-Government and Sustainable Development

Post-1947 India economic growth strategy was socialist in its orientation, but the introduction of economic reform in 1992 brought seismic changes in economic landscape of the country. This was a real game changer, which steered the Indian economy to a new trajectory. As a result, Indian economy became integrated with world economic system. Notwithstanding this new economic stance, the government was also conscious that grass root mobilization and development should also figure in its overall economic scheme of things. Various programmes and projects of long-gestation and medium-*cum*-short duration were started. Some succeeded well, while others produced mixed results. The following programmes need individual elucidation. Some programmes got foreign funding from international bodies, UN affiliates and legion of NGOs too pitched in their mite.

(a) Jawahar Gram Samriddhi Yojana

Jawahar Gram Samridhi Yojana (JGSY) is the restructured, streamlined and comprehensive version of the erstwhile Jawahar Rozgar Yojana (JRY). Launched on 1 April, 1999, it has been designed to improve the quality of life to the rural poor by providing them additional gainful employment. The objectives of the Yojana are: creation of demand-driven village infrastructure including durable assets for increasing the opportunities for sustained employment, and generation of supplementary employment for the unemployed poor in the rural areas. People living in villages constitute the target group of JGSY. The programme is being implemented entirely at the village panchayat level. Village panchayat is the sole authority for preparation of annual action plan and its implementation with the approval of Gram Sabha.

(b) Swarnjayanti Gram Swarozgar Yojana

Swarnjayanti Gram Swarozgar Yojana (SGSY) is the single self-employment programme for the rural poor. Launched on 1 April, 1999, the programme replaces the earlier self-employment and allied programmes—Integrated Rural Development Programme (IRDP), Training of Rural Youth for Self-Employment (TRYSEM), Development of Women and Children in Rural Areas (DWCRA), Supply of Improved Tool-Kits to Rural Artisans (SITRA), Ganga Kalyan Yojana (GKY) and Million Wells Scheme (MWS), which are no longer in operation. The Yojana takes into account all the strengths and weaknesses of the earlier self-employment programmes. It aims at establishing a large number of micro-enterprises in the rural areas. Persons assisted under this programme are known as Swarozgaris and not beneficiaries. A significant aspect of SGSY is that every family assisted under this programme will be brought above the poverty-line in three years and as such the programme aims at creating substantial additional incomes for the rural poor.

(c) Employment Assurance Scheme

Employment Assurance Scheme (EAS) was launched on 2 October, 1993 for implementation in 1,778 identified blocks in the drought prone areas, desert areas, tribal and hilly areas of different States. Later, the scheme was extended to the remaining blocks of the country in a phased manner. The scheme being implemented in all the rural blocks of the country has been restructured from 1 April, 1999.

(d) Rajiv Gandhi National Drinking Water Mission

The Accelerated Rural Water Supply Programme (ARWSP) was introduced in 1972-73 by the Centre to assist the States and Union Territories to accelerate the pace of coverage of drinking water supply. The programme was given a missionary approach with the launch of the

Technology Mission of Drinking Water and Related Water Management, also called the National Drinking Water Mission (NDWM) in 1986. The NDWM was renamed as the Rajiv Gandhi National Drinking Water Mission (RGNDWM) in 1991.

(e) Indira Awaas Yojana

To meet the housing needs of the rural poor, Indira Awaas Yojana (IAY) was started in May 1985 as a sub-scheme of Jawahar Rozgar Yojana. From 1 January, 1996, it is being implemented as an independent scheme. The Indira Awaas Yojana aims at helping rural people below poverty-line belonging to Scheduled Castes/Scheduled Tribes, freed bonded labourers and non-SC/ST categories in construction of dwelling units and upgradation of existing unserviceable *kutcha* houses by providing grant-in aid.

*(f) Credit-*cum*-subsidy Scheme for Rural Housing*

The Credit-*cum*-Subsidy Scheme for Rural Housing has been conceived for rural households having annual income up to ₹ 32,000. However, preference will be given to rural households below poverty-line. Salient features of the scheme are: Subsidy up to ₹ 10,000 per eligible household in plain areas and ₹ 11,000 in hilly/difficult areas. Loanup to ₹ 40,000 per household; and sanitary latrine and smokeless *chulha* are integral part of the house.

(g) Centrally-sponsored Rural Sanitation Programme

Rural sanitation is a State subject. The State Governments implement the Rural Sanitation Programme under State sector Minimum Needs Programme (MNP). The Central Government supplements the States' efforts providing financial and technical assistance through the Centrally-sponsored Rural Sanitation Programme (CRSP). The CRSP was launched in 1986 with the objective of improving the quality of life of the rural people and to provide privacy and dignity to women. The concept of sanitation was expanded in 1993 to include personal hygiene, home sanitation, safe water, garbage and excreta disposal and waste water disposal. The components of the programme include construction of individual sanitary latrines for households below the poverty-line (BPL), conversion of individual sanitary latrines, construction of village sanitary complexes for women, setting up of sanitary marts, intensive campaign for awareness creation, health education etc. The objective of the programme is to accelerate coverage of rural population, especially among households below the poverty-line with sanitation facilities, complementing the efforts in Rural Water Supply.

(h) National Rural Employment Guarantees Act

NREGA is regarded as a lifeline for many who lack sustainable livelihoods.[5] Recently, it was renamed as Mahatma Gandhi National Rural Employment Guarantees Act. The main intention behind the scheme was to provide employment to rural mass. It guarantees minimum 100-days' wages to local people. It has been the key to development process in rural areas. It has been very successful in bringing sustainable livelihood through the involvement of local panchayat. The NREGA not only aims at providing work and wages, but also ensure that it results in the creation of durable assets, which strengthen and enhance the productivity of land and all agricultural resources. The people are involved in the developmental process, which will last for many generations. The work is categorized by the developmental officers who will see the sustainable livelihood of the rural mass. People busy in cutting forest tree, now be entrusted in preserving the forest. People making cow-dung, now will be taught to stop the carbon emission.

Millennium Development Goals and Sustainable Development

In the year 2000, India was among the countries that had signed on to achieve, by 2015, the Unites Nations Millennium Development Goals (MDGs). These goals straddle eight core concerns, including foundational one of reducing poverty and hunger. In many ways, this process is the world's most ambitious social development intervention. It needs people's mobilization in achieving goals.[6]

Large pockets of extreme poverty and hunger persists in Asia, where it is difficult to achieve Millennium Development Goals by 2025. 10 per cent people live on less than $1.25 a day in 19 Asian economies. Around 41.6 per cent people live below poverty line in India.[7] In order to achieve this goal by 2025, all the citizens will have to work collectively especially the village panchayat. Without mobilizing the rural youth, it would be impossible to achieve the millennium goals. The key to this goal is amelioration of poverty.

Forest Conservation and People's Participation

The recorded forest area in the country is 7,65,210 sq. km. (23% of the land area), satellite data indicate forest covers of 6,75,538 sq. km. 20.55 per cent of the total land area). However, 12.68 per cent of total forest areas have crown cover of over 40 per cent and the rest is open forest. About 0.48 million ha are mangrove forests.[8] "At least a third of India's geographical area should be clad with trees for sustainable economic development. The current percentage is less than three."[9]

Practically all of the forest area is under severe stress due to heavy removal of fuel wood, fodder, and timber, non-wood product, manufacturing *bidi* with *tendu* leaf and grazing. In 1976 through the 42nd Constitutional Amendment, the Government of India brought the subject of forest under concurrent list and incorporated Article 48-A (Part IV Directives Principles) for Protection and Improvement of forest and Wild-life by the states. Similarly, Article 51-A (g) Part IV-A Fundamental Duties directs the citizens "to protect and improve the natural environment including forest, lakes, rivers and wildlife and have compassion for living creatures". A new Ministry of Environment and Forest (MoEF) was created in 1985. Protection of biodiversity is important for well-being of the people of the developing countries. Now, it is for the wildlife managers and local people to come forward and protect the forest or get perished. Community participation in sustainable forest management is an age-old practice in India. It has received considerable official support at local levels in many ways since 1970s. In 1990, the Government of India has issued the policy directives of share and care for involving of village community and voluntary agencies to protect and help in the management of forest.

Hurdles in People's Participation in Sustainable Development

Poverty

The World Economic Forum's global competitiveness ranking has put India in fifty-first rank. India has been pushed down to 51st position from 49th due to its poor performance in a range of social sector areas such as education, health and infrastructure. Though India has performed well in complex financial sector areas, attaining the 17th rank globally in terms of its financial markets, 44th in business sophistication and 39th in innovation, it has failed to improve the basic drives of competitiveness.

Thierry Geiger, Associate Director, World Economic Forum, said that in India, there is a widespread poverty, poor health and education facilities and poor infrastructure in rural India. At the same time, India is experiencing rapid growth. India has $293 billion as the balance of payment and poor macro-economic environment. The reasons for India sliding down in the global competitive ranking are : (i) least care for people below poverty line; and (ii) rising inflation and increasing fiscal deficit. In fact, the present government appears to be working on sheer vote bank politics. It is least bothered to take care of the population below poverty line and is striking to reservation based on caste, which should be completely abolished.[10] Poverty level is not uniform in India. It differs from Indian state to state. The FAO and the United Nations World Food Programme announced on September 14, 2010 that 925 million people are estimated to be suffering from chronic hunger in 2010, a small decline from the 1,023 billion estimated in 2009. The new figures on world hunger highlight that the food crisis is still acute for one-sixth of the world's population. Rehman Sobhan, Development Economist and Chairman of Bangladesh's premier public policy think tank, Centre for Policy Dialogue, in his exclusive interview, said, "People go without food because they do not have land, they do not have assets. The relevant right is the right to land..."[11]

At the same time, poverty and population are twin problems affecting sustainable development of India. If we consider poverty as a disease then population is a menace, together these are eating out vital organ of society.

Multiple Communication Revolution

Multi-media communication such as print and electronic media, internet gave a big push to process of globalization. It is due to development of multi-media the poverty, malnutrition and famine like conditions in Third World countries have been in spotlight as never before. This energized and catalyzed many governments to do something to improve the economic deprivation of below poverty level people and political institutional mechanisms came into prominence. Panchayati Raj was the centrepiece of one of many political innovations.

Climate Change

The deleterious effects of development paradigm include carbon footprint resulting from overuse of non-renewable sources of energy like oil, coal, iron, zinc, copper, manganese etc. This affects our climate, environment and as a result, we have either flood or famine in many parts of the world. India is either flooded or face drought-like situation. Farmers, especially in Maharashtra have taken extreme step of committing suicide, as the seed, which they brought, have not yielded desired crops. This might have resulted as the crops could not get enough irrigation facilities. They could not repay the loan they have taken in time. Ultimately, they were forced to commit suicide. The unpredictable climatic changes have become a greatest hurdle for sustainable economic development. The rain pattern has changed globally. Dam constructions are submerging whole villages as a result people are displaced and livelihood is affected. Flood washes away the whole village quite often. People are forgetting how many climates are there in India due to climatic change.

Mobilization of Dispossessed, Disempowered People at Grassroots Level for Success of Panchayati Raj

The corruption and leakage of funds has retarded the developmental process in villages. Our late Prime Minister Rajiv Gandhi has once said if one rupee is sent to village, villagers will receive only 20 paise. The middlemen swallow 80 per cent of the fund. He took initiative to make amendment in the Panchayati Raj Act in order to empower the village *panchayat.* The resource, which is required for sustainable economic development in rural areas, does not reach the target group and marginalized people. Because of the lack of resources, which are already sanctioned, the developmental schemes are not able to start.

U.S. Capitalistic Worldwide Penetration

U.S. capitalistic worldwide penetration along with other European nations has created policy dilemmas in approaches of governments in bringing grassroots transformational changes. International economic organizations like IMF, World Bank, WTO and international trade organizations like MNCs have affected our economy.[12] And to thwart effort of multinational corporations—mining, marketing of seeds and fertilizers etc., special economic zone issues results in retarding our economic development in rural areas. People are dependent on branded seeds and fertilizers for agriculture. Agriculture is becoming the thing of the past. People are not interested in farming. The farmers, who were enjoying ride of bullock cart, today prefer to have ride of big car. For example, Ludhiana city in

Punjab is known amongst many other things to have innumerable Mercedes cars. Urbanization has become the stumbling block in the sustainable economic development in rural areas. People are leaving village and migrating to cities creating slum in cities, which have become a great threat to city development.[13]

Conclusion

Some States have done better than others in implementation of Panchayati Raj and optimizing its potentialities and promises others have fallen on wayside. The very interesting step has been initiated by the Government of Rajasthan to transfer five of its departments, namely primary education, health, agriculture, social justice and empowerment of women and child development to Panchayati Raj Institutions. These elected local self-government institutions will now have full administrative and financial control over the schemes run by these departments, and over the employees responsible for implementing them at local level. Such decentralization of functional and financial powers could tangibly improve the transparency, accountability and delivery of governmental scheme. Transferring operational and financial responsibility to Panchayati Raj Institutions makes eminent sense, and has, in fact, been the spirit behind the Constitutional amendment. But has not been implemented in the real sense for nearly two decades. It is precisely in the 'social sector' and agriculture spheres where Panchayati Raj Institutions can bring about a fundamental change for the betterment in the quality of governance.[14] There is a flip side which cannot be brushed aside or shoved under the carpet as for example the incumbent Chief Minister of Bihar Nitish Kumar of JD (U) has used reservation of jobs etc., in Panchayati Raj Institutions to garner support of backward castes, Muslims and *Mahadalits* in forthcoming electoral battle at the hustings.[15] Thanks to Government of India for creating a separate Ministry at Central Government as Ministry of Panchayati Raj, Rural Development and Urban Poverty.

Gunnar Myrdal, a Nobel Prize winner and writer of *Asian Drama* characterized Indian State as "Soft State".[16] While explaining the functioning of Indian Democracy, J.K. Galbraith, former US ambassador to India termed Indian democracy as "Functioning Anarchy". Economic sustainable development's goal should be inclusive growth and Panchayati Raj has to dovetail its strategy with various stakeholders. Many of the laudable goals enshrined in the Directive Principles of State Policy not only should have statutory legitimacy, but need to be strictly enforced by court. Panchayati Raj Institutions in rural areas will be able to take a lead to forest management, creating biogas plant for the cooking, stopping indiscriminate use of pesticides for more production of grains. The Former Environment Minister Jairam Ramesh proposed to have BT brinjal for sustainable livelihood. Do we need only the present livelihood or want sustainable livelihood as an on-going prospect is a Million dollar question which urgently and piquancy needs an adequate answer brooking no delay.

Notes

1. S. L. Sharma (1997), "Towards Sustainable Development in India: Issue and Perspectives," in S.R. Mehta (Ed.) *Poverty, Population and Sustainable Development*, Jaipur: Rawat, p. 291. Also *see*, Amitabh Sinha, (2010) "*The Copenhagen Guide*" and *Indian Express,* December 6, 2009.
2. Anil Agarwal, (1995), "What is Sustainable Development?" In M.L. Dewan (ed.), *Towards a Sustainable Society*, New Delhi: Clarion Book, p. 21.
3. Shaukat Hassan (1997), "Sustainable Development, Environment Security and Disarmament Interface in South Asia: An Overview", In D.D. Khanna (ed.), *Sustainable Development, Environmental Security, Disarmament and Development Interface in South Asia*, New Delhi: MacMillan India Limited, p. 24.
4. Except Rajasthan and Bihar, all States have passed laws to give effect to the provisions contained in the Act 40 of 1996.
5. Parmela Philipose, (2010), "Time to stand up for the Millennium Development Goals", *Hitavada,* (Nagpur daily) October 10, 2010.
6. *Ibid.*
7. *Indian Express,* (Nagpur Edition) August 22, 2009.
8. Forest Survey of India, (2001), "*State of Forest Report,*" pp. 4-8.
9. *India Today*, September 20, 2010, p. 68.
10. P.K. Vasudeva, "Global Competitiveness", *Hitavada*, (Nagpur daily) October 6, 2010.
11. *Times of India* (Nagpur Edition) October 1, 2010.
12. Abigail Dawn Mcgillivary, (2010), "Indian Economic Reform as an Example of Disaster Capitalism", *Mainstream,* Vol. XLVIII (38), pp. 13-19. September 10-16, 2010.
13. Dhurjat Mukheree, (2010), "Slum on Rise" *Hitavada* (Nagpur daily) October 10, 2010.
14. *Indian Express* (Nagpur Edition), "Devolution & Detail" (Editorial), October 4, 2010.
15. Harihar Swarup, (2010), "JD (U) Overcoming all Hurdles", *Hitavada,* (Nagpur daily) October 11, 2010.
16. Gunnar Myrdal (1968), *Asian Drama*, Pantheon: New York.

12
Sustainable Consumption
Consumer Education and Awareness

Ramaben R. Mavani and *Ramjibhai B. Mavani*

Consumption—Definition

To begin with we may ask the question—who or what is a consumer? Well, this question does not need much explanation or elaboration in the present day context, as we all know what it means and implies. Still in brief, the word 'consumer' can be defined as "any person or body who buys, uses or consumes either for himself or his family and relatives any goods, materials, resources or services, whether produced by nature or man-made." The word consumer just does not mean a person as defined in law or in legal terms for the purpose of legal procedures, but it has a far broader meaning and implications in practice and it covers in its ambit many aspects of consumption such as at individual, community, groups, industrial and commercial levels. Man has been a consumer since his existence. He needs to consume for his survival and sustenance. Not only man, but also all plant and animal life on this planet need to consume in order to survive. In term Sustainable Consumption is defined as "the purchase, use or consumption of any goods, materials, resources or services, whether produced by nature or man-made in such a manner of frugality and prudence so as not to render their supplies and availability to depletion, degradation, total loss and finally, to total exhaustion or extinction, but to let these supplies to continue and even let them get renewed to last for longer and longer times to come for the use of future generations."

Consumption in the Olden Days and Modern Days

The man has been a consumer since his existence, but his consumption patterns have kept on changing over the ages since his existence to the present day. The needs of earliest man were very basic and simple. He hunted, ate raw-food and wore hides and leaves. He drank water from natural water source nearby. But gradually, man began to be civilized. He progressed from Stone Age into Iron Age, Bronze Age, and various other ages, into the present day electronics age. With progression of each age, man began to become a more civilized person and so his consuming needs also increased more than before. With this progressive civilized consumption, man began to need more and more. However, even with these increased needs, the consumption patterns and needs were very simple and basic. These needs were largely limited to the basic needs of "bread, clothing and shelter", i.e. *Roti, Kapda* and *Makan*. There was abundance of everything on this earth, but man was just content with what he had and what he got for his survival. The element of "greed" had still not taken possession of man's fancies to have more and more. The tools, technologies and methods of production and exploitation of whatever natural resources or man-made goods and products, even with gradual improvement and renovations in them, were very basic, simple and manual. This simplicity ensured in itself sustainability of supplies and resources. Man did not have to make any special efforts for it, though he was aware that he was using all the God given resources as a blessing from the God, and to some extent, he was also aware that he should not misuse, overuse or overexploit these resources.

This was the situation until the recent history of last 400 to 500 by-gone years. There was no reason or cause for worrying about sustainability. Then, times changed, and since last 300 to 400 years, there was a sudden increase in consumption patterns by leaps and bounds. Though there may be many known and unknown reasons and factors behind this sudden leap, it can more be attributed to tangible factors like industrial revolution, technological advancement, new inventions and innovations, mechanization, mass production, faster and quicker ways of production etc. These aspects gradually set in and replaced simple tools, simple mechanization and manual work. We all know that this has led to a faster exploitation of supplies and resources on an enormous mass scale. Not only this industrial and technological advancement, but other factors like urbanization, overpopulation, rather population explosion in some parts of the world, capitalism, liberalization in trade and commerce at world level, globalization, advanced commerce and trade practices, jet speed transportation and logistics facilities, super market and mall cultures. corporate manoeuvres to produce and sell whatsoever and by any means to fatten their profit accounts and media advertisements targeted towards gullible consumer groups like women and children have all played their respective roles in changing consumption patterns and driving consumption to an disproportionate gigantic magnitude. Introduction of new products every other day in the market, increased and surplus incomes, increased purchasing powers, materialism, hi-fi lifestyles, attractive purchase offers like "buy now pay later", "buy one get one free", easy loan and installments facilities have also added to this consumption magnitude and are some of the recent factors.

Whereas in the olden days man was content with whatever basic needs he got for his survival, today's man has become more and more materialistic. His greed not just to become rich, but also to possess more and more material things has taken over his prudence. Though we may not be aware of it, and we cannot even be blamed directly or individually for it, we in general want to buy, to possess and to have more and more and still more. It is not that this situation of materialistic tendency prevails in the society at just individual or personal level, but it is prevalent to a much more greater extent amongst the proponents of capitalism, or rather capitalists, industrial, corporate bodies, commercial establishment and multinational companies. Their greed is endless. Now, these factors and tendencies to produce, buy and use more and more, whether there is a genuine need for it or not have combined into one major cause of fathering our today's frightening and burning problem of "Sustainability". Sustainability, today has reached an alarming position. If this situation still continues, we are nearing towards a point of no return.

Consumption quantum has increased many fold since last 300 to 400 years. It was at a very low level then. One of the main reasons was that population at that time was hardly 1/4th of what it is today. Second reason was that there was a lack of fast and effective transport systems. There was no railway, air transport was unheard of, there was little sea and road transport by non-mechanical slow sailing vessels for marine transport and bullock, ox, horse and camel carts for road transport. These basic means of transport plied in the nearby and neighbouring areas only with limited carting capacity. So, the quantity of transported goods was meagre. People mostly used to consume local goods and materials. Export and import of goods as it is known today was almost non-existent. In addition, there were hardly any electrical or electronics goods to use. Use of petroleum and its other by-products was minimal. Cement was unknown. Not just these heavy items, even other humble hundreds of items, which we normally find necessary to use in our daily lives and cannot do without were virtually non-existent in those days. Many of us present here perhaps may not be knowing that we Indians did not drink tea, did not eat bread (with some rare exceptions) and coffee was unknown about 200 years ago. We did not use soap, toiletries, washing powder, toothpaste and hundreds and hundreds of cosmetics items which we used today. Nobody had heard of Coca-cola and Pepsi. But what is the position today? Can we imagine our life today without all the above goods? No we cannot do without our daily necessities of all the above items and many more other items. One may, and especially today's younger generation wonder if people in the olden days did not have any tea or coffee to drink, nor any bread to eat, nor soap to bathe and wash their hands with, then how did they live? Perhaps they did not bathe and never washed their hands? No, it was not like that. People did use to eat, drink and wash, but there were very simple, basic hand-made and home-made alternatives for all these needs, and these alternatives were such that they did not cause a problem for sustainability of resources.

Consumption by Man *vis-à-vis* Plants and Animals

We know that plants and animal life on this earth also consume, but have we ever thought of what do these humble being consume as compared to human beings? Unfortunately (or rather fortunately), they are not gifted by, God of the super brain power that the man is gifted, and so they consume only the basic natural elements like raw food, vegetation, air and water, which are just the very basic needs for survival, and are renewable, and replaceable on their own. No special efforts have to be made for these natural basic things. Whereas what do human beings do? They consume each and everything on this earth on which their eyes fall and to such an enormous magnitude that when this quantum is put into figures it becomes fabulous. If consumption by plant and animal life *vis-à-vis* human beings is compared into ratios, the consumption ratio of humans would be a million times more than consumption of plants and animals. So, we can see that it is the human on this earth who causes problems that endanger the very existence and survival of life on this earth.

Consumption by Developed Countries

If we think of consumption on country level, corporate, industrial level and other mass scale level basis, we see that the consumption in these fields is astoundingly higher in developed countries like USA and some other European countries and use about 60 per cent to 70 per cent of the earth's total resources whereas the rest of the developing and poor countries, all combined use just the remaining 30 per cent. Many consumption patterns in these developed countries are dangerously high, thoughtless and ruthless. To cite just one simple example of ruthless consumption, we can say that some developed countries have wiped off vast and enormous patches of live, green forest covers to exploit timber, just to make chapter for nappies, toilet papers and handkerchief tissues. Some of these countries print newspapers and catalogues which they give out free, containing hoards of advertisements for selling useless things. People hardly even care to open and read these useless newspapers, and they just go to dustbins. Just imagine the number of trees that would have been cut and the amount of other resources and raw materials like power, water, fuel, machinery, manpower and wood that would have been used to produce such useless things, which are just destined to go to the dustbins without a trail of use of a single newspaper and the burden that such useless productions would have exerted on natural resources. There are hundreds and hundreds of examples of such ruthless consumption especially of petroleum products, power, water-supplies etc., consumed by large scale consumers like industries, commercial establishments and corporate bodies. Enormous quantities of natural and man-made resources like minerals, metals, water, power, wood, cement, paper etc. and gigantic machinery are required for industrial production. More the industrial progress, more is the exploitation and consumption; and higher the standard of living more is the demand for consumable goods. Large scale commercial establishments like hotels, super markets, mega malls, railways and transport systems and corporate bodies are consumers of enormous magnitude.

Consumption on Individual Basis

In the olden days, individuals hardly needed anything of their personal belongings apart from their clothing, footwear and a twig of a tree for brushing the teeth and some very few other minor items. All the other items of use were there for the use of the entire family jointly and collectively. But today we all need to have a large number of consumable items which should be for our personal use only like we need to have our personal television, personal telephone and mobile, personal car or scooter, personal computer and laptop, DVDs and VCDs and what not. Not only this, but in some sophisticated families every member of the family needs to have his or her personal room, personal toilet and personal bathroom. Now, just imagine what a great amount of stress this type of consuming patterns excerts on sustainability? This discussion on the pattern of the olden and present day's of individual consumption indicates the way in which consumption patterns have changed and jumped by leaps and bounds over just four hundred to three hundred years and how this excessive consumption has posed a serious threat to sustainability of resources. Excessive consumption has not only posed a serious threat to sustainability, but has given rise to many present day evils like materialistic tendencies and greed for more and more profitability, cut, throat competition, poor and undurable quality of goods, adulteration, unfair trade practices, pollution, floods of advertisements which are baffling consumers everyday, environmental degradation, heaps of rubbish everywhere and municipal dump-yards overflowing with the rubbish causing threat to lives on the planet etc. One of the most serious modern day threat is of which we all hear everyday, i.e. Global Warming. The habit, which has added to all the above evils, is consumption of use and throw items like tins, bottles, disposable dishes, and cups, various sorts of packaging materials, carry bags, which not only put pressure on resources, but are also a great threat on the environment. These have also caused several other problems like clutter and rubbish everywhere and waste, disposal of which has become a headache for municipal authority.

Modern Day Benefits

However, we should not be so ungrateful and forget here to mention the other side of the coin, i.e. many attractive benefits like employment generation, prosperity, saving of labour and time, improved living standards and many other social and infrastructural benefits, which we have derived from the progress made so far. This progress, however, is the very root cause of our modern times' most sensitive and demanding concern for sustainability. We should not mean here to say that we have now to abhor and shun away progress. We do have to make progress, but that should be the progress where sustainability is the primary concern at all levels beginning from exploitation of natural resources, processing these resources, to production, manufacturing and marketing up to the final stage of consumption.

Sustainability: Why is it Necessary?

Why is sustainability necessary? Sustainability is necessary because the resources are here not to last for ever, if ever, if their use continues to go on as it is today. This earth has got abundance of everything to provide amply for survival of humans, animal and plant life on this earth but just as Gandhiji has said, "This earth has got enough to provide for every man's needs, but not enough to provide for his greed." In reality it is not the progress but it is more or less the factor of human greed and excessive consumption that has led to the problem of sustainability. The entire industrial and business world is gripped with these dangerous elements of "greed", though they are not aware of it. In the same way, there is hardly any person from among the millions of individuals who may not been lured and enchanted the factor of "greed".

Consumption: Awareness and Education

Though the terms education and awareness appear easy in their meaning, it is extremely difficult and impracticable to put them into practice. Even then we have to make our best efforts to educate and bring awareness among people, for the sake of sustainability. Consumption cannot be stopped or controlled by law or compulsion. It can be implacable at some stage, when it comes to educating and making individuals aware. Many of us may have experienced that individual persons are so insensitive, hard-headed and stubborn towards not only the general problem of sustainability, but also modern days' other burning problems like adulteration of food, which is a question of life and death for them. To cite just one example, we everyday receive hordes of information through media and other sources about adulteration in food (which is a burning issue like the issue of sustainability), but people hardly pay any attention to this information. When a person is alerted about a particular adulterated item and asked to stay away from, he ignores the warning, purchases and consumes the same adulterated item knowing fully well its ill effects and dangers to his health and life. This is just one example, which shows that people are insensitive, unheeding, and not easy to convince. They just want to keep on with whatever the situation is. One would hardly like to put some innovative, improved consumption pattern into action. This being the drawback it is very essential that individuals are educated and convinced to translate their consumption behaviour into actual practice.

People have to be taught to be more concerned and encouraged to change their consumption patterns to much holy approaches like conscious consuming, real, need related consuming, shunning off "Shopping" instincts, ethical consuming, Gandhian way consuming etc. Some really thoughtful, concerned and understanding individuals can also be taught to put into practice the principle of "Simple Living and High Thinking". Education and awareness programmes through various methods and means like workshops, discussions, dialogues, seminars, street plays, media advertisements etc. can be designed to educate individuals, groups and communities. All these programmes can be made at district, sub-district, and rural levels, and in the regional language of each locality. We should find out the main components that influence consumer behaviour and design ways and means to transit this behaviour into a behaviour aimed at sustainability. Students and children can be educated by introducing sustainability related consumption lessons in their school curriculum.

Our next target group for education and awareness must be industries and commercial establishments, which are comparatively smaller group as compared to millions of individuals, but are major consumers of natural resources. These being smaller and organized entities it is far more easier to educate and bring awareness among them. These groups can also be controlled by compulsion, law and mandate. For example, there should be some mandatory standards for consumption of natural resources like minerals, water etc. and man-made resources like cement, power, machinery etc. Standards for manufacturing sustainable, efficient and eco-friendly and reusable products should also be imposed. Recycling is another very good field to help achieve sustainability. Industries, business and commercial houses must be educated to contain their greed, to shun away from exhibiting alluring advertisements aimed at susceptible consumer groups like women, youth and children, to shun away from manufacturing harmful goods and goods that cause a tremendous strain on resources.

Not just the individuals, industries, commercial establishments and NGOs, but it is actually, the government, which needs to be more concerned about sustainability. It is the government, which has the power to compel, though to some extent, all the above entities to practice sustainability into action. The governments instead of providing all the assistance and encouragement, land, forests and other natural resources to large scale and mega-scale industrial projects, should give more attention and encouragement to small scale, hand-made, cottage and rural level manual industries, all of which automatically lead to sustainability. No special effort has to be made to contain sustainability in the above means.

Conclusion

Lastly, there is no better alternative for a thought than to put it in action. There is no meaning of making rules and regulations, mandates or laws if they just have to remain merely on chapter. They have to be implemented, if some standards have to be achieved. Our country at present lacks in implementation of law and whatever other things that are for the good of our nation. Not only it is the people who lack self-discipline and awareness in many fields, but the governments, administration and implementing authorities lack willingness and awareness in implementing the very task for which they are there. This is one major drawback where much improvement is needed. Time has come to pay serious attention to the problem of sustainability. We all need to resolve to put our thoughts into action, at least to some extent and here we have to contain our greed, be aware and conscious consumer while buying and using materials which we really need and shunning off what we actually do not need. For the sake of sustainability, we have to practice simplicity, ethical and Gandhi on way of life.

13

Trend Analysis of Sustainable Consumption in Corporate Reporting

Anand Acharya and *Bansuri Das*

Introduction

Corporate Social Responsibility (CSR) and Sustainability Reporting is used by companies to inform consumers of their social and environmental values and practices beyond the sustainability characteristics of individual product. Reporting topics include corporate governance, environmental performance, health and safety of employees, community contributions, and supply chain management. But the gap between corporate sustainable reporting and most notions of sustainable consumption is still large, e.g. not many reports look at how the company and its product range supports sustainable consumption. While many companies have a good track record on corporate reporting, this may not necessarily match actual sustainability practices.

The chapter is based on the research aimed at throwing light on companies supporting sustainable consumption in their CSR activities. The focus areas in which corporate implement sustainable consumption were identified and recommendations given to other companies to adopt such CSR activities.

Objectives

The objectives of the study were:

1. to identify corporate social responsibility initiatives of Indian companies which promote sustainable consumption; and
2. to determine the trend in which sustainable consumption activities are being executed.

Methodology

The research was based on secondary data. Corporate Social Responsibility and sustainability reports of various sector specific companies in India were analyzed. A model was developed under which weights were assigned to the companies on the basis of the area and number of sustainable consumption practices. The model is attached under Annexure 1.

Limitations of the Study

1. Not all sustainability reports disclose data pertaining to their CSR activities thus data is not uniform.
2. Companies' capacity and annual revenue are not the criteria for comparing their sustainability report.

Scope

This research shall give guidelines to specific sector companies who want to adopt and promote activities related to sustainable consumption.

Literature Review

Sustainable consumption and production first secured international prominence at the Rio Earth Summit (UNCED) in 1992. At the 1992 United Nations Conference on the Environment and Development (UNCED) in Rio de Janeiro, the Agenda 21 action plan was adopted which is a collection of detailed goals and policies aimed at making sustainable development a reality by eliminating poverty and by eradicating the serious threats to our global and local environment.[1]

Sustainable Consumption is "the use of services and related products which respond to basic needs and bring a better quality of life while minimizing the use of natural resources and toxic materials as well as the emissions of waste and pollutants over the life cycle so as not to jeopardise the needs of future generations."[2] Sustainable consumption is a key step towards achieving sustainable development. The intrinsic relationship between sustainable consumption and the sustainable development paradigm was stressed in the Johannesburg Declaration on "Sustainable Development" which states that: "poverty eradication, changing consumption and production patterns, and protecting and managing the natural resource base for economic and social development are overarching objectives of, and essential requirements for sustainable development."[3]

Sustainable Consumption is about:

- Meeting the increasing needs of people with improved environmental outcomes and more sustainable consumption.
- Using fewer resources and causing less pollution to enable human development in all parts of the world.
- Helping consumers to stimulate suppliers to be innovative, improve competition and promote economic growth and development.[4]

Although companies tend to focus on sustainable consumption related activities internally, but when it comes to their CSR activities or external participation they follow conventional path. There are various definitions of CSR, but this chapter is adopting UNEP's definition of CSR, as mentioned in the Global Compact Environmental Principles Training Package (2005):

> "A values-based way of conducting business in a manner that advances sustainable development, seeking positive impact between business operations and society, aware of the close interrelation between business and society as well as of enterprises, like citizens, having basic rights and duties wherever they operate."

A company can have a good CSR record, but this does not mean that its operations and products are sustainable, nor that sustainability is embedded into the company's culture and decision-making. Core to this is moving beyond an internal frame of reference, coupled with an engagement with key stakeholders, to accept responsibility for the impact of the products and services it sells to consumers.[5]

To find out relations between sustainable consumption of business[6] and its CSR activities various indicators of sustainable consumption have been studied.[7] These include OECD indicators which focus from angle of analyzing economies, UNGC indicators for sustainable consumption[8], UNGC GRI indicators, Indicators of Consumption and Production Patterns (UN CSD).[9] However, none of these specifically look into sustainable consumption in corporate social responsibility activities, so,

Table 13.1 for sustainable consumption and CSR activities has been developed to analyze trend of CSR activities in confirmation with sustainable consumption indicators. Table 13.1 consists of various indicators with sub-indicators as explained below.

Table 13.1: Sustainable Consumption and CSR Activities

Indicator Used with subindicator in brackets	*Description of Indicator*
Green Procurement (Alternate sources of Energy, Cleaner Inputs, Clean Technology)	Focuses on sustainable procurement of electricity, water, raw materials, chemicals, technology transfer etc. from environment-friendly sources.
Material (Reduce, Reuse, Recycle)	Focuses on consumption of various input materials from different usage aspects.
Energy	Focuses on reduction of energy usage within a company.
Water (Reduce, Reuse, Recycle)	Focus is same as for Indicator of Material.
Fuel (Reduce, Treatment)	Focus on judicious use of it.
Waste (Reduce, Reuse/ Recover, Recycle, Environment Friendly Disposal)	Focus on company's varied activities related to it.
Pollution (Air, Noise etc. GHG Gases excluded in this indicator)	Focuses on activities for reducing it.
Green building	Focuses on green building developed by companies for their own use.
Product innovation and design (Biodegradable, R&D, Green Products)	Looks for activities in line with sustainable consumption.
Transport	Looks for various actions to reduce transporation carbon footprint.
Conservation (Habitat, water, trees/soil)	Activities focused on it.
GHG Reduction	Actions taken to reduce GHG emission.
CDM/Carbon Credit	Enrolled/actively.
SC Awareness (Ad&PR, labelling, activities)	Activities related to participation and awareness.
CSR Activities	Specifically promoting Resources use optimization in community external to company.

Sampling

The number of companies whose CSR reports were considered was divided sectorally. A total of 91 companies were reviewed belonging to 11 different sectors. The number of companies reviewed under each sector is illustrated in Fig. 13.1.

Sectoral approach was adopted since it is a significant element in a portfolio to address climate change; it provided a mean to compare best practices, performance standards, environmental performance and use of clean technology by companies to reduce their carbon footprint. To avoid inefficiency and unintended effects, sectoral approach was used to compare CSR reports of companies belonging to a similar sector.

The main benefit of using this approach was to understand the commitment level of companies in a particular area for reducing GHG emissions and to understand the diverse approaches undertaken by companies across different sectors for analyzing the trend in their respective [illegible] to combat climate change.

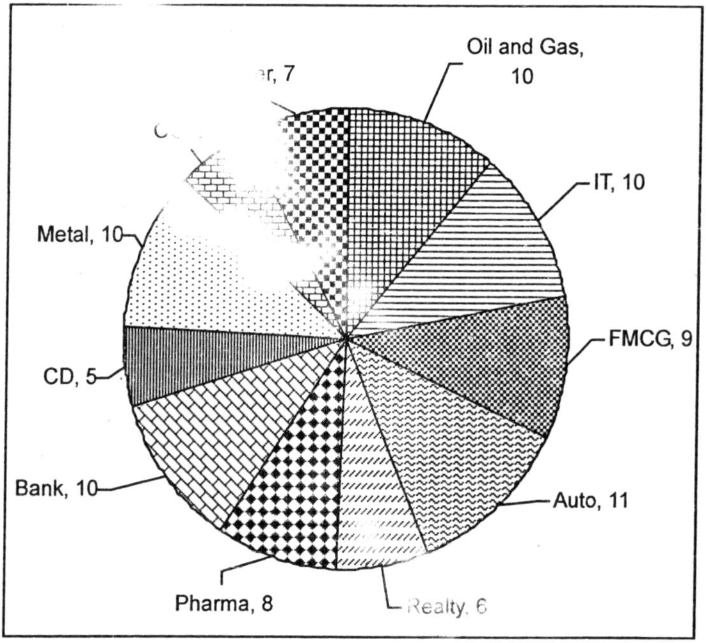

Fig. 13.1: Chart showing the Number of Companies Reviewed in Each Sector

Observations and Analysis

Observations on companies approach tc sustainable consumptions are illustrated below sectorally:

1. Information Technology (*see* Fig. 13.2)
2. FMCG (*see* Fig. 13.3)
3. Automotive (*see* Fig. 13.4)
4. Real Estate (*see* Fig. 13.5)
5. Pharmaceutical (*see* Fig. 13.6)
6. Bank (*see* Fig. 13.7)
7. Consumer Durables (*see* Fig. 13.8)
8. Metal (*see* Fig. 13.9)
9. Consumer Goods (*see* Fig. 13.10)
10. Power (*see* Fig. 13.11)
11. Oil and Gas (*see* Fig. 13.12)

Conclusion

There lies a big gap between companies adopting sustainable consumption practices to reduce their carbon footprint on the environment and mitigate climate change. There exists a big bias across sectors since some companies focus on few indicators of sustainable consumption rather than adopting a holistic approach for reducing carbon footprint especially in respect of companies CSR activities. There is a lack of uniformity in CSR reporting of companies and thus, it is difficult to understand the company's focus area for sustainable consumption.

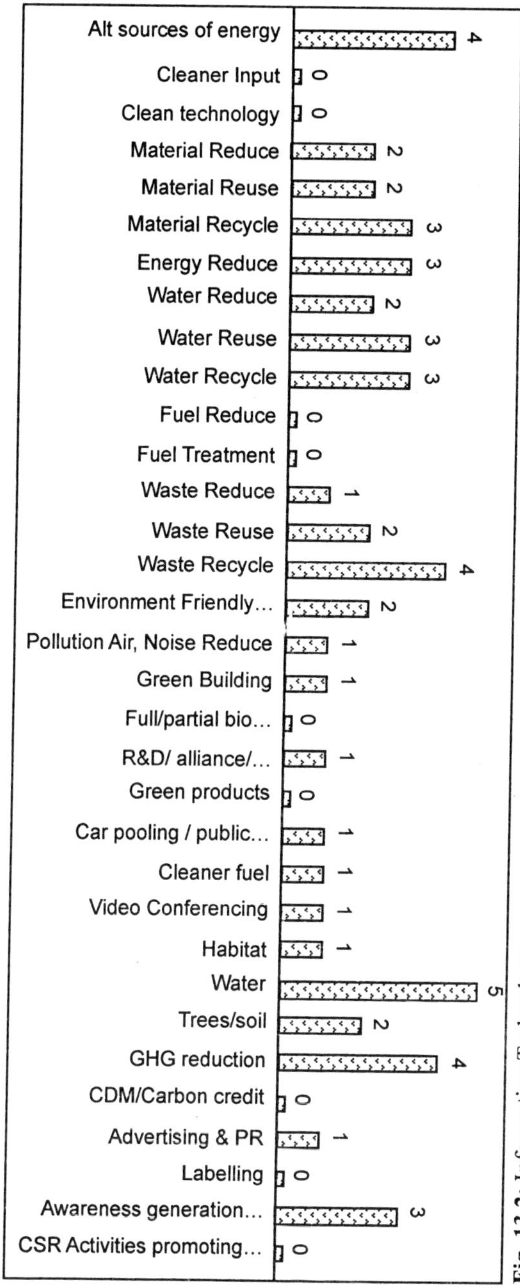

Fig. 13.2: Information Technology.

Analysis

Top 3 Key Areas for adopting Sustainable Consumption in this sector	*Rain water Harvesting* *Waste Recycling* *Adopting alternate source of energy*

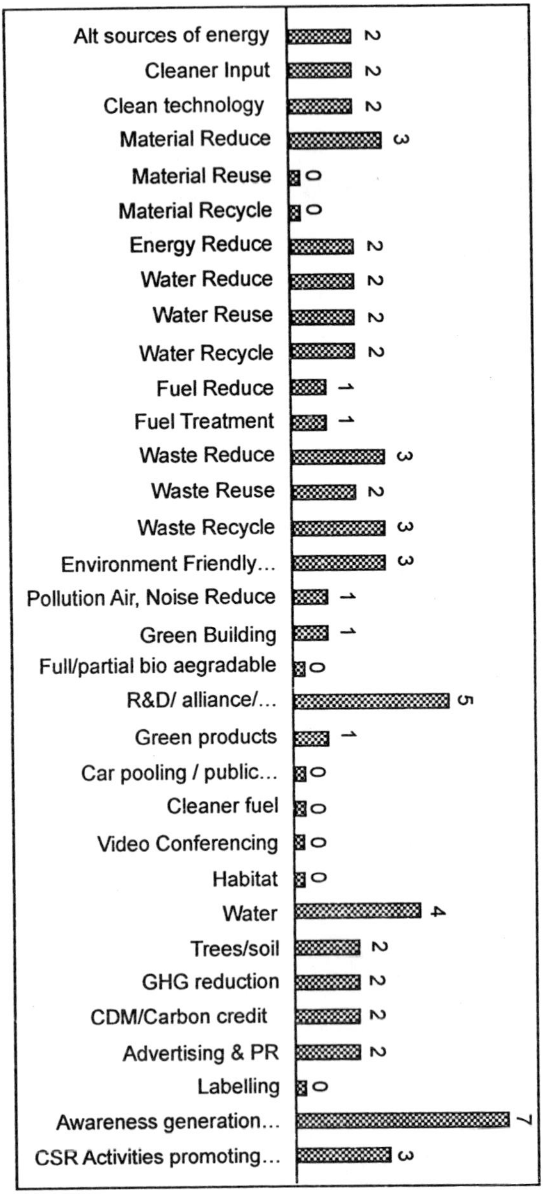

Fig. 13.3: FMCG

Analysis

Top 3 Key Areas for adopting Sustainable Consumption in this sector	*Sustainable consumption awareness generation campaigns* *Research and Development* *Rain water conservation*

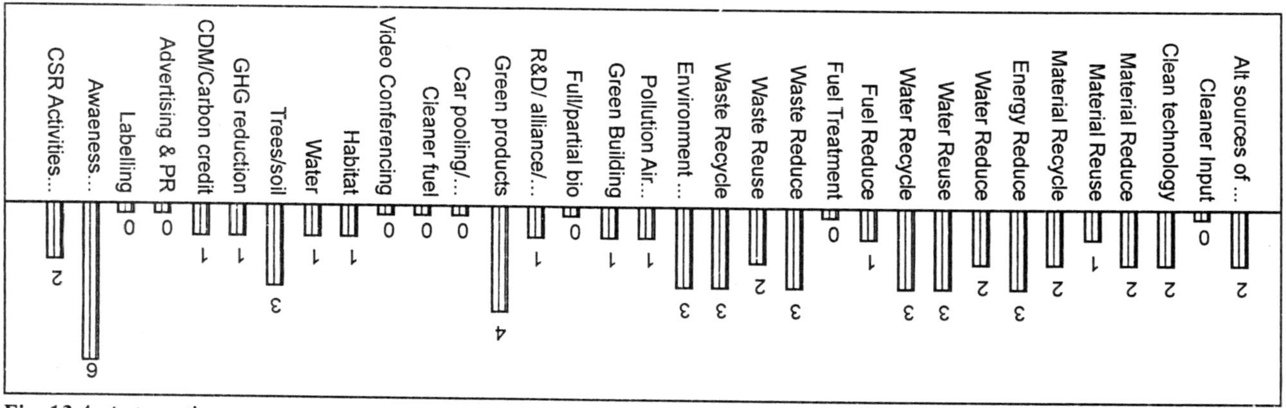

Fig. 13.4: Automotive

Analysis

Top 2 Key Areas for adopting Sustainable Consumption in this sector	*1. Sustainable consumption awareness generation campaigns* *2. Innovation of green products*

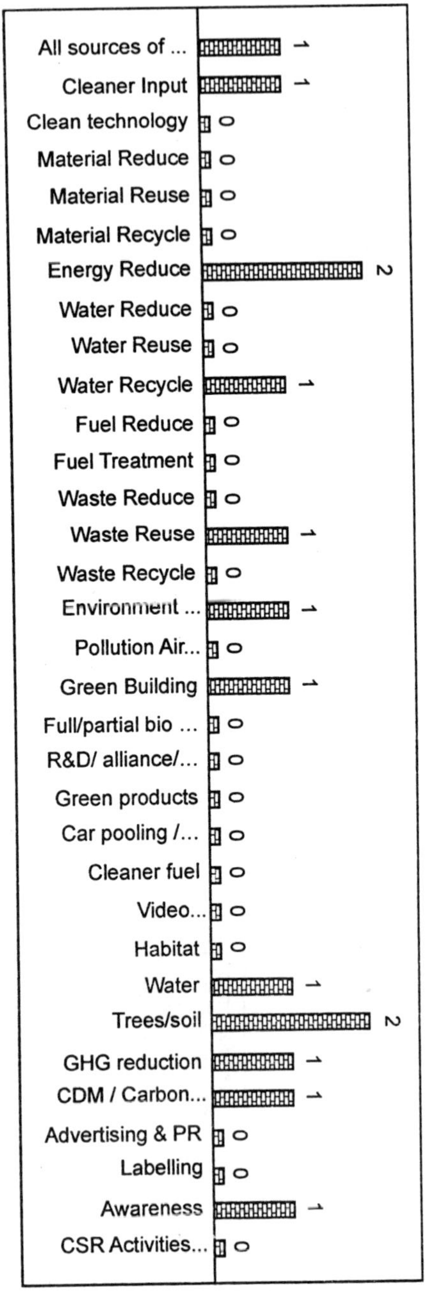

Fig. 13.5: Real Estate

Analysis

Top 2 Key Areas for adopting Sustainable Consumption in this sector	*Tree Plantation* *Energy Reduction*

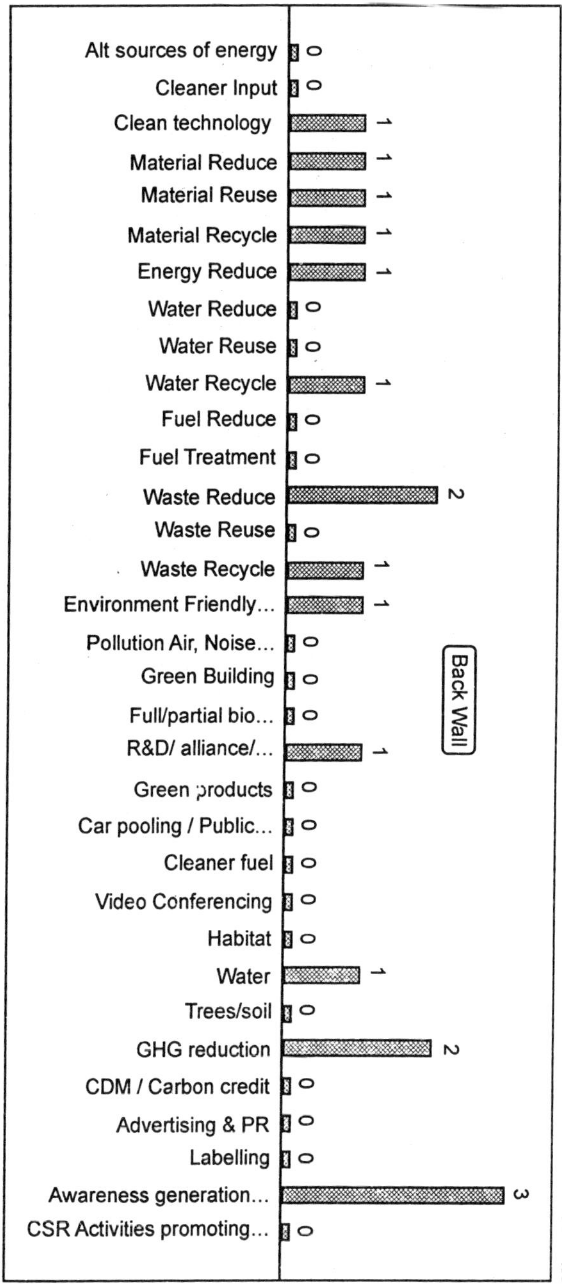

Fig. 13.6: Pharmaceutical

Analysis

Top 3 Key Areas for adopting Sustainable Consumption in this sector	Sustainable consumption awareness generation campaigns GHG Reduction Waste Reduction

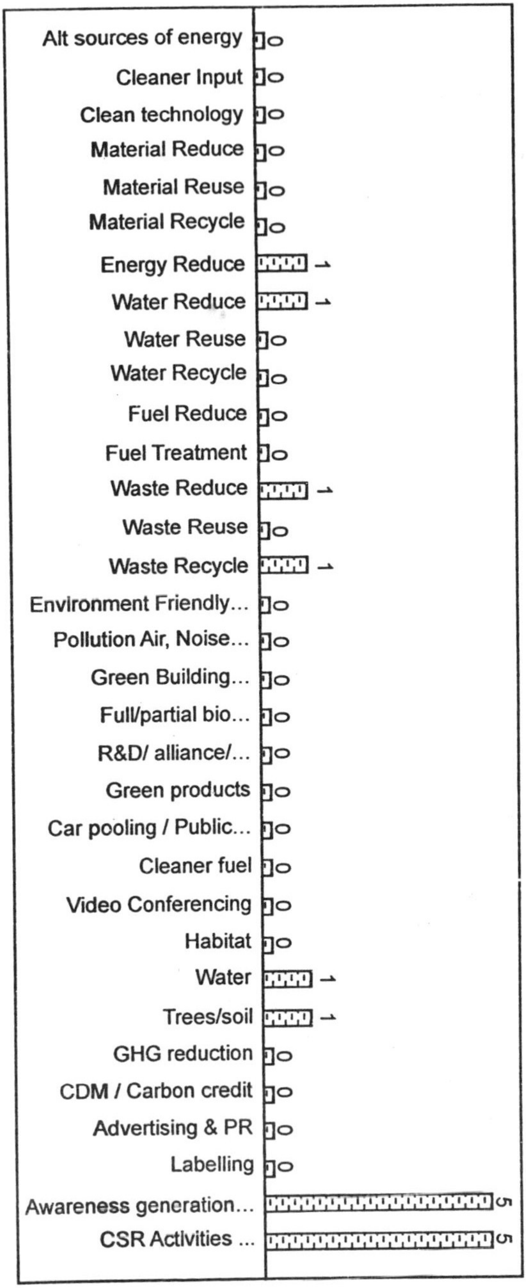

Fig. 13.7: Bank

Analysis

Top 3 Key Areas for adopting Sustainable Consumption in this sector	Sustainable consumption awareness generation campaigns CSR activities promoting sustainable consumption

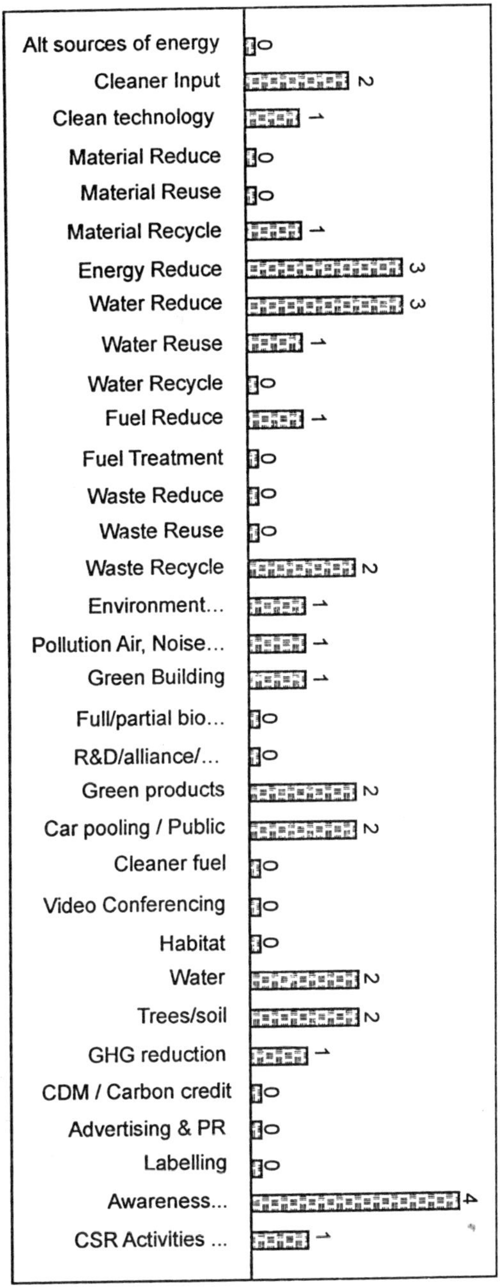

Fig. 13.8: Consumer Durables

Analysis

Top 3 Key Areas for adopting Sustainable Consumption in this sector	Sustainable consumption awareness generation campaigns *Energy Reduction* *Water Reduction*

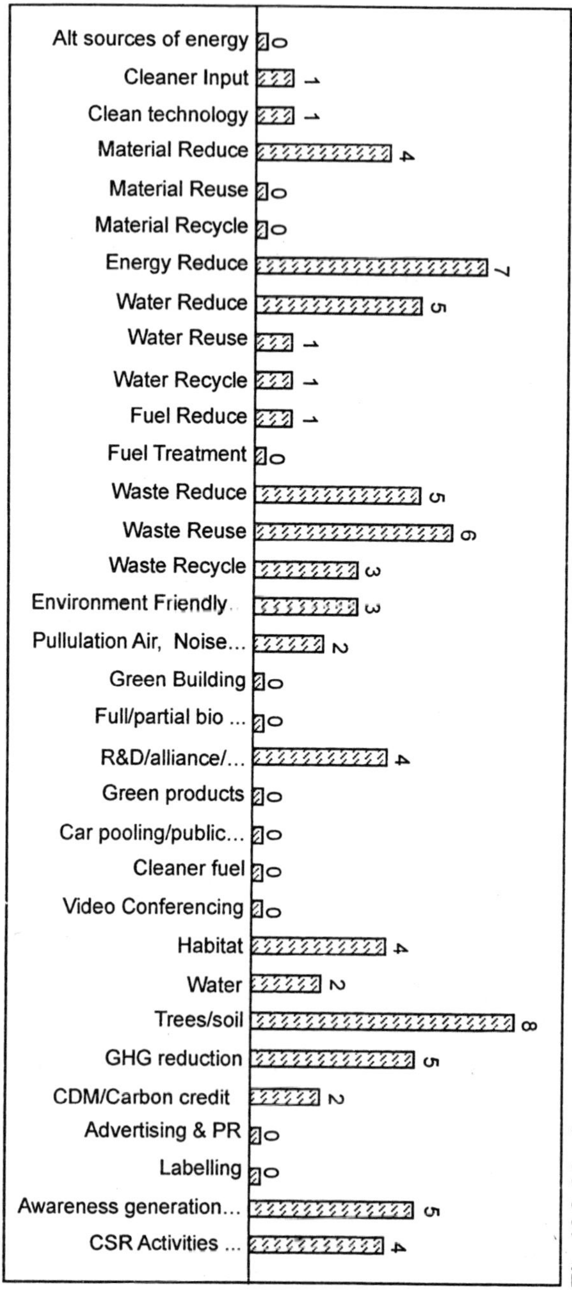

Fig. 13.9: Metal *Analysis*

Top 3 Key Areas for adopting Sustainable Consumption in this sector	*Tree Plantation* *Energy Reduction* *Waste Reuse*

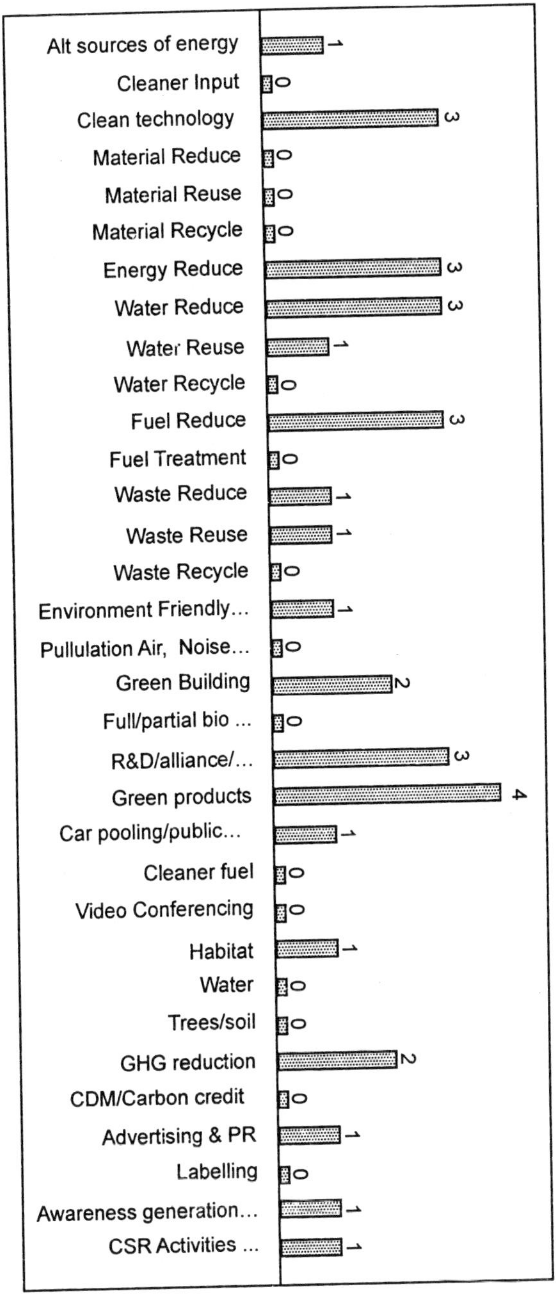

Fig. 13.10: Consumer Goods

Analysis

Top 3 Key Areas for adopting Sustainable Consumption in this sector	*Innovation in green products* *Clean technology adoption* *Energy reduction*

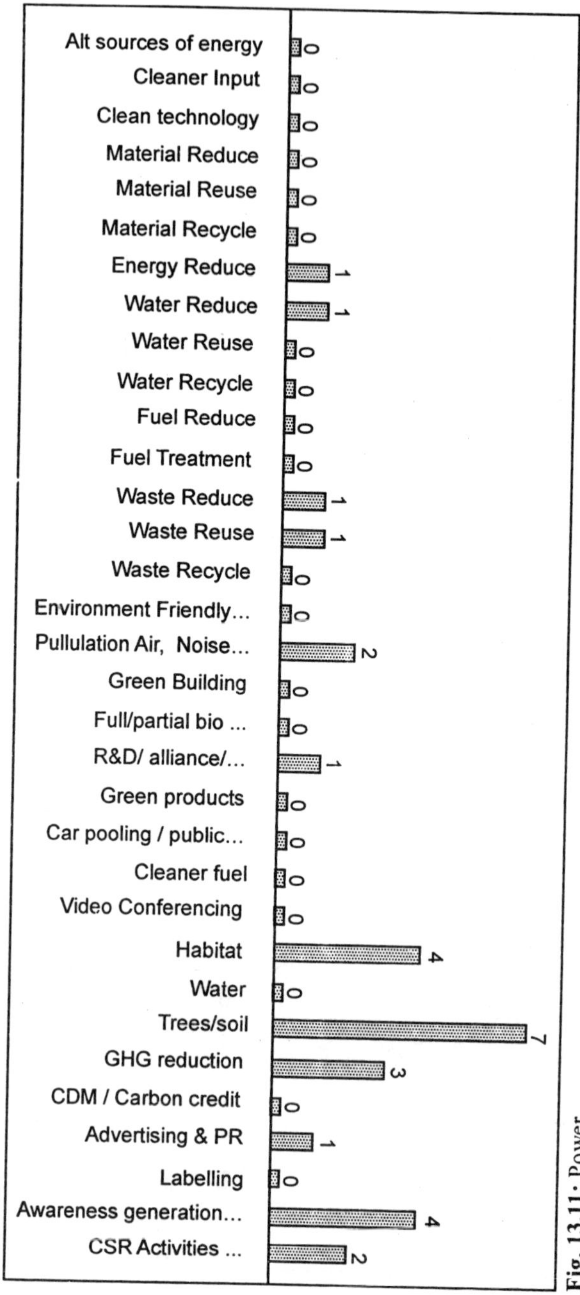

Fig. 13.11: Power

Analysis

Top 3 Key Areas for adopting Sustainable Consumption in this sector	*Tree Plantation* *Habitat conservation* *Sustainable consumption awareness generation campaigns*

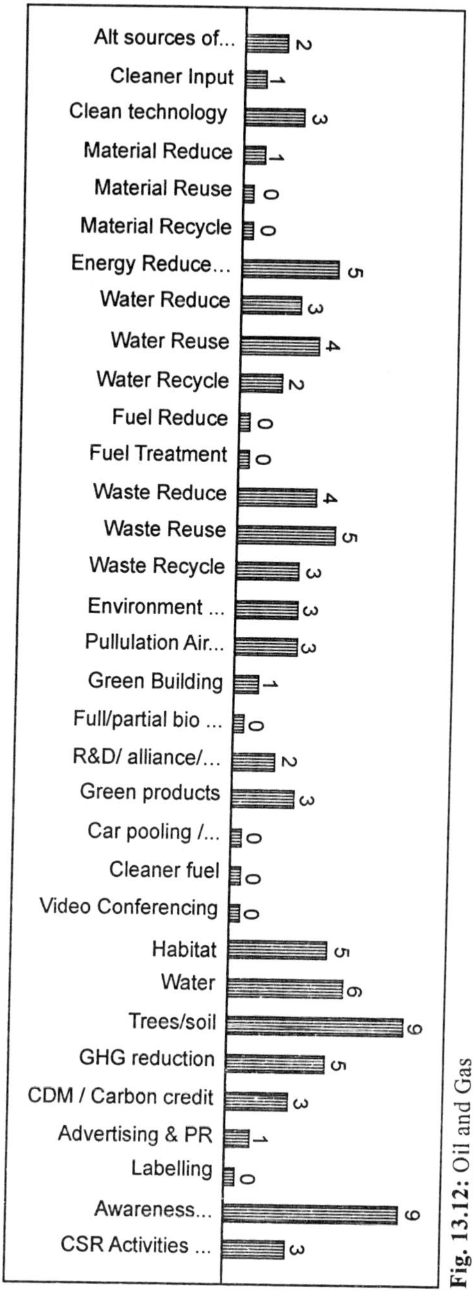

Fig. 13.12: Oil and Gas

Analysis

Top 3 Key Areas for adopting Sustainable Consumption in this sector	*Sustainable consumption awareness generation campaigns* *Tree Plantation* *Rain water conservation*

Annexure 1

Green Procurement	Alternative sources of energy
	Cleaner Input
	Clean technology
Material	Material Reduce
	Material Reuse
	Material Recycle
Energy	Energy Reduce
Water	Water Reduce
	Water Reuse
	Water Recycle
Fuel	Fuel Reduce
	Fuel Treatment
Waste	Waste Reduce
	Waste Reuse
	Waste Recycle
	Environment Friendly Disposal
Pollution Air, Noise	Pollution Air, Noise Reduce
Green Building	
Product Innovation and Design	Full/partial bio-degradable
	R & D/ alliance/ participation
	Green products
Transport	Carpooling/ Public Transport/ Green mode
	Cleaner fuel
	Video Conferencing
Conservation	Habitat
	Water
	Trees/ soil
GHG reduction	
CDM/Carbon credit	
SC Awareness	Advertising & PR
	Labelling
	Awareness generation campaigns
CSR Activities promoting resource optimation	

Notes

1. Swedish Consumer Coalition (2001), *Sustainable Consumption: A Report from the Swedish Consumer Coalition*, Sweden.
2. UN CSD International Work Programme (1995), Http://www.johannesburg summit.org/html/documents/summit_docs/1009wssd_pol_declaration.doc
3. http://www.uneptie.org/pc/sustain/about-us/about-us.htm
4. See, for example, Carbon Trust (2005), *The carbon emissions generated in all that we consume.*
5. Why business could get serious about sustainable consumption I will if you will: Towards sustainable consumption, http://www.sd-commission. org.uk/ file_download.php?target=/publications/down loads/I_Will_If_You_Will.pdf.
6. OECD (1999). Towards Sustainable Household Consumption: Indicators to Measure Progress. http://www.olis.oecd.org/olis/1998doc.nsf/LinkTo/ ENV-EPOC-SE(98)2-Final.
7. Chapter 10, indicators and methodologies for sustainable consumption hands-on sustainable consumption: A training guide for implementing the United Nations guidelines for consumer protection, http://www.consumersinter national.org/media/316122/hands-on%20sustainable %20consumption-%20implementing%20sustainable%20consumption%20 policies.pdf.
8. Figure 13.10 Indicators of Consumption and Production Patterns (UN CSD) Planning For Change Guidelines for National Programmes on Sustainable Consumption and Production.
9. The Sectoral Approach to Climate Change: Introduction and Overview Industry sectoral approaches and climate action: From global to local level in a post-2012 climate framework A Review of Research, Debates and Positions.

Brief List of Companies Analyzed

Companies	*CSR pdf/Link*
Cadbury	http://www.cadburyindia.com/cadtoday/socialresp.asp
Colgate	http://www.colgate.co.in/app/Colgate/IN/Corp/ Environment.cvsp
Marico	http://www.marico.com/abt_marico/csr.html
ITC	Sustainability Report 2010
Britannia	Health and Nutrition Initiatives 2010
HUL	Sustainable development report 2009
Parle	http://www.parleproducts.com/citizen/citizen_ parle_csr.asp
Dabur	http://www.dabur.com/About%20Dabur-Vision
Amul	http://www.amul.com/photogal/pg150808.html
Moser bear	Sustainability Report 2009

(*Contd.*)

Companies	*CSR pdf/Link*
TCS	Environmental Objectives 2009-2010
Infosys	Sustainability Report 2008-2009
Wipro	Sustainability report—executive summary 2008-2009
HCL	http://www.hcl.in/community-initiatives.asp
Patni	http://www.patni.com/
Finanical Technology	http://www.ftindia.com/
Oracle	http://www.oracle.com/index.html
NIIT	http://www.niit.com/Pages/DefaultINDIA.aspx
Mphasis	http://www.mphasis.com/
TATA Motors	Social Responsibility Annual Report 2009-2010
Mahindra Corporation	Sustainability Review 2008-2009
Maruti Suzuki	Maruti Sustainability Report 2008-2009
Ashok Leyland	http://www.ashokleyland.com/green_mission.jsp?name=Green
Apollo	http://www.apollotyres.com/india_community.htm
Bajaj	http://www.bajajauto.com/csr.asp
Hero Honda	http://www.herohonda.com/co_csr.htm
Exide	http://www.exideindustries.com/corporate_social.html
Bharat Forge	http://www.bharatforge.com/index.asp
MRF	http://www.mrftyres.com/MrfSport.aspx
Oriental Bank of Commerce	Directors Report 2008-2009
Canara Bank	Directors Report 2009-2010
Indian Overseas Bank	http://www.iob.in/sakthi.aspx
Yes Bank	http://www.yesbank.in/responsible_climate.htm
HDFC Bank	http://www.hdfcbank.com/personal/default.htm
Axis Bank	http://www.axisbank.com/
ICICI Bank	http://www.icicifoundation.org/
Allahabad Bank	http://www.allahabadbank.com/
Federal Bank	http://www.federalbank.co.in/
Thermax	Sustainability Report 2009-2010
Sony India Ltd.	http://www.sony.net/SonyInfo/csr/environment/

14

Promoting Business Enabling Medicinal and Aromatic Plants in the Indian Himalayan Region

Role of Government, Non-Government and Community Based Organizations

Jyoti Marwah

Introduction

Landscape, people and climate are the three variables that are linked with each other. It has been a long journey of evolution after the disappearance of continental ice-sheets and contraction of mountain glaciers that established Man's dependence on plants.[1] This dependence is now a conflict between man, ecosystems and socio-cultural matrices that has a direct impact on the biodiversity of any region. Climate change is a major concern. The Indian Himalayan Region has been directly impacted for all the reasons mentioned above. This has naturally led to depletion and marginalization of natural resources through loss of vegetation, degradation of soil and water quality and quantity. This work attempts to highlight the efforts being made to overcome these threats by Government initiatives and parallel movements by activists, of whom Eco-Feminism has become a force to reckon with.

Himalayan Syncretism: Man and Plant Life

The Indian Himalayan Region (IHR) spreads across twelve states covering an area about 5 lakh km^2 and forms the northern boundary of the country. It contributes about 16.2 per cent of India's total geographical area, and most of the area is covered by snow-clad peaks, glaciers of higher Himalaya, dense forest cover of mid-Himalaya. The IHR shows a thin and dispersed human population as compared to the national figures due to its physiographic condition and poor infrastructure development, but the growth rate is much higher than the national average. As per 2011 Census, the total population of IHR is 4,69,61,740. They use the natural resources in various ways according to their beliefs, traditions and faith. Most of the regions are rural and inhabited by a number of ethnic and tribal communities. The region has rich plant diversity and these communities in the higher altitudes rely on native plant species for traditional health care systems, as it is the only accessible form for majority of the people logistically and economically.[2] Thus, these medicinal and many aromatic herbs are of vital importance as the main ingredients for local medicines.[3] Aromas since antiquity have had the ability to enhance quality of life, restore strength and vigour, please the Gods and generate a feeling of well-being. Aromatic extracts such as essential oils are a bonus, as besides being fragrant they are medicinal and therapeutic.[4]

IHR supports more than 1748 plant species of known medicinal value, which is 32.2 per cent of the known Indian species.[5] Plants used in folk medicines are listed.[6] Of the 17,500 flowering plants known in India[7] IHR supports about 3,000 for medicinal use. It is unfortunate that 3.5 per cent of the total medicinal plants are in different threat categories as indicated by "The Conservation, Assessment and Management Plan."[8] A collaborative effort for sustainable intervention by Government, Research Institutes, Researchers, Community Based Organizations and NGOs has begun to contribute towards conservation and preservation without halting the commercial gains from the plant species. Himalayan herbs are considered as Divine medicines. The Himalayan medicinal and aromatic plants (MAPs) of different states have been documented and status has been reported.[9] These Medicinal and Aromatic Plants (MAPs) found in the higher altitudes of the Himalaya are recognized for unique biomolecules in view of the environmental stress they are subjected to.[10] It is of some consequence that after years of persuasion UNESCO has given Valley of Flowers a World Heritage Site status to prioritize conservation and preservation of this herbal heritage.

Natural Aromatic Extracts: Economic Value

Industrialization has touched all aspects of modern life. It has even affected the essential oil industry. Growth of multidisciplinary studies and research has resulted in a broad spectrum of new knowledge and understanding of plant extracts. Mr. S.C. Varshney, Former President of Essential Oil

Association of India, in an interview with the *Financial Express on Vision 2005* had rightly said that India's Biodiversity coupled with scientific competence has established her leadership in Aroma business. Essential oils are known to contain alcohols, terpenes, sesquiterpenes, lactones, esters, aldehydes and fats, giving plants the odour and taste unique to each one of them. Synthetic components, as substitutes are ideal in terms of affordability, but the demand for green goods has resulted in a huge market for natural aromatic extracts[11], i.e. flavours, fragrances and extracts of herbs, woods, and spices. Many developed countries have already banned the use of synthetics in flavours and a similar is expected in fragrances for cosmetics and dentifrice.[12]

Today, essential oils, plant concrete, absolutes, plant colour, and aromatic (water) hydrosols are natural and fragrant derivatives which find an important use in the fragrance industry, *agarbattis*, tobacco, food industry, pharmaceuticals, cosmetics and other related industries which combined have a turnover of ₹ 30,000 crore, flavour industry is worth over ₹ 1,000 crore. India, with an annual production of around 24,000 tonnes (18%) of essential oil is third in the worlds' essential oil market which is estimated to have a total production of around 1,20,000 tonnes. In value terms, India ranks second next to USA and its share comes to 24 per cent.[13] The major buyers of Indian Essential Oils are USSR, USA, France, UK, Netherlands, Saudi Arabia, Spain, Morocco, Germany, Australia, Pakistan, Korea, Taiwan etc. However, field research has revealed that due to a number of reasons, there is an adverse effect on the biodiversity, particularly because of the collectors' market orientation, which places heavy pressure on few commercially exploited MAPs. Also there is lack of awareness about sustainable wild harvesting and weak local institutional support.

In the higher altitudes due to prolonged winters, most of these species undergo dormancy. However, with the melting of snow and rise in day temperature they sprout from March onwards, after flowering in June-July and fruit bearing in August the foliage begins to wither after seed setting. This is the time for harvesting; however, to meet the market demand for the pharmaceutical and cosmetic industry these underground parts are uprooted from the wild at any time of the year which results in permanent loss. Increased demand of this wealth has resulted in both legitimate and illegitimate trade. Traditional harvesting methods have declined and reckless extraction continues throughout the year, as livelihood of the locals is dependent on this forest produce. They harvest this produce without making any effort to actually produce it. National

Institute for Rural Development, Hyderabad reports that collectors of MAPs earn around ₹ 5000/HH/year.[14] We must understand that nothing is for ever. The pace at which we are moving in this process of globalization, there looms a fear of future scarcity. Diversified agriculture must receive its share of sponsorship and growth supports. Deforestation has already deprived us of those rare plants from the wild.[15]

Government Initiatives

The importance of maintaining Himalayan biodiversity becomes imperative not only for the present, but for posterity. It has been a source of medicine for millions of people in the country and elsewhere in the world.[16] Recognizing this need, 1970s witnessed several initiatives with UNDP support to promote MAPs. CIMAP, RRL, and FFDC began educating the farmers to popularize the economic viability of its cultivation and value addition. In addition, large number of industrial houses have emerged for large-scale production of essential oils, oleoresins and other extracts. In Himachal Pradesh and Uttarakhand Government Research Institutions like IHBT (Palampur), HRDI (Gopeshwar), CAP (Selaqui), FRI (Dehradun) and CIMAP (Pantnagar) have developed short-term and long-term programmes for preservation, conservation and domestication of MAPs; to this can be added private initiatives. This public-private partnership has resulted in a holistic approach for *in situ* conservation and commercial (PPP) cultivation of medicinal and aromatic plants. Efforts have been made to promote research and development activities for building infrastructure and agronomical techniques. There has been a parallel attempt to conserve traditional medicinal knowledge of the Himalayan region[17] and plants used in folk medicine have been exhaustively listed.[18]

Thus, the need arises to preserve the Himalayan region as a reliable and consistent source of safe herbal materials from cultivated sources as the region is known to support a large number of endemic medicinal and aromatic plants. These cultivated areas require continuous support so as to obtain multiple harvests by regeneration of land, supply of good planting material, availability of water, buy back or marketing facility and wherever possible value addition know-how. The area under MAPs cultivation until now had been limited, scattered and unsystematic due to lack of management and neglect.

MAPs and Uttarakhand

The Government of Uttarakhand identified Medicinal and Aromatic Plants as a potential resource for uplifting the state economy and generating employment for the unemployed. MAPs' cultivation was cited as a success model for mountain development and is viewed as a bridge between sustainable economic development, affordable health care and conservation of vital Biodiversity.[19] Uttarakhand's altitude variation is from 300 to 7817 m above sea level, which gives it a diverse topography, flora, fauna, ethnic communities and tribes like the Bhotias, Rajees, Tharus, Boxas living in synergy with each other.

Hence, the Government of Uttarakhand issued a number of Government Orders (GOs) for the promotion of the herbal sector so as to enhance the socio-economic status of the rural communities through sustainable promotion of MAPs. As a result small and medium enterprises (SMEs) were established for effective commercialization of medicinal and aromatic crops in Uttarakhand. The herbal sector was positively impacted with increased generation of employment and livelihood opportunities. This resulted in enhanced knowledge and market information, which was made available for the small and medium farmers resulting in monetary gains.

G.O. 913/VGVi/2003 was issued for conservation, development and sustainable harvesting of medicinal plants (CDH). This plan was implemented in all divisions of Uttarakhand Forest Department with the joint efforts of HRDI and Forest Department. Through the survey of medicinal plants under this CDH plan, HRDI estimated the actual MAPs diversity especially the critically endangered species and the causes of their depletion. Database was prepared for its conservation support and development in the fragile regions. MAPs were categorized under Medicinal plants, Aromatic crops and Medicinal and Aromatic Tree species. Thereafter, the government institutions of Uttarakhand collected 534 species of medicinal and aromatic plants including the endangered ones from various parts of the region to develop a herbarium during 2004-2007. Ethno-medico-botanical survey of the region was conducted, e.g. the Niti Valley tribal area of Chamoli district based on folklore revealed medicinal use of 95 plants by the Bhotia tribes which includes Artemisia, Pine, Juniper, *Jatamansi* and *Deodara*.[20] Area under cultivation began to grow (Fig. 14.1).

Nursery management is essential for mass production of quality planting material of MAPs. Hence, high quality MAPs have been selected

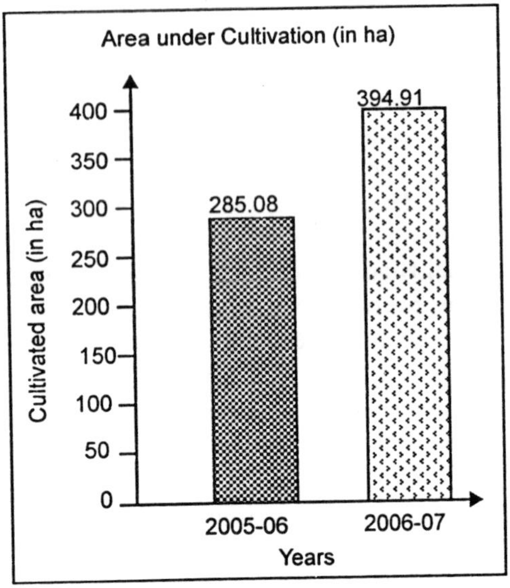

Source: HRDI Report 2005-06, 2006-07.

Fig. 14.1: Area under Cultivation for Medicinal and Aromatic Plants in Uttarakhand

for mass multiplication in seven large nurseries in Uttarakhand and are distributed for cultivation to farmers and growers. These are lemon grass, mint, tagetes, chamomile, *kuth, kutki, kala jeera, chippi, sarpagandha, kalihari*, and coleus. At the outset, 42.60 lakh seedlings were produced on 59.72 acres of land at varying altitudes and agro-ecological and geographical conditions.[21] According to Mrs. Vibha Puri Das, Principal Secretary and Commissioner, Forest and Rural Development, Government of Uttarakhand, the state is divided into four agro-zones—subtropical (Rishikesh), temperate (Dhanolty), alpine (Gangi) and cold desert (Nilong) and is a rich source for medicinal and aromatic plants. Alpine and sub-Alpine species being *kuth*, *kutki*, *van kakri* and *jatamansi*. Temperate plants include rosemary, pyrethrum, artemisia, large cardamom, tagar, *jamboo/faran*, *kala jeera*, *stevia*, *lavender*, and *echinacea*. Sub-tropical plants include chamomile, rose, tagetes, artemisia, *sarpa gandha*, *satawar*, mint, *patchouli*, basil, coleus, clarysage, lemongrass, geranium, citronella, palmarosa, *khus*, and hypericum (Fig. 14.2).

For documentation of the extent of systematic cultivation of medicinal and aromatic plants, the Government of Uttarakhand issued another G.O.

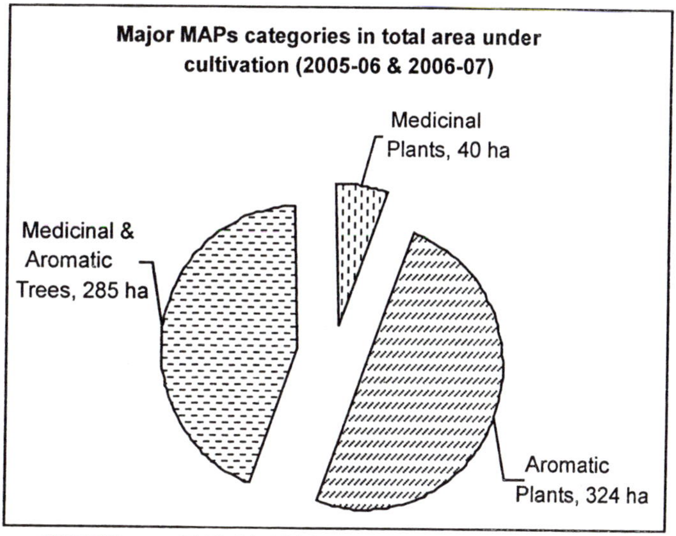

Source: HRDI Report 2005-06, 2006-07.

Fig. 14.2: Total Area of Cultivation for major MAPs' Categories

633/XV/05/5(89)05 in May 2005 for registration of farmers participating in the development of medicinal and aromatic plants sector in the State of Uttarakhand (Fig. 14.3). This was done with several objectives, which were to:

1. make an inventory of MAPs growers of the region;
2. provide training and technical information to farmers and entrepreneurs;
3. provide subsidy and value addition to the farmers produce; and
4. prepare a data base for marketing support and future planning.

In 2002, for the first time, cluster approach was introduced in Rajawala Dehradoon with financial assistance from RGF, New Delhi and Agrisud International, France. This was done for commercialization of the crops as per the agro-climatic zone and crop species in Uttarakhand. In a cluster, 3-4 crops were selected in a radius of 5-6 km to ensure availability of the herb throughout the year for the distillation unit. Seeing the success of this initiative another GO No. 1280/XVI/05/5(168)/2005 giving a subsidy of 95 per cent for establishment of distillation units was issued. 25 clusters of aromatic crops (Lemongrass, artemisia, geranium,

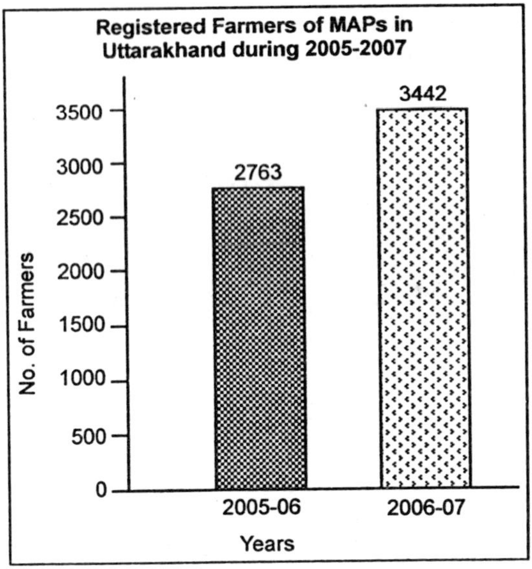

Source: HRDI Report 2005-06, 2006-07.

Fig. 14.3: Registered Farmers of MAPs

mint, stevia, citronella, tagetes, chamomile, palmarosa etc.) and 6 clusters of medicinal plants (*tejpat*, *kuth*, *kala jeera*, large cardamom etc.) were set-up by 2006 with 133 villages and 828 farmers cultivating 208.51 hectare (Figs. 14.1 and 14.4). 15 distillation units were set-up as a result production of essential oils, quality raw materials of medicinal plants as well as crude drugs increased manifold by 2006-07.[22]

Role of CSOs, CBOs and NGOs

Community Development Programme of 1952 (First Five Year Plan) acquired a new phase and became a force at the local level with the 73rd Constitutional Amendment of 1992.[23] The Panchayati Raj Institutions were empowered with authority, financial resources and personnel to carry forward developmental activities. This participatory governance led to:

1. enable people understand their problems and situations;
2. identify their needs and priorities;
3. evolve methods to resolve their needs;
4. mobilize local resources;
5. implementation of programmes with people's participation; and

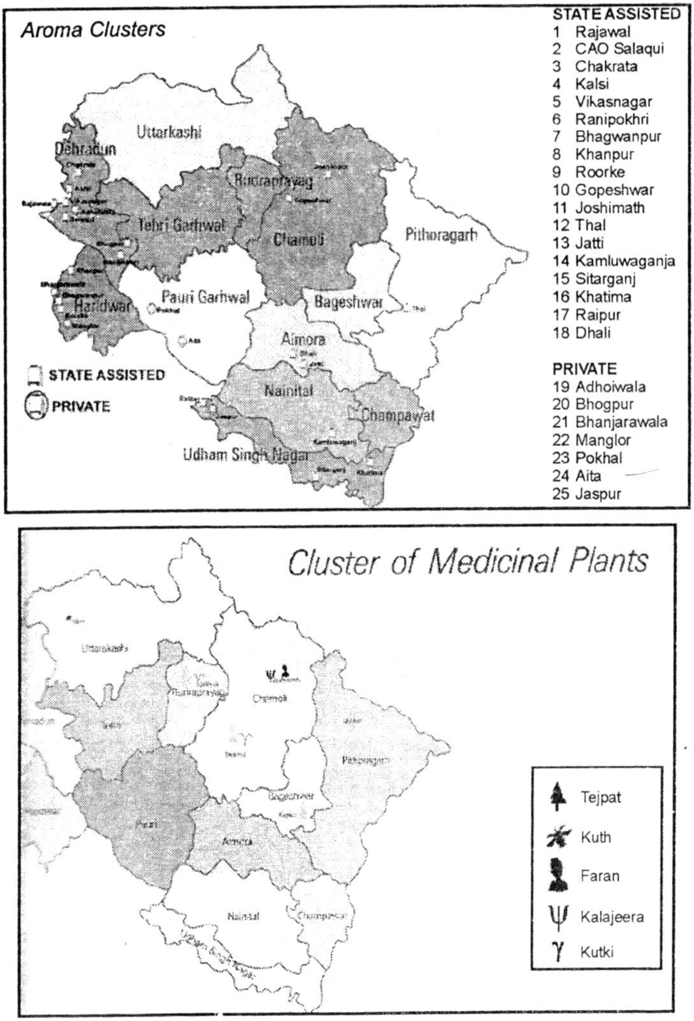

Source: HRDI Report 2005-06, 2006-07.

Fig. 14.4: Area under Aroma Clusters and Medicinal Plants in Uttarakhand

6. self-monitor, evaluate and learn from their efforts.

This enabled civil society and civil society organizations to play a significant role in enabling and empowering the local communities and the marginalized sections of society. So, CSOs like CBOs, professional institutes, people's organisations, social movements, social networks and self-help groups (S.H.Gs) have contributed to overcome lapses in the bureaucratic functioning of the Government. It has helped to improve management of resources and ushered transparency in the process of governance. Thus, the role of CSOs, CBOs and SH Groups in sustainable conservation, domestication and propagation of MAPs cannot be underestimated. Their contribution to the Convention on Biological Diversity (CBD) clearly emphasizes their significant role in environmental management and development through traditional practices. It is widely accepted that traditional knowledge and customary practices related to the use of biological resources must be protected by nations.[24]

Scarcity of Plant Life

Ecological management techniques of some tribes display in-built concepts of conservation of Biodiversity, which is interwoven into their traditional and religious beliefs. They possess incredible knowledge of a number of plant based formulations and this knowledge is generated through age-old experimentation, observation, trial and error. They have devised a symbiotic relation with nature rather than an exploitative one. In Uttarakhand, a large number of plants that are used in primary health care systems are obtained from the alpine zone or the Bughiyals. Harvesting is done during Nanda Ashtami and selected villagers called 'Jagaryas' go to the Bughiyals to collect flowers and plants, which are offered to the Goddess. Collection is not permitted before this ritual. This festival falls in September, which is seed setting time for high altitude plants. Thus, the practice avoids harvesting before seed setting. Only selected men can enter the Bughiyals and also the rules for collection are strict—collection must start early in the morning empty stomach and in a prescribed dress code of a white *Dhoti*. In the cold environs it prevents over-exploitation and in the early hours pollination is least disturbed. Collectors are also required to remove shoes so as to cause minimum damage to the sprouting vegetation. For sustainable harvesting a sample of the produce has to be offered to the deity, this promotes conservation.[25]

Community Based Activism

Navdanya pioneered the movement for seed saving which began in response to the crisis of agricultural biodiversity realizing that this is not possible without participation of the communities who have evolved and protected these plants and animals. Following the Gandhian principles of *Satyagrah*,

Navdanya has launched the *Beej Satyagrah, Anna Satyagrah, Jal Satyagrah* and *Bhu Satyagrah. Navdanya* started the Research Foundation for Science, Technology and Ecology (RFSTE), a participatory research initiative by Dr. Vandana Shiva an environmentalist of international repute. More than 70,000 farmers are primary members of *Navdanya*. In 2004 Vasundhara, an international organic farm and seed keepers gathering of 300 farmers was organized to celebrate diversity and the farmers vowed to keep agriculture and biodiversity free and in the commons.

On June 5,1999 on World Environment Day, *Navdanya* launched the Jaiva Panchayat Movement—the Living Democracy Movement to fight bio-piracy and IPR monopolies. 1000 villagers of Agastya Muni in Rudraprayag, Garhwal, Uttarakhand collected to launch the Jaiva Panchayat. They have begun to record the biodiversity of the village in their own Community Biodiversity Registers (CBR) thus protecting and preserving indigenous data.[26] As a part of the movement more than 4000 village communities have affirmed their rights to biodiversity and have pledged to conserve, rejuvenate and protect plants, animals, trees, cattle, medicinal plants, floral wealth, water, seeds and all biological wealth. This pledge termed the Mandakini Milan Declaration assumes significance as it was taken in Agastya Muni, the sacred land of Rishi Agstaya.

Diverse Women for Diversity was a movement engineered by *Navdanya* to provide women of different regions an alternative voice at World Food Summits, World Bank meetings and Conventions on Biological Diversity. Thus recognizing the fact that for thousands of years women have produced their own food and guaranteed food security for their children and the community at large.

Navdanya's role has been significant in challenging the MNCs and IPR monopolies on life forms and preventing the patenting of *neem, basmati* and wheat. Their role has been appreciable in highlighting the fears of exploitation that India was being subjected to by Monsanto, Cargill, Coca Cola and Vivendi.

The farm has a wide range of Medicinal and Aromatic plants like Geranium, Artimisia, Stevia, Rue, Calendula, Basil, Cinnammon, Fennel, Dil, Lemongrass and Citronella. The value addition, however, is one area of work that the Centre has not undertaken. Their major contribution is in providing organic plant material for extraction of essential oils. However, it is a valuable effort towards conservation and promotion of medicinal and aromatic plants at commercial farms. The Centre is also providing organic sesame oil of good quality, which can be promoted for Aroma therapy.

Parvatiya Jadi Booti Kalyan Sansthan, Mussoorie

Parvatiya Jadi Booti Kalyan Sansthan, Mussoorie, a registered NGO works for the conservation and commercial use of a large number of medicinal and aromatic plants in Mussoorie. Geranium, costus, artemisia, tagetus minuta, *jatamansi*[27], *kachur sugandhi*, rue, stevia, eucalyptus, pyrethrum, lavender, mint and walnut are some of the exotic and threatened MAPs being cultivated by the Sansthan. It works in coordination with Centre for Aromatic Plants at Selaquin, Dehradun providing the centre with seeds of tagetus minuta, stevia, artimesia and saplings of geranium, costus and *jatamansi*. The Sansthan has undertaken efforts in the domestication of wild species of *kapur kacheri* from its own forestland, which has resulted in generation of a cultivar. Burans or Rhododendrons are also the Sansthan's preserve in the forest area. It is immensely valued for its medicinal properties and also for its colour and a unique aroma which is similar to a rose-lavender combine. It has food value and is formulated into exotic jams, syrups and chutneys. It is equally valuable for cosmetic formulations for skin and hair.

Walnut a critically endangered medicinal and fruit bearing species of *Juglans regia* is the Sansthan area of serious concern. The Sansthan received a minor grant for promoting Walnut cultivation, from the Horticulture Board recently, but the Sansthan forest area supports more than 8000 walnut trees for the last 50 years, which are harvested for its fruit. Climate change has affected it quite significantly and the Sansthan is bewildered by the very recent developments in the pattern of fruit ripening. In an interview with Mrs. Veena Duggal, the President opined that a couple of years in the past, fruit was collected in the last week of September and beginning of October, now it has to be done by the end of August, this development is of great concern as this has affected the quality of the fruit. She believes that climate change is the cause for this altered pattern—there is an increase in heat, humidity and change in the pattern of rainfall. It is also of importance to consider the fact that the snowfall, which used to be abundant has now reduced to nominal and for a much lesser period of time. The Sansthan fears the loss of this Herbal Heritage of Mussoorie in the near future. The President of Sansthan painfully added that the couple of Chestnut trees in her forestland, which she has nurtured for the last 50 years, may also see the end of the day due to altered climatic conditions just as the Cherry trees that were lost in the recent past.

The Sansthan has a laboratory where the plants are hydro-distilled for obtaining essential oils and hydrosols, which are used to make products like Aroma therapy, Shampoos, Creams, Lotions, Salves and Balms. The Sansthan promotes the use of these products by participating in the 'Times Wellness' initiative 'Sanjeevini' Exhibition in Mumbai. The Sansthan also promotes the prospects of these plants for economic enhancement among the women and villages in and around Mussoorie by conducting workshops and training programmes. The hilly terrains prevent a fast-paced life in terms of communication and action hence local organisations need to work at a micro-level to develop the sensitivity towards MAPs. The Sansthan was a partner with CAP in their training programme in 2004-05 and introduced the trainees to Lab distillation and cultivars of costus, tagetes minuta, lemon grass, *kapur, cacheri,* artemisia etc. Since, then the Centre has cultivated these plants and harvests them to supply seeds and saplings to the farmers through CAP.

Since May 2009, the Sansthan has initiated the Dhanwantri series of workshop for women cultivators and product users so as to acquaint them with the techniques of cultivation and use of MAPs. This familiarization with MAPs will help promote cultivation of these plants in the environs of Mussoorie. The first one day workshop on Himalayan Jadi Booti, free of any charge for more than 100 women at the site office at Duggal Villa was a phenomenal success. Sri Girish Soman of Nisarg Biotech, Satara Maharashtra was invited to guide and instil a vision in the participants on the value of growing and commercially exploiting MAPs. He himself being an exporter of Essential oils and manufacturer of Aroma therapy, Soaps, *Agarbattis*, Creams, Lotions, Shampoos etc. guided the delegates on the economic viability of growing MAPs and using them for setting up small to medium enterprises. A site visit to the Sansthan's nursery was arranged and the various plants were introduced to them with information on how to grow them in small areas with calculated use of water and shade facilities. The Sansthan has assured the participants a supply of saplings and seeds.

Conclusion

The Sansthan's future plans are based on a threefold agenda and it is suggested for emulation by other regions of the Himalayas, for economic gains and for nurturing the environment and the Biodiversity.

These can be summed up as follows:

1. To give a new life to the rocky and bare mountain stretches of Mussoorie ranges through an environmentally sound and

sustainable programme to green these hills with MAPs. This will also provide people an option for sustainable benefits. History records that Mussoorie was named after the hardy Mansoor shrub with the ability to regenerate in most adverse surroundings. Taking a clue from here, these MAPs were propagated on the hills of Mussoorie to counter the negative impact of environmental degradation due to enhanced tourist traffic and burgeoning population in the last decade. With 20 lakh tourists arriving every year, it is a popular tourist destination. Tourism is an economic asset and need not be looked at with reservations; however, small initiatives by residents can contribute towards conservation. The hills need to be conserved by adding greater greenery so that the charm of the hills can be preserved for posterity.

2. To display the business enabling properties of MAPs, the Sansthan has on its agenda a project to develop a Museum of MAPs. This Museum will generate a greater understanding of this heritage and its business potential.
3. To introduce spice cultivation in and around Mussoorie, the Sansthan experimented with essential oil rich varieties of Turmeric, Ginger and Bush pepper having less fibre, which were obtained from Indian Institute of Spice Kozhikode, Kerala. The results were encouraging and efforts will be undertaken to enhance their cultivation. Increase in humidity has increased the probability of an improved crop.
4. It is as good as redemption that Planning Commission has decided to make Environment Protection a key tenet of governance and will disburse 1,900 crore in 2011-12 on environmental performance by States. Environmental concerns will be a criteria for determining the Central assistance to States based on an index to measure the green performance. This index will be based on the review of air and water quality in the states. The hill states of Sikkim, Uttarakhand, Arunachal Pradesh and Himachal Pradesh can stake better claims as they gain by default. Also it cannot be denied that these states maintain their forest cover at the cost of their economic development and should be provided more funds for the ecosystem services they render to the rest of the country. It is indeed a refreshing change that the environment measures have at last been accepted as a "nationally important target" apart from targets considered till now, such as

population control, elimination of illiteracy, land reforms, timely completion of aided projects, fiscal performance of states, income levels and tax collection etc. Rightly so, the activists observed September 9, 2010 as Himalaya Day and we can hope and pray that this concern has a sincerity of purpose and does not remain to be a political and politicized attempt for short term gains of a few.

Notes

1. Anon. (1992) *Action Plan for Himalayas*, G.B. Pant Institute for Himalayan Environment & Development, Kosi Katarmal, Almora.
   FAQs on Indian Himalayan Region. http://gbpihedenvis.nic.in/PDFs/FAQ/Indian Himalayan.pdf
2. *Ibid.*
3. WHO/IUCN/WWF, (1993) *Guidelines on Conservation of Medicinal Plants*, IUCN Gland, Switzerland.
4. Marwah, Jyoti, "History of the Uses of the Essential Oils through the Ages", 2005, Ph.D. Thesis, University of Mumbai.
5. Samant, S.S., Dhai, U., and Palni, L.M.S., (1998) *Medicinal Plants of Indian Himalayas*, Himavilas Publication, GBPIHED, Kosi Katarmal, Almora.
6. Jain, S.K. (1991) *Dictionary of Indian Folk Medicine and Ethno-Botany*, New Delhi: Deep Publications.
7. Sharma, J.R., Mudgal, V. and Hajra, P. K., (1997) *Floristic Diversity and Conservation Stratgies* (Eds. Mudgal and Hajra), Botanical Survey of India, Ministry of Environment and Forests.
8. *Ibid.*
9. Prakash, V., (2002) *Himalayan Medicinal Plants – Potential and Prospect*, (eds. Samant, S. S., Dhar, B. and Palni, L.M.S.), Nainital: Gyanodaya Prakashan.
10. Sharma, J.R., Mudgal, V. and Hajra, P.K., (1997) *Floristic Diversity and Conservation Stratgies* (Eds. Mudgal and Hajra), Botanical Survey of India, Ministry of Environment and Forests. Dhawan, B.N., (1997). "*Himalayan Biodiversity – Action Plan* (ed. Dhar, U.), Nainital: Gyanodaya Prakashan.
11. Marwah, Jyoti, (2005) *op. cit.*
12. Vashney, S.C., (2001) "Essential oils board to help fight WTO blues", *The Financial Express*, August 20.
13. *Ibid.*
14. NIRD-SRD-504, (2010), *Livelihood and Resources*, University of Hyderabad.
15. Marwah, Jyoti, 2005, *op. cit.*

16. *Navdanya* (Report), "Two decades of service to the Earth and small Farmers", RFSTE, Dehradun.
17. Sharma, J.R., Mudgal, V. and Hajra, P.K., (1997) *op. cit.*
18. Jain, S.K., (1991) *op. cit.*
19. *Ibid.*
20. HRDI, Gopeshwar, *Annual Reports, 2005-06, 2006-07.*
21. *Ibid.*
22. *Ibid.*
23. NIRD-SRD-501, (2010), *Rural Society and Sustainable Development,* University of Hyderabad.
24. HRDI, Gopeshwar, *Annual Reports, 2005-06, 2006-07.*
25. *Ibid.*
26. *Ibid.*
27. NIRD—SRD-501 *op. cit.*

References

Bulchand, Sarada, *Sense of Smell*, National Book Trust, India, 2002.

Castleman, Michael, *The New Healing Herbs*, Bantam Books, 2002.

Chauhan, M. S., A. K. Pokharia and I.B. Singh, Archaeology of Lahuradewa Area, Ganga Plain Pollen Record of Holocene Vegetation and Climate Change from Lahuradewa Lake, National Seminar on Archaeology of the Ganga Plain, Lucknow, 2004.

Christopher, M., "Incense in India", *The Incense*, Journal, 2001.

Dahanulkar, S., Thatte, U., *Ayurveda Unravelled*, National Book Trust, Delhi,

Davies, Patricia, *Aromatherapy A-Z*, Vermillon, 2005

Dimblby, Geoffrey, *Plants and Archaeology: The Archaeology of the Soil*, Paladin, UK, 1978.

Finnermore, H., *The Essential Oils*, Ernest Benn Ltd., London, 1926.

Genders, Roy, *Perfume through the Ages*, G.P. Putnam's Sons, New York.

Gode P. K., *Studies in Indian Cultural History*, Vol. 1, VVRI, Hoshiarpur, 1961.

Gode, P. K., *Indian Science of Cosmetics and Perfumery*, International Perfumer, 1951, No. 3.

Gode, P.K., The Plant-lore of Ancient India, *Aryan path*, Vol. 18, 1947.

Gunther, E., *Essential Oils*, Vols. 1-6, Robert E. Krieger Publishing Company, Inc., Malabar, Florida, 1972.

15

Role of Organic Farming in Promoting Sustainable Agricultural Produce

A Study with Reference to Goa

Santosh B. Patkar and *Henrique Dsouza*

Introduction

Agriculture has been the leading primary activity practiced by man. It has always been the backbone of the Indian economy despite the rapid growth of the industrial and service sector. The Information Technology revolution has brought India at par with the developed nation, although agricultural production is growing, the overall growth is slow. Agriculture still occupies an important place in the Indian economy. It provides employment to around 60 per cent of the total workforce in the country. The increase in population is exerting a lot of pressure on food production. Since 1961, the emphasis shifted to the use of seed-fertilizer-water technology known as the new agricultural strategy popularly known as the green revolution. The traditional agricultural practices were gradually replaced by modern technology and farm practices. The new agricultural technology used resources like fertilizers, pesticides, agricultural machinery etc., which are produced outside the agricultural sector. Large-scale mechanization and irrigation programmes have led of the increase in consumption of electricity and diesel in rural areas. The high use of fertilizers has resulted in increase in production, but there is adverse effect on fertility of soil. This has created environment problems. The use of organic manure is seen as the solution for maintaining a balance between increasing agricultural productivity and the protection of the environment.

Organic farming is a process of comprehensive management approach to improve the health of underlying production of soil. In organic farming stress is given on conventional approach of manures and reducing use of fertilizers, pesticides and chemicals. Regular addition of organic manure improves the soil quality. Organic farming is a productive system which avoids or largely excludes the use of synthetic compounded fertilizers, pesticides etc.

The practice of organic farming, said to be the best-known alternative to the conventional method, also originated in the West, which suffered from the ill-effects of chemical agriculture. However, organic farming is based on the similar principles underlying our traditional agriculture. Organic agriculture aims at human welfare without any harm to the environment, which is the foundation of human life itself.

Organic Farming in India

The conventional farming has helped India not only to produce enough food for own consumption, but also generated surplus for exports. However, the increasing population and income has led to further increase in demand for food and raw materials for industry. The modern system of farming, it is increasingly felt, is becoming unsustainable as evidenced by declining crop productivities, damage to environment, chemical contaminations etc. The necessity of having an alternative agriculture method, which can function in a friendly eco-system while sustaining, and increasing the crop productivity, is realized now. Organic farming is recognized as the best-known alternative to the conventional agriculture.

India has the potential to become a major organic producing country given the international demand for our farm products, different agro-climatic regions for the cultivation of a number of crops, the size of the domestic market and above all the long tradition of environment-friendly farming and living.

The ill effects of the conventional farming system are being felt in India and efforts are made by the government and people to promote organic agriculture in the country. Indian agriculture has traditionally been organic cultivation. The green revolution has transformed the agriculture sector, which increased the production by four fold, and this has helped farmers to increase the production and also productivity. This has resulted in reduction in overall cost of agriculture as compared to overall production of agricultural produce. However, cost of fertilizers has increased. Excessive use of fertilizers during this period has led to new issues of sustainable agriculture production, human health and also environment. Organic farming will be ideal solution for sustainable agricultural produce. In the year 2000, Planning Commission constituted a steering group on agriculture which identified organic farming as national challenge and considered it as a project under Tenth Plan. The National Agricultural Policy (2000) suggested for upgradation of traditional knowledge of agriculture relating to organic farming. The Department of Agriculture and Co-operation (DAC), Ministry of Agriculture constituted taskforce on organic farming in 2000 and this taskforce recommended promotion of organic farming.

The progress of organic agriculture in India is very slow. We have been able to convert only 41,000 ha of area so far, which is a mere 0.03 per cent of the cultivated area and the total number of farms comes to about 5,661. But a comparison of our 41,000 ha to Australia (10.5 million ha), Argentina (3.19 million ha), Italy (1.83 million ha), and USA (0.95 million ha) clearly indicates that organic farming in India has to go very far even to catch-up with that of the leading nations of the world.

Non-Governmental Organizations (NGOs) are spearheading organic farming in India. A Report in 2002 indicates that about 14,000 tonnes of organic products have been raised in India. These include tea, coffee, rice, wheat, pulses, fruits, spices and vegetables. India exports organic agricultural produce to European Union, USA, Canada, Saudi Arabia, UAE, Japan, Singapore and Australia, among others (Table 15.1).

Organic Farming in Goa

Agriculture in Goa is one of the important economic activities in the state. Paddy cultivation is major crop; besides this coconut, cashew nut, areca nut, mango, jackfruit, banana, pineapple etc. are also grown in large scale. Cashew is major cash crop in Goa practiced almost all part of Goa. Goa is dependent for agriculture produce on Karnataka and Maharashtra especially for food grain and vegetables. Many farmers do practice vegetable plantation in small scale such as brinjal, ladyfinger, radish, cucumber, pumpkin etc. Beside these sweet potatoes, chilies, onions etc. are also produced in Goa, but they are seasonal crops and produced on small-scale.

In Goa, agriculture production is followed on traditional methods. Earlier Goan farmers were making use of organic manure. They were making use of leaves from coconut plantation as manure once in a year or alternate. This practice is still being followed by farmers, but with

Table 15.1: Exports of Organic Products from India—2002

Products	*Tonnes*
Tea	3000
Rice	2500
Pulses and Vegetables	1800
Cotton	1200
Wheat	1150
Spices	700
Coffee	550
Cashew nut	375
Pulses	300
Herbal products	250
Oil seeds	100
Total	**11,925**

Source: www.c:\users\organic food exports from India.mht

respect to coconut plantation only. In earlier period, local farmers were giving main stress on seed exchange and free sharing of farming knowledge among the farmers.

In November 2009, TERI has launched a project to help realize the aspiration of a progressive group of farmers to preserve farming—a traditional occupation that is now under threat from rising labour costs, decreasing profits, and changing priorities of people. The key challenge was to find ways to increase earnings from farming and farm-related activities with a view to sustaining agriculture in the village. Farmers are regularly taught new techniques like how to prepare organic inputs from microbial solutions like Effective Micro-organisms (EM), vermicompost, and bokashi-compost made by fermenting rice husk. Such training sessions have been imparted through multi-part programmes, which have entailed practical hands-on experience.

Organic farming has been practiced traditionally by farmers in Goa. Around 625 cashew farmers from Goa including farmers from Bali—Barcem and Canacona areas, have already been registered as organic farmers by Netherland based multinational company SKAL that has office in Bangalore. The farmers get higher price than other farmers in local market too. The potential for organic farming is very high because traditionally Goans had done only organic farming and even now, the use of chemical fertilizers and pesticides is very low in Goa. The spice farm, Pascoal farm, *sahakari* farm are leading farmhouses in Goa practicing organic farming. The tourism industry in Goa is at rise and foreign as well as domestic tourists' arrivals are increasing year by year. Foreign tourists mainly prefer organic farm produce and they pay higher price for the produce. Increasing arrival of foreign tourists will increase the demand of organic farming in Goa. Now-a-days consumers are cautious about health issues and are aware that use of chemicals and pesticides will have adverse impact on their health. Thus, demand for organic farm produce will increase in future.

Sustainable Development and Ecological Concerns

Modern agriculture has grown at the expense of ecology and environment and to the detriment of the well-being of the people. The agricultural practices of the West have proved to be increasingly unsustainable and there is the need to have an appropriate method that suits our needs.

The practice of organic farming is said to be the best-known alternative to the conventional method, which suffers from the ill-effects of chemical fertilizers not only on the farm, but also on the health of all living beings and on the environment. The application of technology, particularly in terms of the use of chemical fertilizers and pesticides all around us has forced people to take action. Their negative effects on the environment are manifested through soil erosion, water shortage, salination, soil contamination, genetic erosion etc.

However, organic farming is based on the similar practices followed by our traditional agriculture. Organic agriculture aims at human welfare without any harm to the environment, which is the foundation of human life itself. Many techniques used in organic farming like inter-cropping, mulching and integration of crops and livestock are not new to various agriculture systems including the traditional agriculture practiced in countries like India. However, organic farming is based on various laws and certification programmes, which prohibit use of almost all synthetic inputs, and health of the soil is recognized as the central theme of the method.

The farming being practiced for the last three decades in India has increasingly been found non-sustainable. The system is oriented towards high production without much concern for ecology and the very existence of man himself. However, among many reservations, the profitability of organic farming in comparison to conventional farming is the crucial one from the point of view of the Indian farmers, particularly the small and marginal.

Organic farming involves management of the agro-ecosystem as autonomous, based on the capacity of the soil in the given local climatic conditions. It is spreading steadily, but slowly all-over the world. India has been very slow to adopt it, but it has made inroads into our conventional farming system. One advantage we have here is the fact that the farming techniques practiced in our country before the advent of the green revolution were basically eco-friendly and they have not faded away from the memories of the present elder generation of our farming community. The Central and State Governments have taken several initiatives to popularize organic farming in the country.

Sustainable agriculture based on technology that combines increased production with improved environmental protection has been accepted as absolutely essential for the maximization of the consumer welfare. The consumers are increasingly concerned about the quality of the products they consume and food safety has become a crucial requirement. Safety, quality and hygienic standards are increasingly being made stricter all-over the world. The mad cow disease and the question of genetically modified food are the recent examples, which have forced countries to tighten the laws. Chemical contamination, unacceptable levels of pesticide residues and environment degradation are the most important issues on which the attention is focused. In order to protect the interests of the consumers, the European Union has taken tough measures including criminal prosecution to ensure food safety.

Ecological and environmental effects have been highly publicized all-over the world. Powerful interests in the developed Western countries have also politicized these issues to take advantage of the poor nations of the world. Efforts have been made to impose trade restrictions on poor nations on the ground of environment protection as a direct result of these campaigns. But the level to which resources have been degraded requires immediate remedial measures without terming the demands for them as the ploys of the rich nations to exploit the poor. The developed countries are to a great extent instrumental in degrading the environment. However, the poorer countries of the world including India cannot delay or ignore the need for remedial measures, which are to be effectively implemented. We cannot ignore the fact that we have also contributed to the degradation of ecology; look at the droughts and floods, disappearance of forests, high noise level and air pollution in the cities.

Sustainable development has caught the imagination and action all-over the world for more than a decade. Sustainable agriculture is necessary to attain the goal of sustainable development. According to the Food and Agriculture Organization (FAO), sustainable agriculture "is the successful management of resources for agriculture to satisfy changing human needs while maintaining or enhancing the quality of environment and conserving natural resources." All definitions of sustainable agriculture lay great emphasis on maintaining an agriculture growth rate, which can meet the demand for food of all living beings without draining the basic resources.

Organically, cultivated soils are in a better position to withstand water stress and nutrient loss. Their potential to counter soil degradation is high and several experiments in arid areas have shown that organic farming could help to combat desertification. It is reported that about 70 hectares of desert in Egypt could be converted into fertile soil supporting livestock through organic and biodynamic practices. India, which has some areas of semi-arid and arid nature in Rajasthan, could also be benefited by these practices.

However, there are a number of myths and fears in the mind of farmers that surround organic farming, both in favour of and against. Some of them are:

1. ***Chemical Farming Produces High Yields:*** The yields in organic farming are, in the long run, far greater than those obtained by chemical farming. In horticulture crops, the effects are even better. Punjab's agricultural yields have remained the same for the past many years while the quantity of agro-chemicals required for maintaining these static yields have steadily increased. In the case of a chemical farm converting to organic, however, there is often a loss in yield and it takes a few years before yields increase and stabilize at a level often higher than that achieved under a chemical regime. It is, therefore, recommended to convert gradually over a period of three to four years if income from the farm is a key issue.

2. ***High Costs Involved in Organic Farming:*** Organic farming involves certain practices such as composting and mulching that involve high costs on account of labour; however, the overall cost of cultivation is usually lower than chemical farming. An important point to note here is that the farmer has to be self-sufficient in his requirement for composts and pest control measures.

3. ***Supply of Nutrients by Using Composts:*** This is a common argument put to use by all detractors of organic farming, especially academicians. The difference in percentages of nitrogen, potassium and phosphorous in fertilizers and composts, is indeed vast. For example, in place 200 kgs. of mixed fertilizers, one needs over 30 tonnes of composts; it is difficult to procure the supply in such large quantity two or three times a year.

4. ***Huge Profits in India:*** Most organic farmers have turned (or in some cases remained) organic because of their beliefs. The "organic

market" exists for a small number of farmers who have access to a few specialized outlets. Otherwise, it is difficult to see every organic farmer getting a premium for his (undoubtedly superior) product. An option for exports has also opened in the last decade, which organic farmers can explore only if they are "certified" as organic. There are a few internationally recognized agencies operating from India who inspect and certify organic farms.

5. *The Non-use of Chemical Fertilizers and Pesticides is Organic Farming or the use of Organic Manures is Organic Farming:* While organic farming is about maintaining soil health ("feeding the soil" rather than "feeding the plant"), it involves producing the highest yields possible, in a sustainable, eco-friendly manner using a number of techniques. Indeed, for any agriculture system to succeed, it must take a responsibility towards feeding the earth. Organic farming entails a lot of hard work and even systems like Do-nothing (or Natural) farming—as propagated by Fukuoka. External inputs, even if eco-friendly or bio-degradable, are ecologically questionable and commercially unsustainable for an organic farm. Work is hence required on-farm to produce inputs such as composts and biopesticides.

Conclusion

The organic agriculture in the country suffers from the absence of linkages between the farmers and markets and absence of financial support from the State and Central Governments. India has the potential to become a major organic producing country given the international demand for our farm products, different agro-climatic regions for the cultivation of a number of crops, the size of the domestic market and above all the long tradition of environment-friendly farming and living. However, an appropriate policy framework is yet to be laid down by the government. The only progress made in this direction is the implementation of National Standards for Organic Production (NSOP) in 2000 and the founding of National Institute of Organic Farming. A few agencies with the assistance of international bodies have entered the field of inspection and certification.

Market forces play a vital role both in providing the engine of economic growth and in responding to the incentives provided by the government. An appropriate National Agriculture Policy, giving a prominent place to organic farming addressing the issues related to its coverage, financial support during the conversion period, creation of linkages among the farmers, processors, traders and consumers, inspection and certification of organic products and increasing the public awareness of the benefits of organic agriculture along with the ill-effects of the conventional system, should be designed. This must be followed by concrete action on the ground if we do not want to miss the far-reaching changes all-over the world brought about by the organic farming movement.

A programme for organic agriculture in these areas must be fully supported by the full compensation both in cash and kind to the farmers in the event of loss of production they would suffer till it reaches the level of the days prior to the adoption of organic farming. A fair, quick and efficient delivery system for such assistance, perhaps by keeping the government bureaucracy at a distance should also be in place beforehand.

Market development for the organic products is a crucial factor to promote domestic sales. Supplies do not match the demand for organic products in the country and the absence of proper links between the two has been pointed out for the slow growth of organic farming in the country. An important role of the government in this direction is to provide various supports to the producers and consumer associations to market the products. To tap the emerging opportunities, Government of India has formulated the National Project on Organic Farming during the Tenth Five Year Plan period with an outlay of ₹ 92 crore. Production, promotion, market development and regulation of organic farming are the major objectives of the project. It envisages setting-up of 50 model organic farms in the country and providing assistance for setting-up commercial production units of organic inputs like bio-fertilizers, fruit and vegetables waste compost and vermiculture. Besides promoting the establishment of commercial production units for organic inputs, the plan would also address issues relating to capacity building in this segment. A National Institute of Organic Farming with six regional offices is also on the anvil.

Organic production support systems are built around standardization of package of practices and facilitation of organized production through farmers groups/NGOs. Organic tea (bio-tea) is produced in India as per national standards, based on the guidelines of Tea Board. Spices Board has standardized package of practices for organic production of ginger, pepper, vanilla, turmeric and chillies. Coffee Board has brought out documents on package of practices for Organic Coffee and guidelines on Production of Organic Coffee. Central Plantation Crops Research Institute (CPCRI) has developed organic production technology for coconut. CICR, Nagpur has standardized package of practices for organic cotton production.

References

Arun Kumar Singh, *Environmental Economics*, New Delhi: Regal Publications.

P. Bhattacharya and G. Chakraborthy (2005), "Current status of organic farming in India and other countries", *Indian Journal of Fertilizers*, Vol. 1(9), December 2005, pp. 111-123.

P.G. Shinde, Pendse, Dongre, *Environment Education*, Mumbai: Seth Publishers.

Rashmi J. Dessai, *Environmental Studies*, Mumbai: Vipul Prakashan.

www.c:\organicfarming in India agropedia.mht

www.c:\users\foundation for organic Agriculture and Rural development

www.c:\users\International federation of organic Agricultural Movement-Wikipedia the free encyclopedia.mht

www.c:\users\organic food Exports from India.mht

www.c:\users\organicIndia.mht

16

Sustainable Eco-Tourism

A Case Study of Beaches in Goa

Badruddin

Background

Eco-Tourism often associated with ecological tourism, is responsible travel to fragile, pristine, and usually protected areas that strives to be low impact and often small in scale. It helps to educate the travellers, provide funds for ecological conservation, benefit the community development, enhances the political empowerment of locals, and foster respect for different cultures. Eco-tourism is held as important by those who participate in it so that future generations may experience aspects of the environment relatively untouched by human intervention. Most serious studies of eco-tourism including several university programmes now use this as the working definition. Eco-tourism may appeal to ecologically and socially conscious individuals. Generally, it focuses on volunteering, personal growth and environmental responsibility. Such process typically involves travel to destinations where flora, fauna, and cultural heritage are the primary attractions. One of the goals of eco-tourism is to offer tourists insight into the impact of human beings on the environment, and to foster a greater appreciation of our natural habitats.

Tourism is a multi-dimensional activity that brings enormous impact for the society by creating a meaningful employment, economic assets, socio-cultural affinities and environmental benefits to the indigenous population. During last couple of years, the subject of tourism has been in considerable debate in various international forums. WTO has declared tourism as the single largest sector.[1] Number of European, South-East Asian and South Asian countries (especially India) are largely benefited from tourism industry.

Goa, a tiny emerald land with its natural scenic beauty, capital of beaches, feasts and festivals and above all hospitable people with a rich cultural milieu, has made it an ideal holiday destination. Eco-lover beaches of Goa provide travel to natural destinations by building environmental awareness, and provide direct benefits to the villagers by respecting local indigenous culture and supporting human rights' movements. At the same time, the International Eco-Tourism Society continues to support Goa tourism. Vast amount of literature on Indigenous Communities and Business Leaders, Eco-tourism Research and Development, Sustainable Business Development, Preserving Eco-tourism Experiences in Destinations, and Educational opportunities for youths and students has been development. Recent initiatives to promote Eco-Tourist Explores, Eco-destinations with their partners and supports, are working with help of several NGOs in Goa. All are helping to understand cross-cultural studies on tourism, emerging issues on educational training, community sensitization and participation activities. Goa's 106-Kilometre coastline is dotted with several world-class beaches which acquire their names after the nearby village or locality. Kissed by the passionate, azure sea, embraced by the land, and shaded by swaying palms, the golden sand sparkling in the sun, these beaches are the most desired places one can ever love on earth. The evergreen eco-friendly destination of Goa is a holiday-maker's paradise. Breathtaking blue beaches, sensuous silvery sands, fabulous flora and fauna, rich cultural heritage, archaeologically captivating churches, temples, feast and festivals, Goa is blessed by all.

Goa was under Portuguese domination for over 451 years. After the liberation of Goa on 19th December, 1961, there was sudden upsurge of tourism due to reduction in taxes on air services. With the emergence of hippie culture in South-East Asia, France, England and some other European countries, Goa became more popular. The "Hippie Trail" became the starting point to develop new ways of tourism in Goa.[2] It added several priority areas including beach tourism, medical tourism, educational tourism, adventure tourism and eco-tourism though most of these remained unimplemented for several years. During eighties, Goa then a Union territory, decided to set-up tourism industry on tentative basis. Due emphasis was given to hotel management infrastructure and soon, Goa became a major tourist destination in South Asia. State Government took serious initiatives only after the formation of statehood in 1987. Government of Goa has already declared tourism as an industry from April 2000.

This backdrop gave rich dividends and significantly helped to increase the number of domestic as well as foreign tourists. It is evident by the manifold increase in the number of tourist from 91,016 in 1972, 8,81,323 in 1990, 12,68,513 in 2000 to 26,42,020 in 2010. International tourism in Goa is directly connected with the number of Charter Flights and the backpackers. The diverse category of charter flights include: Intasun (UK), Lufthansa (Germany), Club Mediterranean (France), Jal (Japan), and Aeroflot (Russia). The Number of charter flights increased substantially from just 24 in 1985-86 to 720 in 2006-07 though there is substantial decrease in number of such flights during the year 2009. During the year 2008-09, the charter flights comprised 40 per cent of the total tourists who visited to Goa.[3] During the year 2008-09, over 615 chartered flights brought 1,45,428 tourists. Some 26-chartered flights brought 64,029 foreign tourists. Goa Tourism Ministry agrees that the increase in the scheduled flights has given flexibility to visitors to decide on their arrival and departure dates. The visitors used to face difficulty during emergencies, as they had to wait for their programmed departure through chartered flight. With the commissioning of scheduled flights, they can leave whenever they want.

While accepting Goa as a major tourist destination, several NGOs have come forward to "Keep Beaches clean, healthy, wealthy, wise and natural" so as to maintain the ethics of "Green Principles". The tourists are encouraged to purchase eco-friendly products built with bamboos and local articles. Goa's naturally filtered resources, collection of articles in natural museums, organization of open air *yoga* camps, hiking, trekking, birds watching, boat cruise water sports, natural waterfalls, mini carnivals, and host of more additional attractions are directly or indirectly attached to the beaches only. Maintenance of turtle nest sites, natural springs, medicinal plants, unattended palm trees, coral reefs, hillocks, waterfalls and springs, naturally preserved animals are important source for sustainable economy.

Movement for Eco-Tourism in Goa

Goa with immense kaleidoscopic eco-system and the wealth of cultural heritage has immense scope for eco-tourism. There is greater need to identify newer areas, sports for eco-tourism and distribution of brochures on eco-ethics related research in Goa. NGOs, large number of environmentalists, teachers, students, professionals and host of other bodies have already joined the mainstream to promote eco-tourism in Goa. Tourist cottages, seafood stuffs and beverages are served in a natural environment. Still there is a greater need to promote the unexplored avenues related to eco-tourism and better infrastructure on beaches, hotel management, road safety, communication networks, and recreational facilities. Goa Tourism Development Corporation (GTDC) and National Tourism Authority (NTA) need to coordinate with local NGOs for sustainable developments.

Needs of Eco-Tourism in Goa

Beach Management Tourism (BMT) in Goa in coordination with GTDC and several NGOs is deeply interested in the protection of coastal lands, territorial waters, fishing and beachside plantation. Four prominent local NGOs: Goa Foundation Mapua (GFM), Goa Peaceful Society (GPS), Goa Desk Resource Centre (GDRC) and *Goa Bachao Abhiyan* are seriously analyzing data about beach management with support of Indigenous People to establish effective partnership. Beach culture in Goa has long been associated with nature and a deep understanding to the maintenance of fragile eco-system through their traditional resources. (World fame beaches like Colva, Calangute, Anjuna, Vagator and Palolem). The indigenous population in the surrounding localities have openly blamed the government bodies to allow hotels, bars, night clubs and host of other attractions wherein no equitable distribution of resources have been locally allocated. Lands have been captured and sold while fishermen have been deprived for their rights. For last couple of years, the beaches of Goa have experienced open violations of human rights in forms of crime that need to be curbed through legislation. Eco-tourism can be promoted at a larger scale to curb the crime in Goa.

Tourist Arrivals in Goa

Goa's population as per the 2001 Census stands 14,57,723 though it does not include seasonal migration. In exceptional cases, tourists stay for more than six months and prefer to stay on isolated beaches to enjoy the sunburns. Goa receives the largest number of tourists from UK followed by Russia, Germany, Finland, France, Switzerland, and USA. In recent years, there is a large number of tourists coming from South-East Asia and Central Asian Republics with an average 5 per cent growth. The domestic tourists come from north mainly Punjab and West Bengal. Table 16.1 shows the number of domestic and foreign tourists who have visited from 2000 to 2010 except 2005 and 2008 due to security reasons.

Table 16.1: Tourist Arrivals in Goa (Domestic and Foreign): 2001-2010

Year	*Number of Tourists*			*Annual Growth (%age)*
	Domestic	*Foreign*	*Total*	
2001	1120242	260071	1380313	8.8
2002	1325296	271645	1596941	15.7
2003	1725140	314357	2039497	27.7
2004	2085729	363230	2448959	20.1
2005	1965343	336803	2302146	–6.0
2006	2098654	380414	2479068	7.7
2007	2208968	388457	2597443	4.8
2008	2020416	351123	2371539	–8.7
2009	2127063	376640	2503703	5.6
2010*	2201020	441000	2642020	17.6

Source: *Economic Survey 2009-10: Government of Goa*, Directorate of Planning, Statistics and Evaluation, Panaji.

* www.goacom.com/joel/news, Accessed on 16 March, 2011.

Goa Tourism: Infrastructure Development (2009-10)[4]

1. Government of India, Ministry of Tourism has sanctioned financial assistance to the tune of ₹ 430 million for the Development of Tourism Jetty and parking lot at Panaji. While Beach Safety Management System continues to work for the development of eco-tourism and Capacity Building.
2. Central Financial Assistance has also been sought for setting-up of Convention Centre at Campal-Panaji. An Institute of Hotel Management is also proposed at Farmagudi, Ponda, Goa with assistance of GTDC. A site for setting a Golf Course was also identified.
3. New Shack Policy has been implemented for smooth running of the temporary shacks on identified basis.
4. Development of infrastructure facilities like beautification of important tourist destinations, improvement of roads, and several safety measures are on.
5. Several eco-friendly areas in and around Temples and Churches of Goa with support of GTDC are already working.
6. Beach cleaning and regulation of the activities to maintain free flow of tourists is being undertaken.

New Tourism Policy[5]

The Tourism Policy and Tourism Master Plan 2011, Goa is a step forward to promote private sectors in the following manners:

1. Diversification and value addition of the tourism product while emphasizing the basic role of the Government to upgrade the infrastructure without disturbing the eco-culture.
2. Encouragement to the existing private tourism initiative through appropriate package of fiscal and friendly taxation measures.
3. Generation of an investor friendly environment for new private initiatives through a combination of prompt process and progressive fiscal policies.
4. Regulatory measures to ensure social, cultural and environmental sustainability have already started.
5. Involvement of local community in the tourism sector for its own benefits and to create trained manpower primarily from the local population at wider scale.
6. Life Safety along the beaches has been given a major thrust in order to reduce the drowning deaths to near zero level with support of Beach Trained Life Guards with necessary equipments. Special Tourist Security Organizations are being provided.

Continuous efforts are being made through promotion in print and electronic media and through participation in various travel related events in India and overseas in order to promote Goa as an ideal tourist destination. This is in view of promoting agro-tourism along with agro-processing and organic farming to generate employment opportunities. As part of Tourism Marketing and Promotion participated in travel related overseas events at Beijing International Tourism Expo-2009, Leisure 2009-Moscow, WTM-2009 London.[6] Besides, the Road Shows at Finland, Denmark, Switzerland, Rome and ITB Asia have immense significance. The domestic events at TF Calcutta, IITM Bangalore, TTF Ahmedabad, Holiday Expo-Travel and Tourism Exhibition at Visakhapatnam etc. are promoting Goa tourism. Goa-tourism is also being promoted in several Western worlds, thanks to Goan Diaspora. The latest event Visit India Travel Mart: International Travel and Tourism Exhibition held from 29 to 31 October, 2010 attracted Dubai Tourism (DTCM), Malaysia Tourism, Gujarat, Rajasthan, Uttarakhand, J&K, Himachal Pradesh, Chhattisgarh, others like makemytrip.com, Discover Motels, Sunrise Leisure System, and all package-related information.

Beach-related Eco-Friendly Attractions in Goa

More vacationers visit Goa every year than other destinations on the west coast of India. It is because of wonderful climate, rich history and large number of unattended beaches. Away from the beaten track, traveller discover the romantic flora and fauna that catch the imagination of visitors that also clued elephant safari, open jungles, wildlife sanctuaries and bird watch islands. But it is unfair to say that eco-tourism flourished in jungles, wild lives, and natural plantation. A broad visionary eco-tourist finds better options in sea-beach related activities like nature friendly dolphin watch, fishing in deep-sea beaches, the habit of sea turtles, bamboo made shacks as relaxed place, and several beach related activities in Goa. Let us briefly examine some of these attractions.

Dolphin Watch

Dolphins are one of the most-loved creatures of the marine world. These are extremely intelligent and playful mammals who delight every visitor with their antics as they play and feed in Arabian Sea. In Goa, dolphin tours include time for stretching out and relaxing, snorkeling and taking pictures. Since Key West guides for Dolphin adventures in Goa are environmentally aware, they prefer to take visitors to observe Dolphins on various beaches. The numbers of Dolphins are not known as these eco-lovers' creatures freely move from one beach to another and across the sea. By a conservative estimate, over 2500 dolphins have been spotted, a combined strength all 27 eco-friendly beaches of Goa. Who can resist the thrill of watching dolphins frolic in their natural surroundings, cavorting in graceful curves above the sea in Goa, really an adventurous experience, probably a rare example in India.

Crocodile Watch in Goa

Crocodile watching in Goa is a unique experience. Stray crocodiles have been spotted at several prominent beaches like Talpona, Galgibaga, Agonda and Palolem while Water Lands of Chorao, Tivim, Siolim and Carambolim are prominent. Galgibaga highest of all beaches has spotted over 39 and Aondia beach is famous for home of Crocodiles. The Syngenta freshwater lakes at Corlim have a small number of 13 crocodiles thriving. Southern Birdwing, a wildlife group which closely monitors the movements of the muggers, as part of the Goa Forest Department's Wildlife Rescue Squad has been involved in the rescue of 38 crocodiles. They also take tourists 'croc-spotting' to the Cumbarjua in a boat that holds many a charm—the meandering river, the whispering mangrove, the wild crocodiles, peregrine falcon or the white collard kingfisher. Goa Foundation, Mapusa continues to analyze critical data on such conservation essential for eco-tourism.[7]

Sea Turtle Conservation

Goa's three prominent beaches least known and often visited by the tourist—Morgim, Agonda and Galgibaga—are fortunate to be home of turtles. These little marine-animals are being frequently found nesting throughout the coast. The Centre for Environment Education Goa (CEEG) has been working on 'Turtle Conservation' since 1984 while large number of environmentalists, teachers and students are being sensitized about such Eco-friendly Sea Turtles and often visit the sites as part of educational tours. Cohabitation activities are being watched by marine researchers.

Beach Shacks: A Relaxed and Comfort Life

Beach Shacks are the essence of Goa Tourism, which have maintained the typical Goan identity. The Conical roof made of eco-friendly coconut palms, the wooden filigree bordering the circular interior, the privately maintained tables and the mouthwatering dishes served hot by courteous smiling faces add to the lasting impression. Tourism shacks is essentially a family business since generations. In 1960s that came from 'hippies' or 'flower children' with a view to promote nature against the materialistic Western culture. Here, the tourists meet the true spirit of Goa. Much before the advent of hotels, the shack culture attracted large number of tourists from Portugal once the Goan colony. These shacks also served the Goan Dish a 'family spirit'—fish curry rice, even now largely served. Several Goans used leafs to enjoy curry rice.[8] Several agencies like Benaulim Environment Trust, Colva Environment Trust, Vagator Beach Management, Anjuna Beach Trust are active.[9] These are working with support of Goan Traditional Shacks Owner Association (GTSOA) and Shacks Owner Welfare Society (SOWS) and Drishti Special Response Services (DSRS).[10]

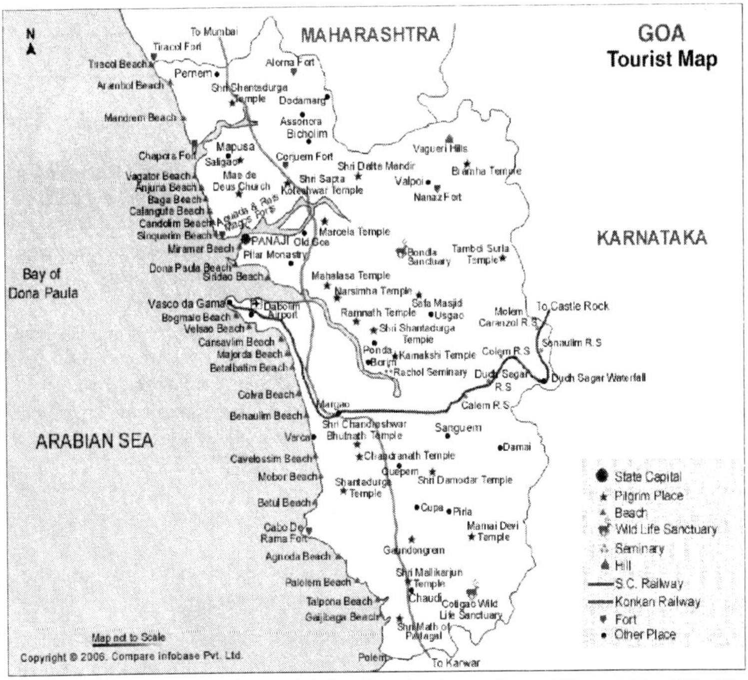

Fig. 16.1: Selected Beaches and Other Tourist Attractions of Goa: A Brief Profile

Goa has large number of famous beaches and islands, which are connected with mainland by various communications. It is a state of seven rivers and their estuaries, there are hills with lush green vegetation, and most of the tourists need to cover large distances to move from one place to other. A list of islands with very brief profile is mentioned in Table 16.2.

Birds Watching in Goa

Large number of islands and presence of large number of local and migratory birds, become the key source of eco-tourism in Goa. Humid forest of Anjediva Sea island and Chorao River island possess extraordinary collection of 300 species of birds. Some of them, viz. sparrow, bulbuls, mynas, house crow are important. Others like quails, jerdons, courser, pintail ducks, winged blackbird, malabar whistling thrust and shams and hill myna are increasing attraction for foreign tourists. Several eco-friendly destinations are being promoted to attract birds watching in Goa.

Table 16.2: Some other Eco-friendly Attractions in Goa

Sl. No.	*Sea/Islands*	*Attractions*
1.	Sao Jorge Island	Desert covered with greenery and some frequently visited wild animals are monkey, dears, etc.
2.	Cambariem	Thickly covered unattended Palm Trees. Some area is also covered by defence personnel.
3.	Grande-I	Thickly green with palm & cashew trees.
4.	Sao Jacinto	Deserted Island—least known.
5.	Anjediva	Least explored green island.
6.	Canacona	Rocky and rare visible crocodile rest habitat.
7.	Chorao (River Island)	Wildlife and migratory birds.
8.	Diwar	Human populated famous for migratory birds and folk culture.

Uses of Mangroves

Mangroves provide a wide range of services and benefits to the mankind. Ecological and economic values of mangroves are recognized world over. They are instrumental in providing ecological stability and livelihood security to coastal regions and people. People in Goa are making use of mangroves by protecting them as a nursery ground for various fish and crab species, which form a part of their daily food. Good use of mangrove areas is also being made for eco-tourism and tourists from India and abroad are taken to these areas for a pleasant trip and crocodile watching. Fallen dried branches of mangroves are also collected in a very limited scale for firewood purpose. However, no bee hives have been reported and these areas are not being used for that purpose. Besides, all the river banks are protected by thick mangrove cover. The general services provided by the mangroves include prevention from soil erosion, stabilization of coasts and beaches, aqua-culture, food beverage and boat making and most important reduction of the effect of Tsunamis.

Miscellaneous Eco-Tourist Attractions in Goa

Goa continues to attract foreign tourists who visit Goa not merely for fun and enjoyment, but also to see the latent natural beauty where other sources and attractions like woodland Birds, Butterfly Diversity and Medicinal and (Ayurvedic) properties are not less significant to promote eco-tourism. Ayurvedic medicine emphasizes hygiene, exercise, herbal preparations, and *yoga* cure ailments. Such treatments rely on herbal medicines, physiotherapy and diet. Ayurvedic medicine is still a popular form of health care in India, especially Kerala, Karnataka and Goa. By a conservative estimate, over 25 per cent Europeans visit Goa for Ayurvedic treatment in an eco-friendly environment.

Unlike moths, butterflies are active during the day and are usually brightly coloured or strikingly patterned. Distinctive features are club-tipped antennae and a habit of holding the wings vertically over the back when at rest. In Goa, such events are not popular, but for the butterflies, eco-zone is an ideal destination. During post-Monsoon, Goa attracts large number of eco-tourist packagers on several beach and river islands. With different eight locations, Goa has collection of 257 butterfly species in various habitats. Such butterflies play an important role in various eco-system.[11]

Besides, several islands have been directly associated with wildlife eco-system where human intervention is least in exception of local communities. The recent move about environment brigade in Goa has declared these zones as "Eco-friendly" where variety of migratory birds are found in astonishing diversity of endemic species, habitats and eco-system, virtually 40 per cent land of Goa is covered by geographical diversity.[12] Goa's three wildlife sanctuaries (Bondla, Cotigao and Salim Ali), sea islands, lakes (Mayem) and natural springs (Kesarwal) are not less important for eco-tourist lovers.

Goa with over 105 long sea beaches with several ideal destinations like tropical forests, islands, rivers and water tributaries has recently come up with new plans called as 'Medical Tourism' where medicinal plants with rich Ayurvedic properties attract over 35 per cent foreign tourists. Several species of herbs like *Karanja, Parisha, Punnaga, Ketaki, Jalapippali, Hamaspadi, Shatavari* and *Langali* are the prominent ones. About 1200 species of plants belonging to different families have been found in Goa.[13]

Conclusion

Goa with its rich heritage, has immense scope for eco-tourism. It is one of the fastest growing activities in state that has yielded unimaginative foreign revenue, cultural assimilation and economic objectives. Goa's well-identified eco-tourist destinations all within the periphery of 50 kilometre sea coast of Goa are immensely important for the tourists. Though the present chapter highlights mainly sea beaches in Goa, apart from various beach related activities, tourists are equally motivated by wildlives, historical churches, temples, natural springs, forts and plantations. Marine related activities are incomplete without giving due consent to hinterland eco-friendly objects that help to learn new styles of living. Large number of tourists visit the plant herbs, trees, flowers, and local products.

Several NGOs and Research organizations like GFM GIRDA, GDRC, GTDC, and GPS increasingly stress the need for sustainability and environment friendly Goa. More recently, Goa was awarded Indian's best beach Tourism destination at a conference in New Delhi. The award was given to Secretary Tourism in Union Ministry of Tourism.[14] It was with a view of keeping beaches in Goa, in the most natural form unlike any other part of India. It has been possible because of several awareness campaigns undertaken to educate people. There is greater need to clean the mind and thinking to promote '*Beach Cleaning Abhiyan*' and '*Goa Bachao Andolan*' as regular practice. More emphasis should be given on the diversification and strict implementation of laws where large number of beach side located industries and hotels cause serious environmental pollution. Usage of biodegradable products should be promoted among the tourists and maintenance of destinations should be under strict control of local NGOs. Education and training programme is the core of eco-tourism that needs vision and futuristic community-based approach.

Today, there is greater need to divert the crowd of tourists from the busiest beaches to hinterland and lopsided beaches like Harmal, Kegadi, Bambolim, Sri Dao, Agassim, Arossim, Velsao, Talpona and Polem which are most natural and blessed with unlimited eco-friendly culture. Unfortunately, tourists either know little or are unfamiliar as the infrastructure has not developed and agencies do not take tourists to these beaches for certain reasons. Interaction between host and guests create new opportunities for peace and greater coordination. So, it is imperative to understand pleasure and hospitality for better results. No doubt, Goa has been developed to serve as one of the world's pleasure peripheries and cultural space for relaxation to preserve local custom. But eco-friendly culture cannot be guaranteed merely by the changes in the value system, traditional lifestyles, family relationship, individual behaviour and community structure.[15] Now, the time has come to move hinterland tourism giving emphasis on 'Rural Tourism' that can better document the history, culture, flora and fauna and can open new avenue for eco-culture. In nutshell, there is a greater need to establish people friendly tourism with greater emphasis on eco-conservation, preservation and protection of land, water and other resources. Upgradation of infrastructure facilities without damaging the environment, culture and sustainable development is must. More emphasis should be given on hospitality industry by promoting the grassroots level and complete ban on the sale of agricultural lands while the legislative bodies should be honest enough to handover the ownership titles to local communities.

Notes

1. Prabhakar S. Angle, (2001), *Goa: An Economic Update* (Mumbai: Goa Hindu Association, p. 107.
2. Avinash V. Raikar, (2009), "Tourism in Goa: Is it Sustainable", *Atharva* (Goa), Vol.4, No.8, August, pp. 4-5.
3. See, "A Bittersweet 09 for Tourism", *Times of India* (Goa), 30 December, 2009.
4. *Economic Survey* 2009-2010: Government of Goa, Directorate of Planning, Statistics & Evaluation, Panaji, pp. 43-47.
5. *Ibid.*, p. 43.
6. *Ibid.*, pp. 43-44.
7. Sujeet Kumar Dongre, *Friday Balcao Synopsis*, January 9, 2004, Vol. 6, No. 1, Centre for Environment Education, Bardez, Goa.
8. Sebastian de Souza, "Beach Shacks: A Struggle for Their rightful place on the beach", *Friday Balcao* Goa Desc Resource Centre, Mapusa, Goa, Vol. 1, No. 1, August 1999 to February 2001.
9. *Times of India*, 10 October, 2010.
10. For the year 2010-2011, *Navhind Times* (Goa), 30 September, 2010, p. 3.
11. "Goa Tourism Bag Best Award", *Navhind Times*, 30 September, 2010, p. 9.
12. Devidas V. Kotkar, " Butterfly Diversities: A Case Study of Mhadei Wildlife Sanctuary Goa", *Atharva* (Goa), Vol. 6, No. 2, February 2010.
13. Sangrama Keshari Das, "Medicinal Plants of Goa" *Atharva*, Vol.3, No. 6, June 2008, pp. 9-10.
14. Devidas Kotkar, "Woodland Birds in Goa", *Atharva*, Vol.5, No.8, August 2010, pp. 2-3.
15. Ritz (2000) "Residents Perception of Socio-Cultural Impact of Tourism at Laks Balaton", in G. Richards & D. Hall, (ed.) *Tourism and Sustainable Community* (London: Rutledge Publications).

References

Bera, Tilak Rayon (2008). *Goa: A Journey & Reminisance* (Kolkata: Woodland Publisher).

Carita, Helder (2000), *Places of Goa: Model Types of Indo-Portuguese Civil Architecture* (Berks, UK : Media Publising Service).

Cunha, Gerard de, (2000), *Houses of Goa* (Hyderabad: Pragati Art Printers).

Delourdes Maria and DeCosta Bravo (2007), *Remembering Goa* (Merces, Goa: L & L Publications).

Fernandez, Pantalep (2006), *100 Goan Experiences* (Benaulim, Goa: World Publications).

Gaude, Surya (2009), *Silent Goa* (Ponda, Goa: Human Resource Development Trust).

Goa: Lonely Planet (Hong Kong: Lonely Planet Publications, 2007).

Goa: Accommodation Directory (Panaji, Department of Tourism, Government of Goa, 2008).

Go Goa: A Perfect Holiday Destination: Goa at a Glance (Panaji: Department of Tourism, 2008).

Goa: Sweet land of Mine (Mapusa: Goa Foundation, 2008).

Gomes, Olivinho J.F., (1996), *Villages Goa: A Study of Goan Social Structure & Change* (New Delhi: S. Chand & Co.).

"Growth of Medical Tourism in Goa: The Booming Medical Tourism", *Navhind Times*, 16 January, 2008.

Hall, Maurice (1995), *Winds on Goa: A History & Guide* (London: Quilter Press).

Lainer, Heinz, (2004), *Birds of Goa: A Reference Book* (Mapusa: Goa Foundation).

Malgaonkar, Manohar, (2004), *Inside Goa* (Hyderabad: Pragati Offset Pvt. Ltd.).

Noronha, Frederick, (2009), *Another Goa* (Panaji: Broadway Book Centre).

——, (2008), *Inside Goa* (New Delhi: Rampa & Co.).

Pandil, Heta (1996), *Walking With Angel* (Pune: Vyama Graphics, Heritage Network).

Pinto, Celsa (1996), *Goa: Images & Perceptions* (Panaji: Rajhans).

17

Fungal Biosorbents and Biosorption

A Review Article

Pawan Kumar Rose and *Rani Devi*

Introduction

Increasing industrialization, urbanization, improvement and advancement in technologies, has caused contamination of our environment. There are many sources of environmental pollution and industries are one of the main contributors among them, especially when they contain heavy metal. Heavy metal(s) are widespread pollutants of great environmental concern, as they are non-degradable and thus persistent (Stratton, 1987). It is well perceived that there is a permissible limit of each metal, above which they are generally toxic (Gadd, 1992), and some are even hazardous. A number of treatment methods for the removal of heavy metals from metal-bearing wastewater have been reported, mainly reduction, ion exchange, electrodialysis, electrochemical precipitation, evaporation, solvent extraction, reverse osmosis, chemical precipitation and adsorption (Gode and Pehlivan, 2003; Lu *et al.*, 2006). Most of these methods have their own limitations like high capital and operation cost, incomplete metal removal, low selectivity, high energy consumption and they generate toxic slurries that are difficult to eliminate (Kapoor and Viraraghavan, 1995 and 1997; Yu and Kaewsarn, 1999). These methods are unstable, especially when metals are present in concentration lower than 100 mg/L (Paknikar *et al.*, 1993).

In this light, biological materials have emerged as an eco-friendly and economic option (Ting *et al.*, 1988). For a long time, peat has occupied the place of prominence among biosorbents, but since, it is not available everywhere, microbial biomass is the other option. Microbial biomass can passively bind large amounts of metal(s), a phenomenon commonly referred to as biosorption (Tsezos and Volesky, 1982; Macaskie and Dean, 1985; Gadd, 1988), thus providing a cost-effective solution for industrial wastewater management (Volesky and Holan, 1995). The uptake of heavy metals by biomass can take place by an active mode (dependent on the metabolic activity) known as bio-accumulation or by a passive mode (sorption and/or complexation) termed as biosorption.

Different types of biomass have been used for the removal and recovery of heavy metals from industrial effluents, such as algae, bacteria, fungi and yeast (Fourest and Roux, 1994). Among them, fungi have been proved to be economic and eco-friendly materials. Fungi possess high metal binding capacity, because polysaccharides, proteins or lipids on the surface of their cell walls contain some functional groups such as amino, hydroxyl, carboxyl and sulphate, which can act as binding sites for metals (Yu *et al.*, 1999). In this review, the biosorption abilities of fungal biomass towards metal ions removal are emphasized. Effect of parameters such as *p*H, metal ion concentration, temperature, physical or chemical pre-treatment of biomass and presence of many ligands in solution, are covered in this study.

Heavy Metal

Heavy metal can be defined on the basis of their physical, chemical and biological properties. The term heavy metal is somewhat imprecise and refers to any metallic element that has a relatively high density and is toxic or poisonous even at low concentration (Lenntech, 2004). Passow *et al.* (1961); Huton and Symon (1986) and Hawkes (1997) defined heavy metals as general collective term, which applies to the group of metals and metalloids with atomic density greater than 5 g/cm^3 or greater than water.

In the periodic table, the heavy metals constitute the Group III transition metals, the actinides series (uranium, neptunium, plutonium and americium), the lanthanide series, and three of the Group IV metalloids (arsenic, tellurium, selenium). The terms 'heavy metals' and 'transition metals' are often used interchangeably, although transition metals strictly refer to Group III elements.

Heavy metal interaction with water exists in two forms:

(a) Water-soluble

Chloride, sulphate and nitrate salts of heavy metals are water-soluble.

These are most common salts of heavy metal ions used in industrial operations. As a dissolved salt, heavy metal ions are in cationic form such as Cd^{2+}, Hg^{2+}, Pb^{2+}, Ag^{+}, Cr^{3+}. Heavy metals can also exist in soluble form as oxymetal anions like chromium, which can also exist as chromate CrO_4^{2-} or dichromate $Cr_2O_7^{2-}$. Another example is arsenic, including arsenate (AsO_4^{3-}), which has an oxidation state of +5, arsenite (AsO_3^{3-}), whereas has oxidation state of +3, as well as selenium (SeO_2^{3-}, SeO_4^{2-}) (Stephengen and Lester, 1987).

(b) Water-insoluble

Oxide, hydroxide, sulphide and carbonate salts of most heavy metals are not soluble or are sparingly soluble in water. Most of the heavy metal cations are divalent (2^+), but some are monovalent (e.g. silver Ag^+) or trivalent (e.g. Cr^{3+}). Many heavy metals can be having multiple oxidation states (e.g. Iron Fe^{2+} or Fe^{3+}).

Heavy metals are present in marine, ground and industrial waste water (Nuhoglu *et al.*, 2002). Heavy metals enter into the environment by both natural and anthropogenic sources. The major causes of emission are the anthropogenic sources specifically mining operations (Hutton and Symon, 1986) and also aqueous waste streams arising from many industrial activities such as metal plating, mining, metallurgy, tanneries, painting, steel industries etc. which are normally contaminated with heavy metals. Heavy metals are often present together with organic pollutants in industrial waste water (Lodi *et al.*, 1998). The effluents from these industrial activities contain dissolved metals such as Cu, Cd, Pb, Zn, Cr, Ni etc. and can pose a serious risk for soil and for groundwater contamination.

Heavy metals are classified into the following three categories on the basis of their use in the field of biosorption (Volesky, 1990 and Bishop, 2002):

1. Toxic metals (such as Hg, Cr, Pb, Zn, Cu, Cd, As, Co & Sn etc.),
2. Precious metals (such as Pt, Ag, Ni, Au & Ru etc.), and
3. Radionuclides (such as U, Th, Ra & Am etc.), whose specific weight is usually more than 5.0 g/cm^3.

Heavy metal pollution represents an important environmental problem due to their non-biodegradability, toxicity and accumulation throughout the food chain, which leads to serious ecological and health problems (Chuah *et al.*, 2005). Discharge and treatment of industrial wastewater containing heavy metals are important issues in environmental protection.

Biosorption

The use of biological materials as biosorbent for heavy metal adsorption and recovery has received a great deal of attention in the past two decades due to their good performance and low cost (Volesky, 1994). Shumate and Strandberg (1985) defined biosorption as "a non-directed physio-chemical interaction that may occur between metal/radio nuclide species and the cellular compounds of biological species." Biosorption can also be defined as the ability of biological materials to accumulate heavy metals from wastewater through metabolically mediated or physico-chemical pathways of uptake (Fourest and Roux, 1994).

The biosorption process involves a liquid phase (solvent, normally water) containing a dissolved species to be sorbed (sorbate, metal ions) and a solid phase (sorbent or biosorbent; biological material) on which it is sorbed. Due to higher affinity of the sorbent for the sorbate species, the latter is attracted and bound thereby different mechanisms. The process continues until equilibrium is established between the amount of solid-bound sorbate species and its portion remaining in the solution. The degree of sorbent affinity for the sorbate determines its distribution between the solid and liquid phases.

The major advantages of biosorption over conventional treatment methods include (Kratochvil *et al.*, 1998): low, cost; high efficiency, minimization of chemical and biological sludge; no additional nutrient requirement, regeneration of biosorbent and possibility of metal recovery.

Micro-organisms uptake the metals in many different ways which implies their complex structure. There are various biosorption mechanisms and are not fully understood. These mechanisms are classified into many types according to various criteria.

Biosorption mechanisms can be divided into two groups according to the dependence on the cell's metabolism:

1. Metabolism dependent, and
2. Non-metabolism dependent.

Biosorption can be classified into three groups according to the location where the metal removed from solution is found:

1. Extra-cellular accumulation/precipitation
2. Cell surface sorption/precipitation; and
3. Intracellular accumulation

In metabolic dependent biosorption, transport of the metal across the cell membrane yields intracellular accumulation. This implies that biosorption may take place only with viable cells and indicate active defence system of the micro-organism, which reacts in the presence of toxic metals.

In non-metabolism dependent biosorption, metal uptake is by physico-chemical interaction between the metal and the functional groups present on the microbial cell surface. Physical adsorption, ion exchange and chemical sorption are some type of non-metabolism dependent biosorption. This type of biosorption, i.e. non-metabolism dependent is relatively rapid and can be reversible (Kuyucak and Volesky, 1988).

Major binding sites are acidic, means these are protonated when neutral, e.g. hydroxyl, carboxyl, sulfhydryl etc. as *p*H increases make available sites for cations. Similarly, some sites are deprotonated when neutral, e.g. amine, amide etc. as *p*H decreases these make available sites for anions.

The process of biosorption is the most promising technique. The most widely used industrial sorbent is activated carbon; however, it is an expensive material. Biosorbents prepared from different types of discarded materials are very convenient material in terms of cost for heavy metal removal from waste water. A number of materials have been tested as biosorbent for heavy metals removal and a number of studies have been reported using fungi as biosorbents.

Fungi as Biosorbent

Biological methods of metal removal, defined as biosorptions have been recommended as cheaper and more effective techniques. In biosorption, either live or dead micro-organisms or their derivatives are used, which bind metal ions through the functioning of ligands or functional groups located on outer surface of cell. Algal, bacteria, fungi and yeast have proved to be potential metal biosorbents (Volesky, 1986).

The application of fungi to remediate the problem of land and water contaminated with toxic compounds have received increasing interest because fungi are ubiquitous in the natural environment and are often the dominant organisms in many soil, particularly those with low *p*H values (Visoottiviseth and Panviroj, 2001).

Fungi have been used for centuries by humans either directly as food or in food processing such as wines, beers, breads and cheeses. *Saccharomyces cerevisae* is used in food and beverage industry (Kuyucak and Volesky, 1988). *R. arrizus* is used in food industry (Tobin *et al.*, 1984). Fungi are also used to produce organic acids, vitamins, enzymes, drugs, antibiotics and alcohol and to modify steroids. *Aspergillus niger* is used to produce citric acid and an industrial enzyme (Kurek *et al.*, 1982).

The potential of fungal biomass in removing metal ions from waste water was recognized by Shumate *et al.* (1978) and Gadd (1986). The uptake of metals by fungi has generated an interest in using them for removal of toxic metals from waste water because of their great tolerance towards heavy metals, their high cell wall binding capacity and high intracellular metal uptake capacity (Gadd, 1987). Both living and dead fungal cells possess a remarkable ability for taking up toxic and precious metals. Immobilization of biomass within a suitable matrix can overcome these problems by offering ideal size, mechanical strength, rigidity, and porous characteristics to the biological material (Trujillo *et al.*, 1995).

Bai and Abraham (1998), recognized the potential of fungal biomass as biosorbents for removal of heavy metals from polluted water. Fungi accumulate heavy metals in amounts higher than the nutritional requirement (Gadd, 1986). Polysaccharides in association with lipids and proteins represent the main constituent of fungal cell wall (Vasudevan *et al.*, 2001). In filamentous fungi, the outer cell wall layers mainly contain neutral polysaccharides (glucans and mannans), while the inner layers contain more of glucosamines (chitin and chitosan) in a microfibrillar structure (Vasudevan *et al.*, 2001). Ligands within these materials include carboxylate, amine, phosphate, hydroxyl, sulfhydral and other functional groups (Vasudevan *et al.*, 2001). Proteins are also associated with metal binding. Polysaccharides constitute up to 90 per cent of fungal cell wall (Ramacle, 1990). Phosphate and carboxyl groups are thought to be responsible for negative charge in the cell wall; amine groups of the chitosan create a positive charge (Ramacle, 1990; Volesky, 1990). Apart from electrostatic attraction to these charged groups, complexation with nitrogen or oxygen donors (e.g. of chitin) may occur (May 1984) since the protein content of fungal cell wall is only about 10 per cent (Volesky, 1990).

The importance of amino acids functional groups in metal uptake is small. Commercial application of these microbial biomass as a biosorbent, however, has been hindered by problems associated with physical characteristics of these material such as small particle size, low density, poor mechanical strength and rigidity, and solid-liquid separation (Volesky and Holan, 1995) (*See* Table 17.1) .

Factors Affecting Biosorption

There are a number of physical and chemical factors which affect the biosorption of metals.

Effect of pH

Several investigators have studied the effect of *p*H on metal ion uptake. It affects the solution chemistry of the metal, the activity of the functional group in the biomass and competition of metallic ions (Friis and Myers-Keith, 1986). Kapoor *et al.*, 1999 observed little or no biosorption of metal ion like Cd, Cu, and Pb at *p*H less than 3.0 using fungal biomass *Aspergillus niger* and metal removal capacity increased very sharply with an increase in *p*H from 3.2 to 4.0. *p*H seems to be the most important parameter in the biosorptive process. Metal biosorption may be brought about by the ionization of negative functional molecular groups which serve as binding sites.

Effect of Metal-ion Concentration

Rate of biosorption is a function of initial concentration of ions. Though percentage metal uptake reduces with increase in initial metal concentration, the total uptake increases. Thus, biosorption is more effective with dilute solution if high percentage of removal is required (Kuyucak and Volesky, 1988; Zhou and Kiff, 1991). At lower concentration of metal ions present in solution could more interact with the binding sites. The per cent biosorption of metal ions to the biomass decreased as the initial concentration of metal ions was increased. This appears to be due to the lack of binding sites for complexation of ions at higher concentration level (Bai and Abraham, 2001).

Effect of Temperature

As adsorption and ion exchange are exothermic reactions only marginal increase in metal uptake is expected up to a limit beyond which the temperature damages the cell wall and leads to decrease in metal binding.

Table 17.1: Biosorption of Heavy Metal by Various Fungal Species

Organism	*Element and experimental details*	*Biosorption capacity (mg/g)*	*Isotherm applicability*
Aspergillus niger	Cu, 2.5 mg/l	1.9	—
Non-Growing	Cu, 2.5 mg/l	5.0	—
A. niger	Cu, 35 mg/l, 1 h	7.22	Freundlich and Langmuir
	Cd, 10 mg/l, 1 h	3.74	—
	Au, 10 to 1000 mg/l	170	—
	Ag, 107 mg/l, 2 h	22.3	Freundlich
	Cu, 63.5 mg/l, 2 h	1.8	Freundlich
	La, 138 mg/l, 2 h	7.5	Freundlich
	U, 71.4 mg/l, 4 h	215	—
	U, 10 mg/l, 1 h	80.7	—
A. oryzae	Zn, 200 mg/l*	17.6	—
	Cu, 6.35 mg/l	13.8	Langmuir
	Cd, 1.1 mg/l, 3 h	2.2	Langmuir
	Cd, 1 h	12.8	Langmuir
A. terreus	U, 30 mg/l*	10	Langmuir and Freundlich
	Th, 30 mg/l*	60	Langmuir and Freundlich

(Contd.)

Organism	Element and experimental details	Biosorption capacity (mg/g)	Isotherm applicability
Penicillium spinulosum			
Non-Growing	Cd, 2.5 mg/l, 2 h	1.5	—
Growing, midlinear phase	Cd, 2.5 mg/l, 12 h	0.4	—
Non-Growing	Cu, 2.5 mg/l, 2 h	2.4	—
Growing, lag period	Cu, 2.5 mg/l, 24 h	3.6	—
Non-growing	Zn, 2.5 mg/l, 2 h	1.3	—
Growing, midlinear phase	Zn 2.5 mg/l	0.2	—
Penicillium notatum	Cu	80	—
	Zn	23	—
	Cd	5.0	—
Penicillium sp.	Al	53	—
	Sn	61	—
	Pb	5.0	—
	Pb, 50 mg/l, 2 h	6.1	—
Penicillium chrysogenum	U, 30 mg/l*	70	Langmuir and Freundlich
Penicillium janthinellum	U, 10 mg/l, 1 h	52.7	—
Penicillium sp.	U, 100 mg/l, 18 h	1.4	—
Penicillium chrysogenum	Th, 30 mg/l*	142	Langmuir and Freundlich
Penicillium *chrysogenum*	Pb, 90 mg/l, 24 h	116	—

(*Contd.*)

Organism	Element and experimental details	Biosorption capacity (mg/g)	Isotherm applicability
Rhizopus arrhizus	Cr	31	—
	Mn	12	—
	Cu	16	—
	Zn	20	—
	Cd	30	—
	Hg	58	—
	Pb	104	—
	U	195	—
	Ag	54	—
Rhizopus arrhizus	Cu, 19 mg/l	17.1	BET
	Th, 30 mg/l*	185	Langmuir and Freundlich
	Th, 696 mg/l, 0.5 h	97	—
Saccharomyces cerevisiae	Cd, 0.5-50 mg/l, 1 h	2.4-31.2	—
	Cd, 22.4 mg/l, 1 h	8.9	—
	U, 10 mg/l, 1 h	33.8	—
	U, 57 mg/l	150	—
	Th, 696 mg/l*, 30 min	119	—
	Cu, 3.2 mg/l, 3 h	1.9	Scatchard
	Cd, 200 mg/l*, 45 min	71	Langmuir

Source: Kapoor and Viraraghavan, 1995.

* The equilibrium metal-ion concentration.

Temperature seems not to influence the biosorption performance in the range of 25-35°C (Aksu *et al.*, 1992).

Effect of Pre-treatment

Physical pretreatment methods such as heating, autoclaving, freeze drying and boiling and chemical pretreatment methods such as using acid, alkali and organic chemical showed enhancement or reduction in metal biosorption, depending on the fungal strains and treatment procedures used (Selatnia *et al.,* 2004). Metal affinity of the biomass can be manipulated by pretreating the biomass with alkalies, acids, detergents, organic solvent, heat and autoclaved which may increase the amount of metal sorbed. Kapoor *et al.* (1999) had investigated the removal of lead, cadmium and copper ions by pretreatment. *Aspergillus niger* was higher than the removal obtained using granular activated carbon. The chemical treatment of biomass with NaOH (0.1M) shows that in the sodium form, the ion exchange sites were more easily able to exchange this cation (Na^+) with ions Ni^{2+} than when the ion exchange sites were protonated (Selatnia *et al.*, 2004). Biosorption capacity was decreased when *Mucar rouxii* was autoclaved as compared to live fungus biomass, this attributed due to loss of intracellular uptake. Acid pretreatment enhanced the metal sorption capacity, HCl was the most efficient. The alkali pretreatment enhanced Cu biosorption, but, Ni sorption remained unaltered. Methanol and hot water pretreatment decreased metal sorption capacity of biomass.

Effect of Co-ions

The presence of anions also affects the biosorption of metal ions. Biosorption is reduced in the presence of ethylenediamine tetra acetate (EDTA) $C_{10}H_{16}N_2O_8$ or $[(HOOCCH_2)_2\ NCH_2]_2$, sulphate, chloride, phosphate, carbonate, glutamate, citrate and pyrophosphate (Zhou and Kiff, 1991; Tobin *et al.*, 1987). The total amount of metal biosorption in multiple metal systems is lower than that in a single metal system (Figueira *et al.*, 1998). As majority of functional groups in the cell wall are non-specific, the outer cations compete for binding sites reducing the uptake of required metal ions from mixed solution. Extent of reduction depends upon the type and concentration of other cations, their increase leading to decrease in metal uptake (Kuyucak and Volesky, 1989).

Conclusion

Thus, biosorption offers an economically feasible technology for efficient removal and recovery of metal(s) from aqueous solutions. The biosorbents can easily be produced using inexpensive growth media or obtained as a byproduct from some industry. However, there is a need to have more knowledge of the basic mechanisms involved in order to develop better and effective biosorbents. More technical and feasibility data is required for a better understanding and effective use of fungal biosorption. The physico-chemical nature of the fungal biosorbents needs to be studied and ways to tailor the nature of fungal cells for increased biosorption capacity of heavy metals needs to be developed. The mechanism of biosorption needs to be further elucidated. The rates of biosorption for various metals, and multi-component sorption, should be studied to serve as a basis for the design of biosorption treatment systems.

References

Aksu, Z.; Sag, Y. and T. Kutsal (1992): The biosorption of Cu (II) by *C. vulgaris* and *Z. ramigera*. *Environ. Technol.*, 13, 579-586.

Bai, R.S. and T.E. Abraham (1998): Studies on biosorption of chromium (VI) by dead fungal biomass. *J. Sci. Ind. Res.*, 57, 821-824.

Bai, R.S. and T.E. Abraham (2001): Biosorption of Cr (VI) from aqueous solution by *Rhizopus nigricans*. *Bioresour. Technol.*, 79, 73-81.

Bishop, P.L. (2002): *Pollution Prevention: Fundamentals and Practice*. Beijing: Tsinghua University Press.

Chuah, T.G; Jumasiah, A.; Azni, I.; Katayon, S. and S.Y. Thomas Choong (2005): Rice husk as a potentially low-cost biosorbent for heavy metal and dye removal: An Overview, *Desalination*, 175, 305-316.

Fourest, E. and J.C. Roux (1994): Improvement of heavy metal biosorption by mucelial dead biomass *Rhizopus arrhizus*, *Mucor miehei* and *Penicillium chryogenum*: *p*H control and cationic activation. *FEMS Microbial*, 14, 325-332.

Friis, N. and P. Myers-Keith (1986): Biosorption of uranium and lead by *Streptomyces longwoodensis*. *Biotechnol. Bioeng.*, 28, 21-28.

Gadd, G.M. (1986): The uptake of heavy metals by fungi and yeast: The chemistry and physiology of the process and application for biotechnology. In *Immobilization of ions by Biosorption*. H.H. Eccles and S. Hunt (Eds.). Ellis Harwood, Chichester, U.K. 135-147.

Gadd, G.M. (1987): Fungal response towards heavy metals. In, R.A. Herbert, G.A. Gadd, (Eds.). *Microbes in Extreme Environments*, London: Academic Press, 84-109.

Gadd, G.M. (1988): in *Biotechnology—A Comprehensive Treatise, Special Microbial Processes* (eds. Rehm, H.J. and Reed, G.), VCH, Verlagsgesell Schaft, Weinheim, Germany, 6b, 401-433.

Gadd, G.M. (1992): *FEMS Microbiol. Lett.*, 100,197-204.

Godc, F. and E. Pehlivan (2003): A comparative study of two chelating ionexchange resins for the removal of chromium (III) from aqueous solution. *J. Hazardous Materials*, B100, 231-243.

Hawkes, J.S. (1997): Heavy metals. *J. Chem. Educ.* 74 (11), 1374.

Hutton, M. and C. Symon (1986): The quantities of cadmium, lead, mercury and arsenic entering the U.K. environment from human activities. *Sci. Total Environ.*, 57, 129-150.

Kapoor, A. and T. Viraraghavan (1995): Fungal biosorption an alternative treatment option for heavy metal bearing wastewaters: A review. *Biores. Technol.*, 53, 195-206.

Kapoor A. and T. Viraraghavan (1997): Heavy metal biosorption sites in Aspergillus Niger. *Biores. Technol.*, 61, 221-227.

Kratochvil, D.; Pimentel, P. and B. Volesky (1998): Removal of trivalent and hexavalent chromium by seaweed biosorbent. *Environ. Sci. Technol.*, 32 (18), 2693-2698.

Kurek, J.; Cztiban and I.M. Bollag (1982): Sorption of cadmium by micro-organisms in competition with other soil constituents. *Appl. Environ. Microbiol.*, 43, 1011-1015.

Kuyucak, N. and B. Volesky (1988): Biosorbents for recovery of metals from industrial solutions. *Biotechnol. Lett.*, 10 (2), 137-142.

Kuyucak, N. and B. Volesky (1989). Accumulation of cobalt by marine alga. *Biotechnol. Bioengg.*, 33(7), 809-14.

Lenntech Water Treatment and Air Purification (2004): *Water Treatment* Published by Lenntech, Rotterdamseweg, Netherlands.

Lodi, A.; Solisio, C. Converti, A. and M.D. Borghi (1998): Cadmium, zinc, copper, silver and chromium (III) removal from wastewater by *Sphaleotilus natans*. *Bioprocess Eng.*, 19, 197-203.

Lu, A., Zhong, S., Chen, J., Shi, J., Tang, J. and X. Lu (2006): Removal of Cr(VI) and Cr(III) from aqueous solutions and industrial wastewaters by natural clino-pyrrhotite. *Environ. Science Technol.*, 40 (9), 3064-3069.

Macaskie, L.E. and A.C.R. Dean (1985): *Biotechnol. Lett.*, 7, pp. 457-462.

Nuhoglu, Y.; Malkoe, E.; Gurses, A. and N Canpolat (2002): The removal of Cu (II) from aqueous solutions by *Ulothei: zonate*. *Biores. Technol.*, 85, 331-333.

Paknikar, K.M.; Palnitkar, U.S.R. and P.R. Puranik (1993): Biosorption of metal from solution by micelial waste of penicillium chrysogenum. Biohydrometallurgical Technologies. Ed. by A.E. Torma, M.L. Apel and C.L. Brierlay, *The Mineral, Metal and Materials Society*, 229-235.

Passow, P.J.; Young, K. and C.A. Sterling (1961): Effect of Heavy metal pollution on plants. *App. Sci. Publishers*, London, 11, 213-279.

Remacle, J. (1990): The cell wall and heavy metals. In B. Volesky, *Biosorption of Heavy Metals*, CRC Press, Boca Raton, Florida. 83-92.

Selatnia, A.; Bakhti, M.Z.; Madani, A.; Kertous, L. and Y. Mansouri (2004): Biosorption of Cd (II) from aqueous solution by a NaOH-treated bacterial dead *Streptomyces rimosus* biomass. *Hydrometallurgy*, 75, 11-24.

Shumate S.E. II, Strandberg, G.W. and J.R. Parrott Jr. (1978): Biological removal of metal ions from aqueous process streams. *Biotech. Bioeng. Symp.*, 8, 13-20.

Shumate, S.E. and G.W. Strandberg (1985): Accumulation of metals by microbial cells. In: Moo Young, M., Robinson, C.N., Howell, J.A. (Eds). *Comprehensive Biotechnology*. Pergamon Press, New York. 4, 235.

Stephengen, T. and J.N. Lester (1987): Heavy metals in wastewater and sludge Treatment Processes. *Sources, Analysis and Legislation*, CRC Press, Boca Raton, Florida, 31-64.

Stratton, G.W. (1987): *Review in Environmental Toxicology* (ed. Hodgson, E.), Elsevier, Amsterdam, 85-94.

Suman, S. and N.R. Bishnoi (2006): M.Tech dissertation work, Department of Energy and Environment Sciences, GJUS&T, Hisar.

Ting, V.P. (1988): Lawson, F. and Prince, I.G., *Biotechnol. Bioeng.*, 34, 990–999.

Tobin, J.M. Cooper, D.G. and R.J. Neufeld (1984): Uptake of metal ions by Rhizoprrs arrhizuz biomass. *Appl. Environ. Microbiol.*, 47, 821-824.

Trujillo, E.M. Sprinti, M. and H. Zhuang (1995): A.K. Sengupta (ed.), *Ion Exchange Technology: Advances in Pollution Control*, Technomic Publishing Company Inc., Pennsylvania, 225.

Tsezos, M. and Volesky, B. (1982): *Biotechnol. Bioeng.*, 24, 385-401.

Vasudeven, P.; Padmavathy, V.; Tiwari, N. and S.C. Dhingra (2001): Biosorption of Heavy metals ions. *J. Sci. Ind. Res.*, 60, 112-120.

Visoottiviseth, P. and N. Panviroj (2001): Selection of fungi capable of removing toxic arsenic compounds from liquid medium. *Science Asia*, 27, 083-092.

Volesky, B. (1990): Removal and recovery of heavy metals by biosorption. In Volesky, B. (ed.) *Biosorption of Heavy Metals*. CRC Press, Boca Raton, Florida, 7-43.

Volesky, B. and Z.R. Holan (1995): Biosorption of heavy-metals, *Biotechnol. Prog.*, 11, 235-250

Volesky, B. (1986): Biosorbent materials. *Biotechnol. Bioeng. Symp.*, 16, 121-126.

Volesky, B. (1990): Biosorption and biosorbents. In Volesky, B. (ed.) *Biosorption of Heavy Metals*. Florida: CRC Press.

Volesky, B. (1990): Biosorption by Fungal biomass, in Volesky, B., (eds.), *Biosorption of Heavy Metals*, CRC Press, Inc., Boca Raton, FL, 139-172.

Volesky, B. (1994): Advances in biosorption of metals: Selection of biomass types. *FEMS Microbial. Rev.*, 14, 291-302.

Volesky, B. and Z.R. Holan (1995): *Biotechnol. Prog.*, 11, 235-250.

Yu, Q. and P. Kaewsarn (1999): Binary adsorption of copper (II) and cadmium (II) from aqueous solutions by biomass of marine alga Durvillaea potatorum. *Sep. Sci. Technol.*, 34(8),1595-1605.

Zhou, J.L. and R.J. Kiff (1991): The uptake of copper from aqueous solution by immobilized fungal biomass. *J. Chem. Technol. Biotechnol.*, 52, 317-330.

18

Media and Environmentalism

Coverage, Claims-Making and Framing of Environmental Issues

D.S. Poornananda and *K.G. Vasuki*

Introduction

For a problem to enter into the arena of public discourse or become part of the political process media coverage is crucial. The mass media have been attributed a major role as a forum for public debate in general, where various social groups, institutions, and ideologies struggle over the definition and construction of social reality (Guruvitch & Levy, 1985: 19). Hall (1979) suggests that the mass media serve three major functions in our society. First, the media selectively construct social knowledge. Second, the mass media not only reflect diverse aspects of our society, but also selectively rank and arrange social knowledge, offering preferred meanings and interpretations. In other words, the mass media provide tools of interpretation, or frames. Third, through the process of argument, exchange, debate, consultation and speculation, the mass media lead social consensus on a specific social issue. Although news media try to achieve principles of objectivity, neutrality, impartiality, and balance in reporting, some events, particularly risk issues, are inherently dramatic, sensational and thus newsworthy (Molotch & Lester, 1974).

The mass media are often held-up as the cause for the higher awareness of environmental issues (Mazur, 1985). People had been aware of the environmental deterioration in a limited localised context for a long time, but in the recent past the media have played an important role in broadening that awareness and transforming many discrete problems into a major public issue. What had previously been perceived as individual difficulties were redefined as part of a more general problem of 'the environment'.

A widespread recognition of the environment as an issue by the Western media was noticed in the early 1970s. When the Earth Day was celebrated in 1970, the mass media afforded the environmental issue 'instant and widespread recognition' (Gottlieb, 1993). The interpretation of the Earth Day as 'Day one' of the new environmentalism was widely embraced by the media. The environment moved from being a fringe issue to an issue of paramount concern to the public. By the time the UN Conference on Human Environment was held in 1972 at Stockholm there was considerable rise in the press coverage of the environmental issues with some major newspapers employing journalists on 'environmental beat'. Mass media coverage led to a rise in public awareness about the environment (Hannigan, 1995).

The Indian media largely ignored environmentalism until the 1980s. Very few correspondents of the Indian newspapers went to cover the Stockholm Conference in 1972. The environmental concern was dismissed as a Western fad irrelevant to the Third World countries (Guha, 1992). The attitude of the press was in line with Prime Minister Indira Gandhi's defence of development over environment at the Conference.

The developing countries were initially sceptical if not hostile to environmentalism. During the Stockholm Conference representatives of poor countries observed that their problem was too little rather than too much industry, and that some smoke in the air would be a small price to pay for lifting the multitudes from their gross deprivation. The Government of India and Brazil were vocal in their defence of 'development over the environment.' Former Indian Prime Minister Indira Gandhi delivered a stirring speech arguing that if pollution was the price of progress, her people wanted more of it. The conference was termed as a 'sinister conspiracy' to prevent the developing world from developing further (Guha, 2000). There was a widespread belief that environmentalism was a product of the move towards 'post-materialist' values among the populations of North America and Western Europe. Whenever environmental questions were raised they were brushed aside as 'bourgeois deviations'. The assumption was that poor societies had to become prosperous first before they could find green movements in their midst. Guha (2000) has disputed the view that the societies of the Third World are too poor to be green. He has shown that vibrant and growing environmental constituency exists in societies such as Brazil, India and Thailand, where a large majority of the people are still poor (Guha, 2000).

Because the mainstream media did not cover environmental struggles taking place in places far away from big cities it was assumed that environmental concern was lacking among the people. The urban-centred development-obsessed media did not take notice of such grassroots movements. The environment as an issue figured marginally in the psyche of Indian journalists (Chapman *et al.*, 1997). Nehru's project of building a modern and industrial nation was dear to many publishers and journalists. For them India was too underdeveloped to worry about environmental pollution (D'Monte, 2005).

The Bhopal Gas Disaster of December 1984 proved to be the turning point in environmental news coverage (Akhileshwari, 1989) in India as also environmental activism. The decade witnessed many environment-related events that attracted the attention of the press. It was only after this disaster that newspapers began paying attention to the seriousness of the environmental pollution. The magnitude of the disaster shook many newspapers out of their indifference to environmental problems (Krishnatray, 1989). Hundreds of correspondents descended on Bhopal to cover the worst ever-industrial disaster. The disaster continued to make news for years as the victims launched a long struggle for medical treatment, compensation and rehabilitation. Guha (1992) has observed that it was only in the 1980s that Indian newspapers took note of ecological degradation in different parts of India, and the human suffering that followed in its wake.

By the beginning of the 1990s, the newspapers had realised that environment was one of the issues that the nation had to address. When the Earth Summit was held in Rio de Janeiro in 1992, a large number of Indian media persons were sent to cover it. Two decades after the Stockholm Conference, the Indian media began realising that a global policy was needed to address environmental problems and that they were not the concerns of people in the developed countries alone. The environmental movement spread to many parts of India. Some of the environmental groups had achieved small victories with some controversial projects being shelved. As the environmental movement expanded, the media began covering protests in different parts of the country. By the late 1980s, the environment became a broad and definable area of public concern, which was recognisable in the same way that disparate events are recognised as relevant to the 'economy' or 'education'.

However, there are still many media persons in India who dismiss environmentalism as a fringe concern. The environment has never been a major issue in the electoral politics. Unlike some European countries (Austria, Belgium, Luxembourg, the Netherlands, Germany, Sweden and Switzerland) where there are active green parties with their representatives in national legislatures and in the European Parliament. The environment has never been on the agenda of political parties in India. There is no example of a politician winning an election either to the Parliament or a State legislature on environmental issues.[1] Evidence from the past suggests that attempts to involve politicians in the environmental problems affecting their voters have failed. The political parties have viewed the environmental question largely in development *vs.* environment frame, which is evident in their economic policy statements. Gadgil and Guha (1995) have found that the interest of politicians in environmental issues is, by and large, inversely proportional to the size of their constituency. They say, "In our experience, Members of Parliament appear to care the least, members of the State legislatures a little more, members of district councils a little more still, and members of *mandal panchayats* emphatically the most" (p. 190). What is ironical is that those who have greater interest in environment are not involved in the decision making process. In the absence of political parties with green agenda, the environmental issues had to be raised by communities of affected people and environmental groups.[2] Though environmentalism in India has not succeeded in effectively influencing policy shifts in a big way, it has played an important role in placing the environmental issues on the agenda of the public and the media (Chapman *et al.*, 1997).

Studies have shown that the press has rarely taken initiative in reporting environmental issues (Kumar, 1996) because of which the 'issue entrepreneurs' (Schoenfeld *et al.*, 1979) and traditional networks have played an important role in bringing press attention to the issues. Issue entrepreneurs are the public interest groups and public-spirited individuals who discover issues and attempt to get the public involved address those issues. The traditional networks such as village and tribes are used to highlight an issue. This is evident in the environmental struggles in Madhya Pradesh, Uttar Pradesh, Chhattisgarh, Rajasthan, Karnataka and Maharashtra. These struggles include many forms of collective action. Gadgil and Guha (1995) have argued that these forms of protest get press attention as they provide dramatic news even though the issues are not comprehensively covered. Getting an issue reported in the media involves a process in which many actors are involved.

This chapter examines the coverage given to environmental news in daily newspapers across time, representation of claims makers in the news stories and framing of environmental news.

Coverage of Environmental News

A content analysis of four major newspapers[3], *The Hindu*, *The Times of India*, *The Indian Express* and the *Deccan Herald*, showed that the coverage of environment as an issue increased between 1984 and 2008.[4] The coverage which was only 0.77 per cent in 1984 went-up to 2.07 per cent in 1992 (Fig. 18.1).

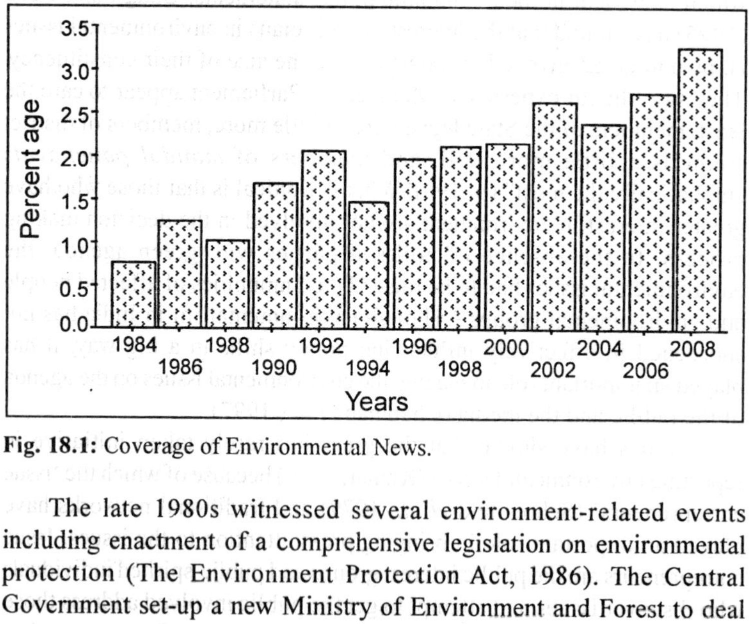

Fig. 18.1: Coverage of Environmental News.

The late 1980s witnessed several environment-related events including enactment of a comprehensive legislation on environmental protection (The Environment Protection Act, 1986). The Central Government set-up a new Ministry of Environment and Forest to deal matters related to environment. Bhopal Gas Tragedy in 1984 and the Chernobyl accident in 1986 had been widely reported in the media. Environmental movement gathered momentum in the late 1980s as environmental organisations sprang-up in different parts of India (Mohan, 2007). Environmental coverage increased in volume after the year 2000. A programme of establishing special economic zones (SEZs) to promote faster growth in exports came under severe criticism by environmental groups. Protests against environmental consequences of special economic zones began even in those states where environmental movement had not been active.

The content analysis has shown that no single problem dominated environmental news coverage. The issues covered seem to go through the 'issue attention cycle' (Downs, 1972). Deforestation has received significantly higher coverage throughout the period compared to the other environmental issues. Air pollution and water pollution received higher coverage between 1984 and 1992. There was a significant increase in the coverage of nuclear hazard from 1986 and a decline from 1994. The Chernobyl disaster seems to have greatly contributed to the dramatic increase in the coverage given to the environment in 1986. The effect of the disaster on environmental coverage was not only witnessed in India but also in many other countries. Suhonen (1993) had found that environmental coverage reached a peak in the Finnish Press after the Chernobyl disaster. Gooch (1996) also reported a similar trend in the Baltic Press. There were nation-wide protests against the construction of nuclear power plants in India throughout the late-1980s. The environmental consequences of big dams appeared more frequently in the newspapers from the year 1994. Although news about global warming appeared in 1988 a significant increase in its coverage was found only in the year 1998 and the issue continued to receive greater coverage in the following years (Fig. 18.2).

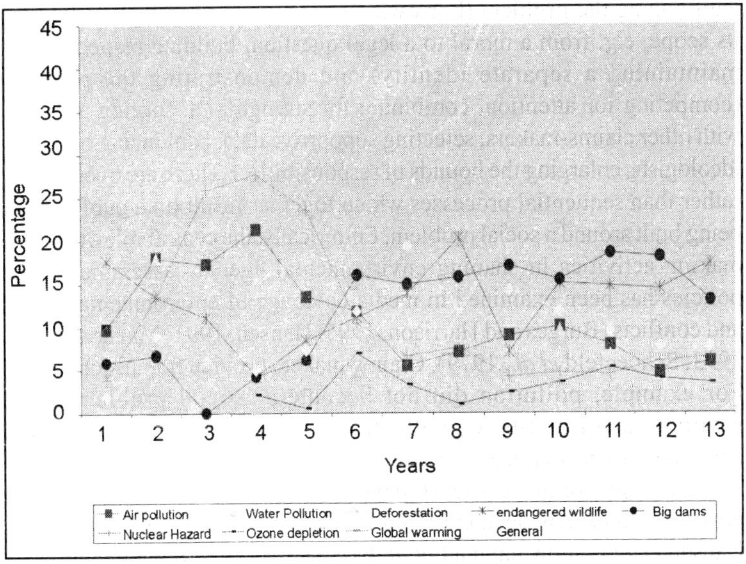

Fig. 18.2: Coverage of Environmental Issues.

It is interesting that news about environment in general was accorded higher coverage than some of the environmental issues. These were the items that reported about environmental destruction in general without focusing on a specific problem. Writing about the environment in general involves no controversies. News stories on specific issues require greater effort in understanding and explaining the complexities involved.

Claims-making and the Coverage

The media provides a series of arenas in which symbolic contests are carried out among competing sponsors of meaning. This symbolic contest has two basic issues: who gains access to media representation and what themes emerge in the media treatment of an issue. Claims-makers are those who gain media representation. The idea of the claims-maker is being operationally defined as the quoted source. Environmental problems by and large depend for their public visibility on complex processes of claims-making activity. As initially conceptualized by Spector and Kitsuse (1977) claims are complaints about social conditions which members of a group perceive to be offensive and undesirable. Claims-making process involves animating the problem (establishing rights, developing constituencies, funnelling advice and imparting skills and information); legitimizing the problem (borrowing expertise and prestige, redefining its scope, e.g. from a moral to a legal question, building respectability, maintaining a separate identity) and demonstrating the problem (competing for attention, combining for strength, i.e. forging alliances with other claims-makers, selecting supportive data, convincing opposing ideologists, enlarging the bounds of responsibility). These are overlapping rather than sequential processes which together result on a public arena being built around a social problem. Empirically, the central role of claims-making activities in shaping environmental agenda, assessments and policies has been examined in media coverage of environmental issues and conflicts (Burges and Harrison, 1993; Hansen, 1991; Mazur and Lee, 1993; Schoenfeld *et al.,* 1979). Claims-makers provide frames for stories. For example, pollution did not become a 'social problem' until environmental activists were able to convince others to show concern about conditions that had actually existed for some time.

The nature of the relationship between the media and environmental pressure groups has been explored by Cottle (1993), Anderson (1993), Hansen (1993) and Chapman *et al.* (1997). It is only in the recent years that environmental claims-makers have taken the form of professional social movements with paid administrative and research staffs, sophisticated fund-raising programmes and strong institutionalized links. In India, a majority of the environmental groups lack such organisational structures. Most of their claims-making activities are confined to the districts or states from where they operate. As a result, it is hard for them to get space and time in the national media. They attract media attention only when they create events close to media centres (Chapman *et al.*, 1997). Since officials and scientists are easily accessible to the media their views get reported more often than those of the smaller environmental groups.

With regard to who largely influence the frames newspapers use for environmental issues it was found that officials and scientists dominated environmental news converge as sources for several years. Officials accounted for nearly fifty per cent of the sources quoted in the environmental stories in the year 1984. While the percentage of officials and scientists declined over the years the other sources increased their presence in the newspapers (Fig. 18.3).

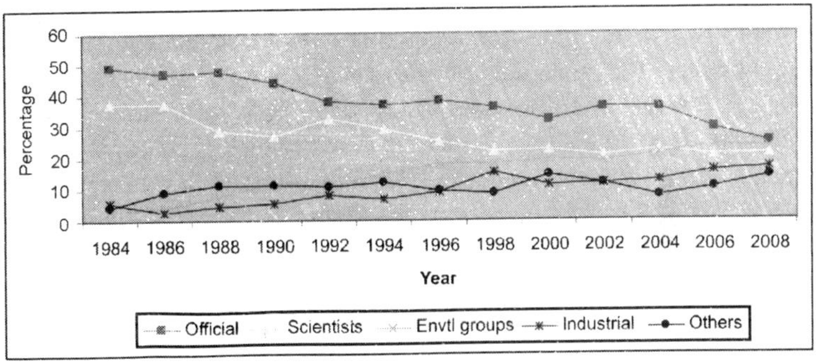

Fig. 18.3: Sources of Environmental News.

Environmental groups, industrial and other sources (politicians, victims and unidentified persons) have increased their presence in the newspapers. Although official sources and scientists continue to be major sources their influence as claims-makers seems to have declined. Increased media representation gained by the environmental groups was visible. The claims-making activities of the environmental groups seem to have increased after the 1990s. For many years sources other than official and scientific sources were always looked at with scepticism (D'Monte, 2005).

That the newspapers gave credence to officials and scientists as sources was also evident in the fact that they were quoted as single sources in the news stories. Environmental groups were rarely quoted as single sources. They were often quoted along with official and scientific sources, sometimes with industrial sources. Politicians were not frequently quoted as sources. The view that environmental pollution is a small price to pay for development is still dominant among mainstream politicians (Gadgil & Guha, 1995). While they show concern for the environment, in general they do not take pro-environment stand when it comes to specific environmental issues.

Studies suggest that sources exercise substantial control over story frames (Dunwoody & Griffin, 1993; Gandy, 1989; Einsiedel, 1988; Greenberg *et al.*, 1989; Wang, 1988; Hansen, 1991; Nohrstedt, 1991; Anderson, 1993; Einsiedel & Coughlan, 1993; Gooch, 1996) and that credibility is a crucial factor governing source-media relations. If the environmental groups are to attract favourable media coverage they must be viewed as legitimate and authoritative. The low profile of environmental groups as primary definers in actual media coverage indicates that it is to the fora of 'public authorities' and 'science' that journalists turn for validation of such claims. Consequently, both continued media coverage and the wider elaboration of certain environmental problems hinge crucially on the extent to which they become part of, and articulated through, the agendas of these other established fora (Hansen, 1991). The claims of the pressure groups are presented along with the sources that have "obvious credentials and well-established credibility" (Goodell, 1986). Hall *et al.* (1978) argue that powerful 'accredited' sources, such as government departments, enjoy privileged access to the media. They command greater access to the media by virtue of their claims to expert knowledge, their powerful position in society, or their representative status. Thus, the powerful sources become over-accessed by the media. While information given by officials and experts is usually published without responses from the environmentalists, the views of the environmentalists were seldom carried without the reactions of the officials or experts. That the journalists doubted the credibility of non-authoritative sources was evident in how they were quoted. While officials 'said', 'explained', 'clarified' and 'reiterated' environmental groups 'claimed', 'argued', 'alleged', 'charged' and 'contented' were often used whenever environmental groups were quoted. Use of such terms suggests what is authentic and what is questionable.

In the year 1984, environmental groups accounted for only three per cent of the sources quoted in the news stories. By the year 2006 as much as 23.75 per cent of the sources quoted were environmental groups. The environmental groups have not only grown in number but also in their organizational capacities. Some of the groups have units that plan media strategies to gain positive coverage. There is a significant positive correlation between the quantity of coverage of environmental issues in the newspapers and the use of environmental groups as sources. Over the years environmental groups have increased their representation in the newspapers. They address media conferences, issue press statements, publish status reports, hold demonstrations and conduct seminars. A perception that is very dominant among the media is that if they frequently use environmental groups as sources they may move towards advocating environmental causes. Advocacy[5] with regard to environmental issues is not a favoured practice as journalists see themselves as neutral and ironic voice, willing to produce news only if the scientific evidence concerning environmental problems is sufficiently powerful and unambiguous. Since, there are very few media investigations of environmental issues, the responsibility has shifted to the environmental groups to dig out information about environmental destruction. Many of the issues would never have been reported but for the efforts of environmental groups. That the environmental groups are more frequently represented in the recent years is an indication of their importance as claims-makers.

Framing of Environmental Issues

Media Frame is a concept adapted by several media sociologists in the late 1970s and early 1980s (Getlin, 1980; Tuchman, 1978) from Erving Goffman's work on small group interaction. Since, the process of news production involves the mechanism of how mass media select and organize the reality, the concept of frame is important in investigating how media cover environmental issues. Frames, like news angles, are organizing devices that help both the journalist and the public make sense of issues and events and thereby inject them with meaning. In short, they furnish an answer to the question 'what is it that's going on here?' (Benford, 1993: 678). When expressed over duration of time, frames are known as 'story lines' (Gamson and Wolfsfeld, 1993: 118). The process of selection, which is the central concept in media frames, delimits the scope of a news story. In addition, the same elements of news may tell different stories depending on the way of organizing. According to Entman (1993), framing involves selection and salience. Thus, to frame is to select some aspects of a perceived reality and make them more salient. Frames are manifested by the presence or absence of certain key words, stock phrases, stereotyped images, sources of information, and sentences that provide thematically reinforcing clusters of facts or judgements (Entman, 1993: 52).

Even when the details of an event are not disputed the event can be framed in a number of different ways. Both claims-makers and their opponents routinely compete to promote their favoured frames to journalists as well as to potential supporters. At the same time, news workers forge their own frames largely for reason of efficiency and story suitability. Gamson and Wolfsfeld (1993) depict the interaction between the movements and the media as a subtle 'contest over meaning' in which sources attempt to 'sell' their preferred images, argument and story lines to journalists and editors who, more often than not, prefer to maintain and reproduce the dominant mainstream frames and cultural codes.

The sample news stories on environmental issues from 1984 to 2008 were examined to understand frames.[6] Frequently used words were identified and then interpreted as frames. The most dominant frame found was the 'event orientation' frame. Event orientation allows news sources to control the establishment of story frames and absolves journalists from attending to the bigger environmental picture. When the rising waters of the Narmada dam submerged tribal hamlets in the year 1994, the issue was framed as 'drowning' and 'rescue' operation. The larger issue of destruction, displacement and rehabilitation was ignored as the newspapers relied heavily on official sources.

Event orientation was not confined to disasters alone, but also spread to slow onset environmental hazards like global warming, ozone depletion, acid rain and so on. In order to fit these latter phenomena into news agenda, newspapers framed them as the recent outcomes of an event rather than the inevitable outcome of a series of political and societal decisions. While event-centred coverage has the advantage of raising public awareness of otherwise ignored environmental topics, it also has a negative side. By focusing on discrete events rather than on the contexts in which they occurred, the newspapers tend to give news consumers the impression that individuals or errant corporations rather than institutional politics and social developments were responsible for those events.

'Development *vs.* Environment' frame was another frame that was noticed during the period. This frame was found more often from 1984 to 1996 and less often after 1998. The issue of environment was presented as an issue between proponents of development and opponents of development.

The coverage of issues was often characterised by conflict between individuals or between institutions and individuals. It was often reduced to "a conflict of authorities and even personalities quoted in the media." Unable to explain the scientific and political complexities associated with a given environmental problem and similarly unable to investigate the inter-correlations between issues, the environment became a personality conflict. The entire issue of the Narmada Project was presented as a war between Medha Patkar, the leader of the Narmada Bachao Andolan (Save Narmada Movement) and the Chief Minister of Gujarat State.

Furthermore, newspaper stories on environmental hazard events favoured monocausal frames rather than frames involving long and complex causal networks. For example, when the Cauvery river in Karnataka State almost dried up in the summer of 2004 it was attributed to a simple natural phenomenon—drought conditions—rather than to a combination of factors including destruction of forests and unregulated drawing of huge quantity of water for various purposes upstream. Monocausal frames appeared more often in stories that had officials as single sources. This monocausal framing occurs because newspapers are reluctant to implicate several powerful institutional actors—the state bureaucracy, timber contractors and the industry (Prasad, 2007).

Conclusion

Newspapers that rejected environmentalism as a Western fad in the 1970s began to see pollution incidents as part of a more general problem of 'the environment' by the 1990s. A significant increase in the coverage of environmental news was noticed in the year 1986. The volume of coverage increased in the next two decades. Of the major environmental issues deforestation received the highest coverage. Global warming as an issue found significant space in newspapers from 2004. Officials and scientists dominated the news on environmental issues as sources. Although environmental groups are more frequently used as sources in the recent years officials still play a key role in influencing the frames of environmental news. A significant positive correlation exists between the volume of coverage of environmental issues and the use of environmental groups as sources. Environmental issues are often framed as events and conflicts without providing depth. There is also a tendency among the newspapers to equate a movement with the personality of a leader and present an issue as a conflict between individuals. A more comprehensive coverage could be possible if there is a balanced use of sources.

Notes

1. Shivaram Karanth, a well-known literary giant and environmentalist, lost the elections in Karwar Parliamentary constituency in 1989 in Karnataka State. Karanth had been a vociferous anti-nuclear campaigner and had drawn huge crowds during the protest rallies. Despite overwhelming support for the movement against the nuclear plant voters did not see the issue as an electoral issue.
2. Any association/organization/community group that has the primary objective of mobilizing public opinion and resisting any policy/plan/project harmful to the environment is considered an environmental group for the purpose of analysis here. The association may have been formed by affected persons of by people with public concern. The groups here include even those groups that have no formal organizational structures.
3. The four dailies are among the newspapers that have had considerable influence on policy decisions and public opinion in India (Jeffrey, 2000).
4. Three constructed weeks (Budd *et al.*, 1967) constituted the sample for each year. A total of 1092 issues of the four newspapers formed the sample (21 issues × 4 dailies × 13 years = 1092). Only the contents appearing in the main sections of the sampled issues were analysed. All supplements issued with the main sections of the newspapers were excluded.
5. Detjen (1991) has argued that though the media coverage of environmental issues is often lacking, advocacy journalism is not an answer. He believes that "advocacy journalism, if it means one-sided and unfair reporting, is misguided and in the long run counter-productive. If major newspapers, magazines and broadcast stations adopt an advocacy philosophy, the media will be treading on dangerous ground that could alienate readers and viewers and cause them to stop trusting the media. Journalists who have spent their careers establishing reputations for fairness and accuracy could suddenly find their credibility evaporating" (p. 94). He prefers traditional approaches of media—such as investigative reporting, agenda setting and mass education—to advocacy.
6. Semetko and Valkenburg (2000) assert that there are two possible ways of content analyzing frames in the news: inductive and deductive. The inductive approach focuses on analyzing a news story without any concrete pre-conceptions of these frames. On the other hand, the deductive approach is related to predefining certain frames as content analytic variables to verify the extent to which these frames occur in the news coverage. The deductive approach requires a clear idea of the kinds of frames likely to be in the news, because the frames that are not defined can be overlooked in the process of content analysis. A number of studies have identified the importance of certain frames in news coverage by focusing on their consequences for the public's interpretation of the events and issues (i.e. Graber, 1988; Hannah *et al.*, 2006, Iyengar & Simon, 1993). The current study involves inductive approach to content analysis.

References

Akhileshwari, R. (1989). Environment and the media. *Vidura*, 26(3), 11-13.

Anderson, A. (1993). Source media relations: The production of the environmental agenda. In A. Hansen (Ed.), *The Mass Media and Environmental Issues* (pp. 51-68). London: Leicester University Press.

Beder, S. (1998). *Global Spin: The Corporate Assault on Environmentalism.* Vermont: Chelsea Green Publishing Company.

Budd, R.W., Thorp, R.K., and Donohew, L. (1967). *Content Analysis of Communications*. New York: MacMillan Co. (P) Ltd.

Chapman, G., Kumar, K., Fraser, C., and Gaber, I. (1997). *Environmentalism and the Mass media: The North-South divide*, London: Routledge.

Cottle, S. (1993). Mediating the environment. In A. Hansen (Ed.), *The Mass Media and Environmental Issues* (pp. 134-149). London: Leicester University Press.

D'Monte, D. (2005). The greening of India scribes. In N. Rajan (Ed)., *Practicing Journalism: Values, Constraints, Implication* (pp. 89-102). New Delhi: Sage Publications.

Detjen, J. (1991). The traditionalist's tools (And a fistful of new ones). In C.L. LaMay and E.E. Dennis (Eds.), *Media and the Environment* (pp. 91-101). Washington, DC: Island Press.

Dunwoody, S. and Griffin, R.J. (1993). Journalistic strategies for reporting long-term environmental issues: A case study of three superfund sites. In A. Hansen (Ed.), *The Mass Media and Environmental Issues* (pp. 22-50). London: Leicester University Press.

Dunwoody, S. (1986). The scientist as source. In S.M. Friedman, S. Dunwoody and C.L. Rogers. (Eds.). *Scientists and Journalists* (pp. 3-16). New York: Free Press.

Einsiedel, E., and Coughlan, E. (1993). The Canadian press and the environment: Reconstructing a social reality. In A. Hansen (Ed.), *The Mass Media and Environmental Issues* (pp. 134-149). London: Leicester University Press.

Entman, R.M. (1993). Framing: toward clarification of a fractured paradigm. *Journal of Communication*, 43(4), 55.

Gadgil, M., and Guha, R. (1992). *The Fissured Land: An Ecological History of India*. New Delhi: Oxford University Press.

Gadgil, M., and Guha, R. (1995). *Ecology and Equity*. New Delhi: Penguin.

Gamson, W., Modigliani, A. (1989). Media discourse and public opinion on nuclear power: A constructionist approach. *American Journal of Sociology*, 95 (1), 1-37.

Gans, H.J. (1979). *Deciding what is news*: A study of CBS evening news, NBC nightly news, Newsweek and Time. New York: Pantheon Books.

Gitlin, T. (1980). *The Whole World is Watching*. Berkeley: University of California Press.

Gokhale, V. (1991). Indian media's response to global warming. http://www.veenago.com/nonfiction/Indian_Media_Envrio_Issues.pdf

Gooch, G.D. (1996). The Baltic Press and the environment: A study of the coverage of environmental problems in Estonian and Latvian newspapers 1992-93. *Geoforum*, 26(4), 429-443.

Gotlieb, R. (1993). *Framing the Spring: The Transformation of the American Environmental Movement*. Washington DC: Island Press.

Graber, D. (1988). *Processing the News: How people tame the information tide* (2nd ed.). New York: Longman.

Greenberg, M.R., Sachman, D.B., Sandman, P.M., Salomone, K.L. (1989). Risk, drama and geography in coverage of environmental risk by network TV. *Journalism Quarterly*, 66 (2), 267-76.

Griffin, R.J. (1995). Impacts of information subsidies and community structure on local press coverage of environmental contamination. *Journalism and Mass Communication Quarterly*, 72 (2), 271-84.

Guha, R. (1992). Coming of age. *Critique*, 1 (5), 23-24.

Guha, R. (2000). *Environmentalism: A Global History*. New Delhi: Oxford University Press.

Guruvitch, M. Levy, M. (1985). Introduction. In J.A. Anderson (Ed.), *Mass Communication Review Yearbook 5*. Beverly Hills: Sage Publications.

Hall, S., Critcher, C., Jefferson, T., Clarke, J., Roberts, B. (1978). *Policing the Crisis: Mugging, the State, and Law and Order*. London: MacMillan Co. (P) Ltd.

Hannah, G., Cafferty, T. (2006). Attribute and Responsibility Framing Effects in Television News. *Journal of Applied Social Psychology*, 36 (12), 2993-3014.

Hannigan, J.A. (1995). *Environmental Sociology: A Social Constructionist Perspective*. London: Routledge Publications.

Hansen, A. (1990). Socio-political values underlying media coverage of the environment. *Media Development*, 37 (2), 4-6.

Hansen, A. (1991). Television news coverage of environmental issues. A haher presented at the seminar on "Environment and development issues: What sort of television?" Falmer: Unversity of Sussex.

Hansen, A. (1991). The media and the social construction of the environment. *Media, Culure and Society*, 13 (4), 451-462.

Hansen, A. (1993). Greenpeace and press coverage of environmental issues. In A. Hansen (Ed.), *The Mass Media and Environmental Issues* (pp. 150-178). London: Leicester University Press.

Herman, E.S. and Chomsky, N. (1988). *Manufacturing Consent: The Political Economy of the Mass Media*. London: Vintage.

Hungerford, S.E., and Lemert, J.B. (1973). Covering the environment: A new 'Afghanistanism'? *Journalism Quarterly*, 50(3), 475-482.

Iyengar, S. and Simon, A. (1993). News coverage of the Gulf crisis and public opinion: A study of agenda setting, priming, and framing. *Communication Research*, 20, 365-383.

Jeffrey, R. (2000). *India's Newspaper Revolution*. New Delhi: Oxford University Press.

Killingsworth, M.J. and Palmer, J.S. (1992). *Ecospeak: Rhetoric and Environmental Politics in America.* Carbondale, IL: Southern Illinois University Press.

Krishnatray, P. (1989). Environmental Journalism. *Vidura*, 26 (3), 13-15.

Kumar, K.J. (1966). Mass media and environmental awareness: A research perspective. *Vritta Vidya*, April 1996, 11-13.

Lowe, P., and Morrison, D. (1984). Bad News or Good News: Environmental politics and the mass media. *The Sociological Review*. 32: 75-90.

Mazur, A. (1985). The mass media in environmental controversies. In A. Brannegan and S. Golderberg (Eds.), *Social Response to Technological Change* (pp. 135-151). Westport, CT: Greenwood Press.

McCombs, M. E. (1977). Newspapers *versus* television: Mass communication effects across time. In D.L. Shaw and M.E. McCombs (Eds.), *The Emergence of American Political Issues: The Agenda Setting Function of the Press.* (pp. 120-142). St. Paul: West Publishing Company.

McCombs, M.E. and Shaw, D.L. (1972). The agenda-setting function of mass media. *Public Opinion Quarterly*, 36, 176-187.

McCormick, J. (1991). A green world after the cold war? In C.L. LaMay and E.E. Dennis (Eds.). *Media and the Environment* (pp. 198-203). Washington, DC: Island Press.

Mohan, M. (2007). *Environmental NGOs: A Critical Perspective*. Mumbai: Manthan.

Molotch, H., and Lester, M. (1974). News as purposive behaviour: On the strategic use of routine events. *American Sociological Review*, 39(1), 101-112.

Prasad, A. (2007). Mediating the environment. In A. Sahu (Ed). *Environmentalism and Development in India* (pp. 57-69). New Delhi: Rawat Publications.

Semetko, H.A., and Valkenburg, P.M. (2000). Framing European politics: A content analysis of press and television news. *Journal of Communication*, 50(2), 93-109.

Sigal, L.V. (1973). *Reporters and Officials: The Organisation and Politics of Newsmaking*. Lexington: Heath.

Spector, M. and Kitsuse, J.I. (1977). *Constructing social problems*. Menlo Park, CA: Cummings.

Stocking, H; Leonard, L. (1990). The greening of the press. *Columbia Journalism Review*, 29, 37-44.

Trumbo, C. (1996), Constructing climate change: claims and frames in US news coverage of an environmental issue; *Public Understanding of Science*, 5, 269-283.

Tuchman, G. (1972). Objectivity as strategic ritual. An examination of newmen's notion of objectivity. *American Journal of Sociology*, 77 (4), 660-79.

Tuchman, G. (1973). Making news by doing work: routinising the unexpected. *American Journal of Sociology*, 79 (1), 110-131.

Valiverronen, E. (1992). *Environmental Controversies: The Role of Experts and Legitimation of Science in the debate on forest damages in Finland.* Paper presented to IAMCR Conference, August 16-21, Sao Paulo, Brazil.

Wiebe, C.D. (1973). Mass media and man's relationship to his environment. *Journalism Quarterly*, 50 (3), 427-432.

Wilkins, L. and Patterson, P. (1987). Risk analysis and construction of news. *Journal of Communication*, 37 (3), 80-92.

19

Business Approaches to Sustainable Consumption With Reference to Entrepreneurship Development and Innovation Perspective

Shrikrishna S. Mahajan

Introduction

The challenge of sustainable development is global phenomenon. Businesses can play vital role in fostering more sustainable levels and patterns of consumption, to meet this global challenge. The business has important opportunity to help consumers to choose and use their goods and services, which are sustainable. As a social responsibility of business on one hand and the corporate ethics (or commitment with stakeholders) on the other hand, business must create sustainable value for consumers and simultaneously they should respect environmental limits and common values. This chapter aims to discuss the business approaches to sustainable consumption in the context of climate change and also tries to cover the entrepreneurship development and innovation perspective of this issue. In the first section of this chapter, an attempt has been made to review the conceptual framework in respect of sustainable consumption, climate change, entrepreneurship development, innovation etc. In the second section, the business practices in terms of corporate social responsibility, corporate governance, professional ethics, environment management, environmental accounting etc. have been analyzed. The third section, comes up with the conclusion and suggestions to move forward for sustainable consumption.

The Statement of the Problem

Environmental problems like climate change should be conceptualized as problems of consumption and not only production pattern. The role of business in mainstreaming the sustainable consumption is significant. For this purpose, the business approaches to sustainable consumption may be categorized into three groups: (i) Innovation, (ii) Choice Influencing and (iii) Choice Editing.

The Objectives of the Study

The main objective is to explore the business approaches to sustainable consumption with reference to entrepreneurship development and innovation perspective. The specific objectives are as follows:

1. To discuss the business approaches to sustainable consumption in the context of climate change.
2. To study the entrepreneurship and innovation perspectives of the sustainable consumption.
3. To analyze the business practices in terms of corporate social responsibility, corporate sustainability, environment management etc.

I
CONCEPTUAL BACKDROP

Sustainable Development

"Sustainable Development is development that meets the need of the present without compromising the ability of future generations to meet their needs."[1] It is a process of change in which the exploitation of resources, the direction of investments, the orientation of technological development, and institutional change are all in harmony and enhance both current and future potential to meet human needs and aspirations. It balances the need for economic growth with environmental protection and social equity. Natural energy resources like coal, petroleum etc. should be prudently used and wastage should be avoided so that future generations can have these energy resources for their survival also. Four fundamental principles of sustainable development are:

1. Principle of Intergenerational Equity;

2. Principle of Sustainable Use;
3. Principle of Equitable Use or Intergenerational Equity; and
4. Principle of Integration.

Sustainable Consumption

The definition proposed by the 1994 Oslo Symposium on Sustainable Consumption defines it as "the use of services and related products which respond to basic needs and bring a better quality of life while minimizing the use of natural resources and toxic materials as well as emissions of waste and pollutants over the life cycle of the service or product so as not to jeopardise the needs of future generations."[2] Sustainable consumption is not always equivalent to liveable conditions. In the United States, for the most part, technology and capital are available to find or invent replacement resources and for people to find new occupations that are less destructive to the environment. The United States can start becoming a more sustainable society.[3] On the other hand, many developing countries do not have the ability to reduce their consumption of resources and are often subordinate to a more powerful government. Developing countries may receive necessary imports such as food from outside sources and furthermore may not be able to control the exploitation of their own natural resources by international companies.[4]

Climate Change

Global environmental problems like climate change should be conceptualized as problems of consumption and production patterns. Consumption rather than a production-based vision for environmentally sustainable economic growth would make the design and implementation of climate protection, as well as other environmental problems, more effective.[5]

Innovation

From the perspective of business, innovation is an essential driver of more sustainable consumption. The goal of sustainable innovation is to deliver high levels of emotional and functional value, while minimizing resource use and environmental impacts. Innovation is well-known core business function. Business innovation responds to the challenge of sustainable consumption through: eco-friendly measures, product innovation and design, production and supply chain management, and business model innovation.

Corporate Social Responsibility

Social responsibility of business means the obligation of business enterprises to make decision and follow lines of action, which are desirable in terms of the objectives, and values of society. Decisions may affect environment, consumers and the community. *Sakal,* a Marathi newspaper made appeal to the public for planting trees and launched the campaign for tree-plantation in Kolhapur city which got overwhelming response from all corners of the society.

Discussion

It is evident that there are massive and persistent inequalities between consumption in the developed countries of Europe and the US (or the north) and the developing countries (or the south). Per capita consumption rates in Germany, for example, are 15 times those in India.[6] Addressing these inequalities is a vital issue as well as a mechanism for achieving sustainability and preserving the natural environment. Business can play an important role in fostering sustainable consumption by delivering sustainable value to society and consumers, helping consumers to choose and use their goods and services sustainably, and promoting sustainable lifestyles that help to reduce overall consumption of materials and resources.

Climate Change and Consumption

The climate change can be seen in the form of unsustainable consumption as it represents one of the factors as global carbon dioxide emissions.

Table 19.1 shows that 10 countries have major contributions to world's total carbon dioxide emissions. It was 71.39 per cent in 1990, which reached to 73.83 per cent by 2003. Table specially indicates the increase in share of carbon dioxide emissions by US, China and India. The problem of climate change has aroused due to unsustainable consumption of resources like energy.

Table 19.2 reveals that the consumption of primary energy (oil equivalent) is distributed unevenly and inequitably among few countries.

Table 19.1: Share in Global Carbon Dioxide (CO_2) Emissions (%)

Countries	*1990*	*2003*
United States	23.04	23.06
China	10.41	14.07
Russia	9.67	6.38
Japan	4.54	4.79
India	2.63	4.07
Germany	4.24	3.35
Canada	2.19	2.39
United Kingdom	2.76	2.24
Italy	1.91	1.85
France	1.80	1.63
Rest of the World	38.61	36.17

Source: United States Department of Environment.

Table 19.2: Consumption of Primary Energy (Million of Tonnes of Oil Equivalent)

Country	*1990*	*2005*	*2030*	*Increase during 1990-2005*	*Increase during 2005-2030*
World	8755 (100%)	11429 (100%)	17721 (100%)	2674 (100%)	6292 (100%)
OECD	4518 (51.6%)	5542 (48.5%)	6800 (38.4%)	1024 (38.3%)	1258 (20%)
China	874 (10%)	1742 (15.2%)	3819 (21.6%)	868 (32.5%)	2077 (33%)
India	320 (3.7%)	537 (4.7%)	1299 (7.3%)	217 (8.1%)	762 (12.1%)
China+ India	1194 (13.6%)	2279 (19.9%)	5118 (28.9%)	1085 (40.6%)	2839 (45.1%)

Source: International Energy Agency (IEA), World Energy Outlook, 2007.

Sustainable Consumption

Global consumption patterns and trends are putting unsustainable and increasing stress on the earth's ecosystems, the supply of material resources needed for industrial growth, and human social systems and well-being. Thus in order to meet the personal ambitions of increasing affluence, particularly among the rapidly growing middle class of the developing world, development must not only be decarbonized, but also dematerialized. Consumption must become more sustainable.

The key issues regarding sustainable consumption for consideration by business are: (a) making it easy and affordable for the consumer to make sustainable purchasing decisions, as they increasingly report a willingness to do so; (b) making sustainable products available and comparable—without compromising on performance and at no extra costs; and (c) leveraging the unprecedented power of consumers to share information about companies, products and services via social networks, to promote sustainable products, usage, consumption and lifestyles.

Corporate Sustainability

Corporate sustainability is considered to be a business and investment strategy that seeks to use the best business practices to meet and balance the needs of current and future stakeholders.[7] Corporate sustainability encompasses strategies and practices that aim to meet the needs of stakeholders today while seeking to protect, support and enhance the human and natural resources that will be needed in the future.

Corporate Sustainability Performance and product differentiation and innovation are related. High growth firms have more opportunities to implement sustainability principles into their expanding operations. Low growth firms on the other hand have already made a sunk cost investment in existing production technologies and have less scope to pursue product differentiation or innovation strategies that incorporate sustainability principles.[8]

The global enterprises today enjoy unprecedented opportunities, but they also face some uncomfortable challenges. On the one hand, many companies are doing well, achieving new levels of reach, innovation and brand awareness. On the other, operating at global scale means they come face to face with the world's most pressing problems—including climate change, poverty, resource depletion, inequality, fast-growing populations in developing countries and ageing populations in developed ones.[9]

II
THE ROLE OF BUSINESS IN MAINSTREAMING SUSTAINABLE CONSUMPTION

The business approaches to sustainable consumption can be categorized into three broad categories as:

1. ***Innovation***: Business process for the development of new and improved products, services and business are shifting to incorporate provisions for maximizing societal values and minimizing environmental cost.
2. ***Choice Influencing***: The use of marketing and awareness-raising campaigns to enable and encourage consumers to choose and use products more efficiently and sustainably.

3. ***Choice Editing*:** The removal of "unsustainable" products and services from the marketplace in partnership with other actors in society.

Some efforts worldwide are being made one of them is of NEN. Nippon Ecology Network (NEN) in Japan focuses on ensuring safe and fairly priced foods and other goods. It is supplemented by the Green Purchasing Network bringing together over 1,000 companies, public authorities and citizen groups to promote the choice of sustainable goods and services across Japan. The NEN is women's initiative and has become a big movement in Japan.[10] But corporate sustainability efforts are criticized by some people. Market forces will never meaningfully reduce consumption. The myth that they can or will is an attempt to protect the ideology of growth against the threat posed by its increasingly evident consequences.[11]

Consumerism *vs.* Sustainable Consumption

Globalization through its consequences like individualism, unbridled freedom and consumerism is throwing big challenges over sustainability. An over-consumption leads to over-production which eventually leads to environmental problems like climate change. In religious or cultural context, people behave in such a manner that can be exploited as an opportunity by the businesses especially in developing countries like India. Diwali Offer, Vijayadashami Offer or Christmas Offer increase the level of consumption. Even people who have no purchasing power borrow money and celebrate festivals. Celebrating festival is not objectionable, but the way of celebration should be sustainable.

***Capitalistic Approach*:** The consumerism leads to excessive use of goods and services due to prestige for maintaining so called status and feudal tendency. It also leads to discrimination between different strata of the society and causes injustice to usc who have no purchasing power parity.

***'Use and Throw' Approach*:** The product design is made in such a way that people should adopt the 'Use and Throw' Approach.

***'Old is Gold' Approach*:** When the product is developed it has a provision for repairing and reusing the products during its useful life and even some cases this useful life can be increased by making renovation or repairs.

***Engineering Approach of SPC*:** The product or service should be designed in such a way that the consumers should be motivated for sustainable consumption which can be adopted as strategy for the Sustainable Production and Consumption (SPC).

III
CONCLUSION AND SUGGESTIONS

Conclusion

The business houses have challenges in this regard but they have options for change. There is need of dialogue with stakeholders and between businesses to define sustainable products and lifestyles and to formulate plans of actions to move forward for sustainable consumption in particular and sustainable development in general. As our world is facing the problems such as rising fuel prices, serious issues of hunger and poverty, scarcity of water, arable land and other natural resources, it needs to foster sustainable and responsible consumption from a business perspective. The entrepreneurs are the people who can systematically address this issue through technological and social innovations. It needs the combination of American approach to technical innovation, Japan's approach to social innovation and India's approach to knowledge society and Chinese approach to equitable distribution of resources. Lord Buddha's most practical approach of liberty, equality and fraternity would survive the world. The question before us is "how we can encourage the development of sustainable technologies to become commercially viable?" The appropriate technology is the answer for this question. To be able to lead sustainable lifestyle based on informed purchasing decisions and changes in behaviour, consumers need the support of all actors: business, government and civil society. Intensive effort is needed to strengthen and test methodologies for sustainable production and consumption.

Suggestion

Any recommendation or strategy to steer production and consumption in a sustainable direction must follow a multi-pronged approach since multiple forces and factors influence and govern the progress. Business, government and civil society must all transform with their different accountabilities and capacities, towards the single goal of sustainable human progress.

Notes

1. *Our Common Future,* Report of the World Commission on Environment and Development (The Brundtland Report, 1987).
2. Norwegian Ministry of the Environment (1994) *Oslo Roundtable on Sustainable Production and Consumption.*
3. Bauer, Joane (2006). Forging environmentalism, New York: M.E. Sharp.
4. Cobb, John (1992). *Sustainability*, New York: Orbis Books.
5. Sanwal, Mukul (2008). Sustainable development perspective of climate change, *Economic and Political Weekly*, April, 12, p. 49.
6. von Weizsacker, E., A.B. Lovins and L.H. Lovins (1997): "Factor four: Doubling wealth, halving resource Use", *Earthscan*, London quoted in Gopalan, Radha (2001), Sustainable food production and consumption agenda for action, *Economic and Political Weekly*, April, 14, p.1210.
7. Report of the United Nations World Commission on Environment and Development, 1987.
8. Tracy Artiach, Darren Lee, David Nelson and Julie Walker (2010). The determinants of corporate sustainability performance, *Accounting & Finance*, Vol. 50, p. 49.
9. Odd Gullberg (2006): *The Role of Business in Tomorrow's Society*, WBCSD, Geneva, Switzerland at www.wbcsd.org.
10. Gopalan, Radha (2001). Sustainable food production and consumption agenda for action, *Economic & Political Weekly*, April, 14, p.1216.
11. Michael Hannis (1998): *The Myth of Green Consumerism: Consumption, Community and Free Market*, Lancastar University MAVE Programme, http://www.lancs.ac.uk/users/philosophy/mave/mh_2.htm quoted in Gopalan, Radha (2001), Sustainable food production and consumption agenda for action, *Economic and Political Weekly*, April, 14, p.1211.

20

Greening the Marketing Mix

Rethinking Competition during Climate Change

Praveen Goyal and *Zillur Rahman*

Introduction

Recent studies show certain facts; those prove immense changes in the global climatic conditions. One of the major changes is global warming. Global warming, a significant part of climate change is mainly an outcome of accumulation of greenhouse gases (GHGs) in the environment. These gases are resultant of the unsustainable emission of the industrial countries. It is the dangerous threat for the survival of the human being. Earth's average surface temperature has increased by 0.74°C between 1906 and 2005. This change is leading to lower agriculture output, damaging droughts, floods and storms and increase in the sea level. In the present scenario, climate change is not only the matter of environmental concern, it is also becoming one of the biggest challenges for the development of the world.

Developing countries have only recently set out on the path of industrialization. That is the reason why their per capita emissions are still comparatively low. An analysis of India's emissions shows that its per capita emission of carbon is one-fourth of the global average. Even the top 10 per cent of urban population emits well below the global average per capita emission. But it does not mean that we are neither responsible nor we should concern for the changing climatic condition. Protection of environment is the primary responsibility of each and every individual.

Climate Change and Consumers

Government is running various awareness programmes to make people aware about the climate change and its harmful impacts. Eco-consciousness is increasing in India in the form of positive attitude for green attitude. Currently, middle and upper-class citizens are the most environmentally concerned segment of the Indian population. Apart from that, Government is also organizing various awareness programmes to make common man aware about the harmful impact of global warming and pollution. Resultant to these efforts, Green is becoming a big trend, invented by our need to become eco-friendly and to survive in harmony with our environment.

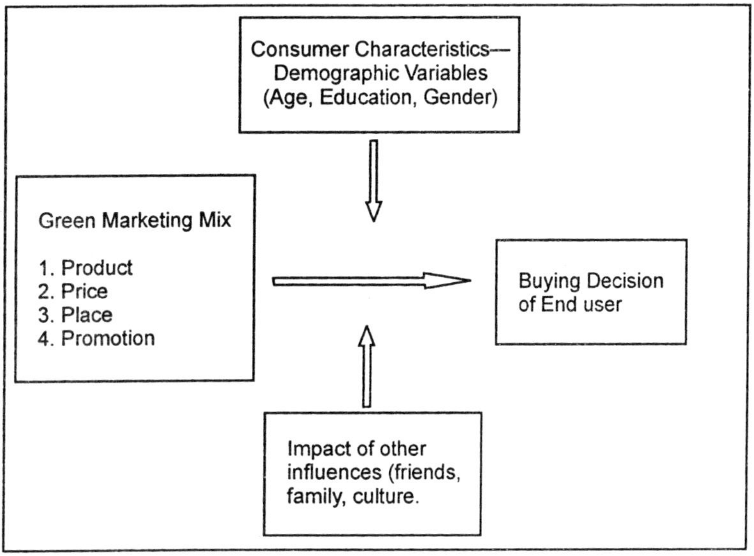

Fig. 20.1: Consumer Purchase Decision—Conceptual Model

Source: Wanninayake and Randiwela, 2008.

There are number of examples of companies those adopted the environment friendly practices to satisfy their consumers' need in better and efficient manner. Consumers' purchase decisions are affected by the marketing mix adopted by the companies (Fig. 20.1) and the various demographic variables like age, sex and education level. To remain in the competition, companies modify their marketing mix so that they can attract more customers and can enhance their market share.

Impact of Climate Change on Business

In this competitive era, to retain its position it is becoming important for an organization to cope with the changing expectations of all stakeholders. Government being an important stakeholder has formulated first National Action Plan on Climate Change on June 30, 2008. The main focus of this plan is on the functioning of the businesses in the nine energy intensive sectors. Business leaders increasingly recognise the signs of change and are preparing to take action on their own. 13th Annual Global CEO Survey done by PricewaterhouseCoopers in 2009 shows that 25 per cent CEOs consider climate change as a threat. In order to go green, a company's top management and employees must believe in the concept and commit themselves to implement it. Companies across the industries and across the border are facing increasing rigorous environmental regulation, as well as pressure from the stakeholders. The companies are compelled to work on triple bottom line concept to ensure the sustainable development of the economy and reduce the impact of climate change. Due to the significant increase in consciousness for green, companies are now facing pressure to make required changes in their production process and products from its stakeholders.

Companies are redesigning their promotion campaigns and focusing on the green benefits of their products. Every brand in world will have to become green, as the response to climate change is crucial for the sustainable development. This is largely green is already a force to be reckoned with in the West and because it is beginning to make business sense for Indians.

Changing Marketing Practices

Today every company in each industry is trying to integrate environmental concerns in their existing products as well as new product and service development. On this aspect, different types of information disclosures can be seen on website of every company like sustainability report, environmental initiatives, corporate social responsibility etc. Companies have realized that they have to provide information to their stakeholders about the environmental impact of their products and processes. Consumer is becoming aware about the various issues like global warming and depletion of natural resources. As the result of this awareness, consumer is preferring the products that are having zero or less impact on the environment. The expectation to reprocess, biodegradable packaging, and introduce green innovation are increasing. If the companies want brand loyalty, it is required to develop a comprehensive environmental strategy.

These changes in the environment concern impose financial burden to adopt better technology. At the same time, companies can increase their profits by maintaining and increasing the customer base. To convert this opportunity into profit, it is important to communicate the environment friendly practices to the consumer. Now-a-days, Indian brands have taken on the green challenge by aligning themselves with a green cause, by introducing green products, taking steps to reduce energy consumption, reduce costs, waste minimization and by implementing green as a business critical success factor.

Green has become the essence of the company's marketing strategy to capture greater market share. But even after the increase in concerned for the environment a significant gap between demand and supply is observed, and most of the products failed early in the introduction stage of the product life cycle due to unavailability, higher cost and lack of green concern. This reduced demand for the green products forced the companies to rethink their actual concern and redesign their strategies. Researches have proved that organizations need to set up long term goal to educate, maintain a long term customer relationship, to develop a positive brand image and increase the acceptability of green products.

Literature Review

The green awareness began in 1960s and early 1970s with increasing concern about the negative impact of consumption pattern, economic and population growth on the environment (Cohen, 2001). But, a serious concern for green marketing appeared in the late 1980s with a rapid increase in the consumer awareness for the green products. The increasing awareness in environment friendly products, their willingness to pay for these products, increased concern for these products encouraged companies to show interest in the green marketing (Peattie and Crane, 2005).

Green marketing practices generally promoted as the genuine concern for the nature of inputs as well as outputs, waste reduction and the impact of these upon the environment and society as a whole in both present and future (Walker and Hanson, 1998). According to American Marketing Association, green marketing is the marketing of products that are presumed to be environmentally safe. It includes various activities like waste reduction, changes in the product, and modifications in the communication mix. Although there were some insights developed by explaining some of its features like a holistic and systemic approach, an open-ended time frame, global perspective that prefers environmental sustainability rather than economic effectiveness is the demand of contemporary era. It is mostly linked with the greening of the different facets of traditional marketing. This involves 'green' new product development, 'green communication' methods, for sale to 'green' consumers (Kinbourne, 1998).

Green marketing mainly focuses on four issues. These issues are: first, importance of green marketing; second, impact of green marketing on firms' competitiveness and performance; third, recognition by consumer; and fourth, improving effectiveness of green marketing. During 1990s, the concern for environment increased and resulted in increased challenges for the companies (Johri and Sahasakmontri, 1998).

Different reasons might have prompted different people to adopt this new trend of being green, but it surely has proved popular. It is advised that a proactive green marketing strategy concentrate needs of stakeholders without compromising the needs of future generations with diffusion of innovation (Peattie and Crane, 2005). There are few reasons, which enforce a marketer to adopt the green marketing as an important part of strategy. It is also necessary to keep in mind that customer do not compromise on traditional product features like quality, ease in availability, performance etc. (Ginsberg and Bloom, 2004). This change in the consumer mind set is putting a new competitive pressure on business (Deveshwar, 2009).

Classification of Companies

According to Ginsberg and Bloom, Companies can be classified on the basis of utilisation of these elements in four categories:

1. ***Lean Green***—These companies adopt the green practices, but they do not focus to publicise these initiatives. They implement the environment friendly practices just for the cost reduction and improving the efficiency.
2. ***Defensive Green***—This kind of marketer use green marketing as a precaution to avoid the crisis situation or to counter the competition. They use green marketing to create the positive brand image. Environment initiatives may be sincere, but temporary just to differentiate from the competitors.
3. ***Shaded Green***—The companies, which adopt shaded green strategy, invest in long-term, environment-friendly processes that

require a significant financial and non-financial dedication. They differentiate their product on the basis of greenness.

4. ***Extreme Green***—Extreme green companies adopt green marketing mix in the holistic manner. They integrate environmental concern in overall marketing strategy. The greenness is the main driving force for the companies. Concept of life cycle assessment, total environmental quality management, waste reduction, and environment friendly promotion are deeply embedded in the company's philosophy. They serve the niche segment of the market.

Indian FMCG Industry: An Overview

This sector is one of the important sectors for the Indian economy. This sector is related to each and every individual that is why it plays an important role in the growth of an economy. The main strength of the FMCG industry is its existence in both urban and rural markets of the country. India's FMCG sector is the fourth largest in the economy and provides employment opportunities for more than three million people. This sector mainly includes Household Care, Personal Care and Food Beverages. The key players in FMCG Industry are Hindustan Unilever Limited, Dabur India Limited, Procter Gamble Hygiene and Health Care Limited, Nirma Limited, Emami Limited, Colgate Palmolive India Limited, Godrej Consumer Products Limited etc. The total FMCG market is of more than INR 85,000 crore.

The current growth of sector is in two digits and it is expected to continue. The important attributes of the FMCG industry is well-defined distribution channels, low operating cost, low per capita consumption and extreme competition. In the first and second quarters of financial year 2008-09 industry sales increased by more than 15 per cent. Companies enjoy the great profit with the modifying the packaging and the product mix, as well as introduction of environment friendly practices like waste reduction, recycling, reuse etc.

Financial Express of 20 April, 2009 has reported that the Indian FMCG industry is set to record double-digit growth despite recession. The report added that the industry is expected to register a value growth of 14 per cent in January-March 2009 as compared to the corresponding period of 2008. CRISIL is anticipating that FMCG sector could touch around INR 1,40,000 crore by 2015.

Greening the Marketing Mix: A Discussion

To make greenness effort profitable, it is necessary to show it in the tangible form, that is why companies are changing their marketing strategies. They are including green in their promotions and redefining their marketing mix. Marketing mix can be defined as the combination of certain tools companies use to achieve their marketing objectives. These are also known as four Ps of marketing. These four Ps are Product, Price, Place and Promotion.

It is evident that Indian FMCG companies are adopting the way of green marketing to sustain in the current competitive era. Companies are trying to reduce the carbon credits of their products. Researchers have analyzed marketing mix of the FMCG companies in context of green from last few years. Major changes have been observed in the products and promotion of the companies.

FMCG companies are redesigning their marketing strategies by introducing the concept of green and big player like ITC, HUL, P&G are indulging in the greening of their marketing mix. The subsequent discussion of the research paper is based on the different news articles related to environment initiatives taken by the industry to modify their marketing mix.

1. ***Green Product***—The product is based on the need of an environment friendly consumer. Companies are introducing various changes to make their product green. These changes are becoming necessary as level of environmental awareness is increasing. They are earning the carbon credit by reducing the emission of CO_2. India's largest FMCG player HUL submitted a proposal to earn carbon credits by changing refrigerant for the ice cream at retail stores. The refrigerator will be more efficient and will reduce the electricity consumption. These will have less impact on the climate (Mint, October 7, 2008, CMIE). ITC has earned 57,000 carbon credits for 3,000 hectares of plantations (*Business Standard*, December 7, 2008, CMIE).

Other method to make green product is by minimizing the waste from the manufacturing process. According to Hindustan Unilever (HUL), after setting-up a cross-functional waste management team, its energy consumption has fallen by 34 per cent, carbon dioxide emissions are down by 25 per cent and its water consumption has fallen by 9 per cent (*Times of India*, December 14, 2009, CMIE). The Godrej group of companies including Godrej Industries Ltd. (GIL) and Godrej Consumer Products Limited (GCPL) collaborated with Ernest and Young (E & Y) to develop future clean development mechanism to reduce greenhouse gas (GHG) emission and to earn carbon credits (*Times of India*, February 4, 2008, CMIE). Dabur India Limited has also tied up with a Belgium firm to reduce carbon emission in company's plant. Company has invested ₹ 5 crore for this purpose (*Business Standard*, January 13, 2010, CMIE).

Another recommendation given by experts to make the 'green product' is to use renewable energy sources like wind energy, solar energy or conservation of energy. It is reported that 96 per cent of the ITC's energy requirements are fulfilled from internal sources with more than 24 per cent of energy generated from renewable resources (*Business Line*, September 29, 2008, CMIE).

Ruchi Soya Industries Limited is also indulged in wind power generation. Company has installed windmills in Madhya Pradesh, Tamil Nadu, Maharashtra, Gujarat and Rajasthan with a combined capacity of 59.10 MWh as of the end of last financial year (Green Energy, http://www.ruchisoya.com/Green_Energy.html). Glaxosmithkline Consumer Healthcare Ltd. introduced various energy conservation techniques, which resulted in reduction of around 22 per cent in cost of steam generation per ton of product (GSKCH Annual Report, 2009, http://www.gsk-ch.in/downloads/GSK_Annual_Report_2009.pdf).

Companies are making the process free from the harmful chemicals to minimise the harmful impact on the environment as a one more strategy for green production. ITC Ltd. completed its Chlorine-Free (ECF) Pulp and Chapter Project in April 2008. The commercial production has commenced with a capacity of 2 lakh tonne of paper per annum. This new environment friendly technique lowered water consumption and improved the efficiency. It has led to cleaner effluent discharge and superior strength properties (CMIE, May 19, 2008). Company also tied-up with Ramky Infrastructure (one of the leading player in municipal solid waste management) for its waste collection initiative in many cities. (*Hindu Business Line*, September 14, 2009, CMIE).

2. *Green Price*—Consumer is always ready to purchase the product that gives more benefit than the cost he incurs. The more benefit is possible by the better quality, performance, design or appearance. Companies should keep this thing in consideration so that they can charge premium for green products. On the other hand, company can save cost by waste management, energy efficiency quality of the product.

Companies are enjoying more profit after introducing green initiatives in their strategy. In an attempt to give back to the society, ITC, a diversified company has introduced various green initiatives. The company's energy efficiency and eco-sensitivity proved a profitable corporate strategy (*Economic Times*, November 12, 2009, CMIE). The company reported a great improvement in profit margin, i.e. 15 to 30 per cent (*Business Standard*, December 7, 2009, CMIE). HUL another big player implemented ploughshare-mixing technology in its soap manufacturing plant and enjoyed the estimated cost reduction by 30 per cent. The technology also reduced the energy requirement, which resulted in cost and emission reduction (*Business Standard*, July 7, 2008, CMIE). Nestle India is also working on various projects to reduce use of natural resources and cut costs. One of the steps involves, utilising steam generated in its boilers for substituting fresh water (*Business Standard*, June 11, 2009, CMIE).

3. ***Green Place***—Companies are reducing the transportation expenses by applying different supply chain techniques. They are using local inputs for production to reduce the cost and carbon emissions and consequently carbon footprints. Companies are reframing their distribution system in order to make them green. They are using software to optimise the transportation system to reduce the fuel consumption resulting in reducing the negative impact on environment. ITC Limited invested in the automated information technology systems to keep track of stocks, reduce the distribution costs and to optimise the distribution system (*Business Standard*, August 14, 2008, CMIE). HUL also changed its inventory management cycle practice to reduce process cost and to regain the lost market share (*Economic Times*, July 4, 2009, CMIE).

4. ***Green Promotion***—Promotion mix contains different type of promotion methods. These methods are advertising, sales promotion, direct marketing etc. Companies are now using signage, billboards those work on solar energy, environment-friendly papers in the posters and boards. Before designing environmental promotion, companies must study the consumer's perception for green. The green promotion should possess enough information related to corporate concern for environment but should not be exaggerated. Involvement in the community welfare is another "Green" marketing strategy devised as an approach to catch the attention of environmentally aware consumers. The project 'Samriddhi' by HUL, *e-choupal* by ITC are the various examples of these initiatives.

For success of green marketing initiatives, it is required to match the company's brand attributes with the customer's perception for green. For this purpose companies are educating about their product's feature in context of green with the help of new promotion campaign. ITC's mission '*Sunehra Kal'* includes its sustainable development initiatives (*Business*

Line, September 29, 2008, CMIE). Nestle India is also involved in the various community works like support to local schools, help in the maintenance of public parks, green belts, blood donation camps and health awareness programmes. Company is spreading awareness for conservation, hygiene, health and wellness of society to fortify the relationship between Nestle India and the community. To ensure the sustainable development of society Glaxosmithkline Consumer Healthcare Ltd. organised number of health camps for the local people at its various sites (GSKCH Annual Report, 2009).

Statistical Analysis

For the purpose of analysis, sample of companies have selected that are listed with BSE FMCG Index and CNX FMCG Index, with some adjustments, using CMIE Database. The annual sales, advertising expense and distribution expense data have also been extracted from the same database. In this section of the chapter, the analysis of the different Ps of marketing mix of the FMCG companies those are involved in the green marketing practices in any manner has been presented. Different ratios have been calculated with the available data for the analysis purpose.

The annual sales of the FMCG companies in India is given in the Table 20.1.

Table 20.1: Annual Sales of FMCG Companies

(In Rs. cr.)

Company Name	Mar-06	Mar-07	Mar-08	Mar-09	Mar-10
Dabur India Ltd.	1372.52	1641.57	2128.17	2435.93	2892.42
Glaxosmithkline Consumer Healthcare Ltd.	1092.28	1236.56	1430.61	1747.35	2086.23
GCPL	692.26	799.42	923.28	1135.37	1301.58
Hindustan Unilever Ltd.	12108.87	13189.7	14895.56	21949.17	18462.34
ITC Ltd.	16236.65	19505.06	21467.38	23247.84	26399.63
Marico Ltd.	1046.47	1375.6	1578.1	1923.92	2031.9
Nestle India Ltd.	2643.96	2944.2	3647.49	4472.04	5232.59
Nirma Ltd.	2244.5	2548.08	2651.15	3378.01	3329.68
Procter and Gamble Ltd.	742.64	599.5	556.02	655.57	775.67
Ruchi Soya Inds. Ltd.	7504.79	8591.01	11014.27	12154.23	13508.45
Tata Global Beverages Ltd.	971.01	1056.38	1136.45	1363.35	1705.62
United Spirits Ltd.	3601.37	4678.74	5518.93	7470.72	9205.97
Total	**50257.32**	**58165.82**	**66947.41**	**81933.5**	**86932.08**

Source: CMIE Database.

Table 20.1 provides the total growth of the FMCG industry in the last 5 years. The companies like ITC, HUL are able to retain their market share in the period of global crisis due to their green strategy and adoption of green marketing mix. ITC enjoyed the growth of 63 per cent in the last five years from the total sale of ₹ 16,236.65 crore to ₹ 26,399.63 crore. In the same period, HUL realized the growth of near 54 per cent. Although growth rate of other companies are more than these big players, but percentage share in total market is with the ITC and HUL. Total market share of both these companies is more than half of total market share. Adoption of environment concern, community welfare schemes, growth in the rural market with help of different initiatives provide growth opportunities for the FMCG companies in India.

The total advertising expenses of the FMCG companies in last five years is given in Table 20.2.

Table 20.2: Annual Advertisement Expenditure

(In Rs. cr.)

Company Name	*Mar-06*	*Mar-07*	*Mar-08*	*Mar-09*	*Mar-10*
Dabur India Ltd.	151.66	197.6	248.1	284.93	390.03
Glaxosmithkline Consumer Health-care Ltd.	126.3	143.16	164.1	194.04	302.09
Godrej Consumer Products Ltd.	53.42	53.78	61.4	63.15	101.69
Hindustan Unilever Ltd.	1005.67	1272.88	1440.22	2130.92	2391.43
ITC Ltd.	225.73	288.15	377.54	502.3	514.66
Marico Ltd.	128.72	178.48	180.47	169.56	221.65
Nestle India Ltd.	135.94	149.09	172.21	194.36	267.51
Nirma Ltd.	36.46	41.57	40.96	44.25	54.35
Procter and Gamble Hygiene and Health Care Ltd.	56.05	52.00	57.95	68.84	89.56
Ruchi Soya Inds. Ltd.	9.05	7.74	9.5	7.08	10.54
Tata Global Beverages Ltd.	89.99	92.75	100.2	90.96	127.57
United Spirits Ltd.	223.44	290.86	303.01	346.77	473.54
Total	**2242.43**	**2768.06**	**3155.66**	**4097.16**	**4944.62**

Source: CMIE Database.

According to Table 20.2, the advertising expenses of HUL are highest in the FMCG industry. HUL is having nearly half share in the Advertising expenses of the sum of all the given companies. Advertising expense of HUL increased from ₹ 1005.67 crore in the financial year 2005-06 to ₹ 2391.43 crore in the financial year, i.e. 2009-10. The reason behind the increasing expense is the investment in the environmental awareness campaigns in the print and broadcast media. ITC's tag line—'greener ways to clean and save' is one of the examples of investment in the green campaign.

The total distribution expenses of the FMCG companies are given in is Table 20.3.

Table 20.3: Annual Distribution Expenses

(In Rs. cr.)

Company Name	*Mar-06*	*Mar-07*	*Mar-08*	*Mar-09*	*Mar-10*
Dabur India Ltd.	40.5	48.5	52.42	50.07	52.88
Glaxosmithkline Consumer Healthcare Ltd.	45.38	57.62	65.79	77.88	89.95
Godrej Consumer Products Ltd.	25.25	30.7	46.06	51.75	61.83
Hindustan Unilever Ltd.	573.8	651.47	731.41	1136.68	867.62
ITC Ltd.	352.21	456.51	548.4	625.01	608.17
Marico Ltd.	42.14	55.52	68.54	90.44	90.16
Nestle India Ltd.	117.72	133.72	160.84	203.55	240.37
Nirma Ltd.	15.23	146.29	136.91	159.12	170.49
Procter and Gamble Hygiene and Health Care Ltd.	27.09	29.56	37.24	31.07	42.72
Ruchi Soya Inds. Ltd.	167.83	205.04	273.4	283.5	201.05
Tata Global Beverages Ltd.	23.86	25.53	26.33	32.1	34.67
United Spirits Ltd.	53.13	51.65	60.55	83.65	108.29
Total	**1484.14**	**1892.11**	**2207.89**	**2824.82**	**2568.2**

Source: CMIE Database.

Table 20.3 shows the changing pattern of the distribution expenses of the industry. Distribution expenses of ITC increased from ₹ 260.97 crore in 2005-06 to ₹ 608.17 crore in 2009-10 that is nearly 73 per cent. But in the last two financial years, it can be seen that there is a huge reduction in industry's distribution expenses. The distribution expenses from ₹ 2824.82 crore for year 2008-09 reduced to ₹ 2568.2 crore in the last financial year; thanks to different transportation model and the supply chain management techniques adopted by the companies.

Comparative Analysis of Marketing Mix

The comparative analysis of the different element of the marketing mix is given in Table 20.4. The table indicates the ratio of advertisement expenses to sales for the FMCG companies.

Table 20.4: Advertisement Expenses to Sales Ratio

Company Name	*Mar-06*	*Mar-07*	*Mar-08*	*Mar-09*	*Mar-10*
Dabur India Ltd.	0.110	0.120	0.116	0.116	0.134
Glaxosmithkline Consumer Healthcare Ltd.	0.115	0.115	0.114	0.111	0.144
Godrej Consumer Products Ltd.	0.077	0.067	0.066	0.055	0.078
Hindustan Unilever Ltd.	0.083	0.096	0.096	0.097	0.129
ITC Ltd.	0.013	0.014	0.017	0.021	0.019
Marico Ltd.	0.123	0.129	0.114	0.088	0.109
Nestle India Ltd.	0.051	0.050	0.047	0.043	0.051
Nirma Ltd.	0.016	0.016	0.015	0.013	0.016
Procter and Gamble Hygiene and Health Care Ltd.	0.075	0.086	0.104	0.105	0.115
Ruchi Soya Inds. Ltd.	0.001	0.001	0.001	0.001	0.001
Tata Global Beverages Ltd.	0.092	0.087	0.088	0.066	0.074
United Spirits Ltd.	0.062	0.062	0.054	0.046	0.051

Source: CMIE Database.

Table 20.4 shows that amongst all, Ruchi Soya Industries limited is showing the uniformity in the ratio values. The trend remain same for the last five years, i.e. 0.001. It means that company's expenditure for the advertisement is very low in comparison to sales. Apart from that ratio is constantly increasing for other industries. The reason for this growth is, simply to maintain the market share. It is necessary to educate the consumer about the various initiatives taken by the companies to create a positive brand image and to earn consumer's loyalty.

The ratio of distribution to advertisement expenses for the FMCG companies is given in Table 20.5.

Table 20.5: Distribution to Advertisement Expense Ratio

Company Name	*Mar-06*	*Mar-07*	*Mar-08*	*Mar-09*	*Mar-10*
Dabur India Ltd.	0.267	0.245	0.211	0.176	0.136
Glaxosmithkline Consumer Healthcare Ltd.	0.359	0.401	0.401	0.401	0.298
Godrej Consumer Products Ltd.	0.472	0.571	0.750	0.819	0.608
Hindustan Unilever Ltd.	0.570	0.512	0.508	0.533	0.363
ITC Ltd.	1.560	1.584	1.453	1.244	1.182
Marico Ltd.	0.327	0.311	0.380	0.533	0.407
Nestle India Ltd.	0.865	0.897	0.934	1.047	0.899
Nirma Ltd.	0.418	0.311	3.343	3.596	3.137
Procter and Gamble Hygiene and Health Care Ltd.	0.483	0.568	0.642	0.451	0.477
Ruchi Soya Inds. Ltd.	18.545	26.491	28.779	40.042	19.075
Tata Global Beverages Ltd.	0.265	0.275	0.263	0.353	0.272
United Spirits Ltd.	0.238	0.178	0.199	0.241	0.229

Source: CMIE Database.

Table 20.5 shows that distribution to advertisement ratio has a different trend across the industry. Ruchi Soya Industries limited has largest ratio as compared to other companies. This ratio is showing both increasing and decreasing pattern in the study period. Except Proctor and Gamble and HUL, each company is having highest ratio in the financial year 2008-09. Interestingly, in financial year 2009-10 the ratio has decreased across the companies in the industry. Companies have adopted various initiatives like adoption of automation to track the stock record, transportation system to reduce the fuel and energy consumption in the distribution system resulting in the reduction in the distribution expenses.

Table 20.6 shows the distribution expenses to sales ratio of the industry in the study period.

Table 20.6: Distribution Expenses to Sales Ratio

Company Name	*Mar-06*	*Mar-07*	*Mar-08*	*Mar-09*	*Mar-10*
Dabur India Ltd.	0.029	0.030	0.025	0.021	0.018
Glaxosmithkline Consumer Healthcare Ltd.	0.042	0.047	0.046	0.045	0.043
Godrej Consumer Products Ltd.	0.036	0.038	0.049	0.046	0.048
Hindustan Unilever Ltd.	0.047	0.049	0.049	0.052	0.047
ITC Ltd.	0.022	0.023	0.026	0.027	0.023
Marico Ltd.	0.040	0.040	0.043	0.047	0.044
Nestle India Ltd.	0.044	0.045	0.044	0.045	0.046
Nirma Ltd.	0.007	0.057	0.051	0.047	0.051
Procter and Gamble Hygiene and Health Care Ltd.	0.037	0.049	0.066	0.047	0.055
Ruchi Soya Inds. Ltd.	0.022	0.024	0.025	0.023	0.014
Tata Global Beverages Ltd.	0.025	0.024	0.023	0.024	0.020
United Spirits Ltd.	0.015	0.011	0.011	0.011	0.012

Source: CMIE Database.

Table 20.6 shows that the ratio of the distribution expenses to sales of the companies are almost constant except for few. The companies are investing on research and development to explore new ways to make their distribution channel greener and to reduce the impact of the industrial activities on the climatic condition of the planet.

Conclusion

Significant change in the climatic conditions results in a threat for the survival of the society. This threat is shifting the buyer's consumption pattern from unsustainable to sustainable. This shift is changing the buying behaviour of individuals because their needs are changing from environmental harmful products to environment friendly products. They are more concerned about the environment protection. This transformation in consumer's behaviour is compelling corporates to think about the harmful impact of their activities on the natural environment of the world. The rapid increase for the environment concern in last two decades is stressing companies to prove the change to ensure the sustainable growth of the society. Organizations are now aware about the fact that without adopting green in the core of their strategy they cannot survive in the present competitive era.

Indian FMCG companies are also adopting 'green' to retain their image in the market. The companies are involved in various activities to show their concern for environment as well as society. Companies like HUL, ITC started publishing Sustainability Report of the company to achieve benefit and to develop a positive brand image as it is required that benefit should be visible to the consumers. Companies are trying different ways to get benefit from their green efforts. They are redefining their marketing mix by introduction of green products and processes.

But at the same time it is necessary for the companies to understand that Green marketing should not overlook the economic aspect of marketing. Customer is ready to pay the eco-premium but they have to enhance the performance of their product and focus on the retention of the customer. Green Marketing is still at the childhood stage in the Indian companies. Green marketing helps in the effective outcomes like cost cutting, employee satisfaction, waste minimisation, society welfare for the companies as well for society also. Only thing required is the determination and commitment from all the stakeholders of the companies. It is the right time to adopt the concept of sustainable development in the marketing mix of the companies and integrate them to save the planet from the upcoming risk.

References

Balasubramanian, D. (2008), "I T C Ltd.'s Chlorine-Free (ECF) Pulp and Paper Project is completed", 19 May, CMIE.

Business Line (2008), "ITC Forms Unique Business Models Focused on Rural India", 29 September, CMIE.

Business Standard (2010), "Dabur ties up with a Belgium firm to become more energy efficient", 13 January, CMIE.

Business Standard (2008), "HUL's Ploughshare Tech Likely to Reduce Costs by Per cent", 7 July, CMIE.

Business Standard (2008), "ITC Limited to Invest in Automated Information Technology Systems", 14 August, CMIE.

Business Standard, (2009), "ITC's Green Initiatives Add to Profits", 7 December, CMIE.

Business Standard, (2009), "Nestle to Reduce Costs by Going Green", 11 June, CMIE.

Cohen, M. (2001), "The Emergent Environmental Policy Discourse on Sustainable Consumption", *Exploring Sustainable Consumption: Environmental Policy and the Social Sciences*, Cohen, M.J. and Murphy, J. (Ed.), London: Pergamon, pp. 21-37.

Deveshwar, V.C. (2009) "New Paradigm of Competitiveness: Positioning ITC for the challenges of tomorrow", *Outlook*, Vol. XLIX, No. 32, pp. 18-23.

Economic Times (2009), "HUL Shifts to Monthly Inventory Management Cycle", 4 July, CMIE.

Economic Times (2009), "ITC Green Initiatives Showcase a Profitable Corporate Strategy", 12 November, CMIE.

Feldman, L.S. and Stachler, S.M. (1996), "Green Marketing: Do Corporate Strategies Reflect Experts' Advice?", *The Journal of Marketing Management*, Vol. 5, Issue 1, pp. 20-28.

Ginsberg, J.M. and Bloom, P.N. (2004), "Choosing the Right Green Marketing Strategy", *MIT Sloan Management Review*, Vol. 46, No. 1, pp. 79-84.

GSKCH Annual Report, (2009), available at http://www.gsk-ch.in/downloads/GSK_Annual_Report_2009.pdf, (accessed on 13 October 2010), pp. 9.

Hermens, M. and Das, B. (2009), "A Green Evolution", *Business Outlook*, June 13; available at http://business.outlookindia.com/article.aspx?102268, (accessed on September 30, 2010).

Hindu Business Line, (2009), "ITC Ties Up with Ramky for Waste Chapter Collection Project in Chennai", 14 September, CMIE.

Indian CEOs poised to respond to climate change, (2009), available at http://*www.pwc.com/en_GX/gx/sustainability/.../india-ceo-climate-change.pdf* (accessed on October 5, 2010).

Johri, L.M. and Sahasakmontri, K. (1998), "Green Marketing Of Cosmetics and Toiletries in Thailand", *Journal of Consumer Marketing*, Vol. 15, No. 3, pp. 265-81.

Kilbourne, William E. (1998), "Green Marketing: A Theoretical Perspective", *Journal of Marketing Management*, Vol. 14, pp. 641-55.

Kotler P. and Keller K.L. (2006), *Marketing Management*, Delhi, India: Pearson Prentice Hall Publication.

Menon, A. and Menon, A. (1997), "Enviropreneurial Marketing Strategy: The Emergence of Corporate Environmentalism as Market Strategy", *Journal of Marketing*, Vol. 61, pp. 51-67.

Mint (2008), "Domestic home appliance makers hope to earn carbon credits", 7 October, CMIE.

Narain, S.; Ghosh, P.; Saxena, N.C.; Parikh, J. and Soni, P. (2009), "Climate Change: Perspectives from India", available at http://www.undp.org.in/content/pub/ClimateChange/UNDP_Climate_Change.pdf, (accessed on 5 October 2010).

Parikh, J.K. and Parikh, K. (2002), "Climate Change: India's Perceptions, Positions, Policies and Possibilities", available at http://www.oecd.org/dataoecd /22/16/1934784.pdf, (accessed on 30 September, 2010).

Peattie, K. and Crane, A. (2005), "Green Marketing: Legend, Myth, Farce or Prophesy?", *Qualitative Market Research*, Vol. 8, No. 4, pp. 357-70.

Polonsky, M.J. and Rosenberger, P.J. (2001), "Re-evaluating Green Marketing: A Strategic Approach", *Business Horizons,* Vol. 44, No. 5, pp. 21-30.

Prasad, H.A.C. and Kochher, J.S., (2009), "Climate Change and India-Some Major Issues and Policy Implications", Available at http://finmin.nic.in/WorkingPaper/Workingpercent20paperpercent20Climatepercent20Change.pdf.

Raghavan, L. and Vahanvati, G. (2008), "Going Green in India Embracing the Environmental Imperative", available on http:// www.landor.compdfsk9L Raghvan_25Jul08.pdf, (accessed on 5 October, 2010).

Schwepker, C.H., Jr. and Cornwell, T.B. (1991), "An Examination of Ecologically Concerned Consumers and Their Intention to Purchase Ecologically-Packaged Products", *Journal of Public Policy and Marketing*, Vol. 10, No. 2, pp. 77-101.

Times of India (2008), "Godrej Group Turns to Ernest and Young to Earn Carbon Credits", 4 February, CMIE.

Times of India (2009),"HUL Cuts Cost through its Waste Management Team", 14 December, CMIE.

Vaccaro, V.L. (2009), "B2B Green Marketing and innovation theory for competitive advantage", *Journal of systems and Information Technology*, Vol. 11, No. 4, pp. 315-30.

Walker, R.H. and Hanson, D.J. (1998), "Green Marketing and Green Places: A Taxonomy for the Destination Marketer", *Journal of Marketing Management*, Vol. 14, No. 6, pp. 623-39.

Wanninayake, W.M.C.B. and Randiwela, P. (2008), "Consumer Attractiveness Towards Green Products of FMCG Sector: An Empirical Study", chapter presented at Oxford Business and Economics Conference Program, 22-24 June, Oxford, UK, available at *www.gcbe.us/2008.../W.m.c.b.percent20Wanninayake*, percent20Pradeeppercent20Randiwela.doc. (Accessed on 7 October, 2010).

Index